PENGUIN BOOKS

THE NEW AMERICAN POVERTY

Michael Harrington is a widely respected writer, lecturer, and political activist, whose other books include *The Other America*, *The Accidental Century*, *Twilight of Capitalism*, *The Vast Majority*, and *The Politics at God's Funeral*. He is co-chair of Democratic Socialists of America.

THE NEW AMERICAN POVERTY

Michael Harrington

PENGUIN BOOKS

PENGUIN BOOKS
Viking Penguin Inc., 40 West 23rd Street,
New York, New York 10010, U.S.A.
Penguin Books Ltd, Harmondsworth,
Middlesex, England
Penguin Books Australia Ltd, Ringwood,
Victoria, Australia
Penguin Books Canada Limited, 2801 John Street,
Markham, Ontario, Canada L3R 1B4
Penguin Books (N.Z.) Ltd, 182–190 Wairau Road,
Auckland 10, New Zealand

First published in the United States of America by
Holt, Rinehart and Winston 1984
Published by arrangement with Holt, Rinehart and Winston
in Penguin Books 1985

LIBRARY OF CONGRESS CATALOGING IN PUBLICATION DATA
Harrington, Michael.
The new American poverty.
Reprint. Originally published: New York:
Holt, Rinehart and Winston, c1984.
Includes index.
1. Poor—United States. 2. Economic assistance,
Domestic—United States. I. Title.
HC110.P6H37 1985 305.5'69'0973 85-3486
ISBN 0 14 00.8112 7

Printed in the United States of America by
R. R. Donnelley & Sons Company, Harrisonburg, Virginia
Set in Century Schoolbook

To the memory of Selma Lenihan
A vibrant, magnificent member of
The pilgrimage toward our humanity

Contents

Acknowledgments

The sources for statistics and other facts are given in the text itself.

Portions of Chapter 3 appeared, in different form, in *Harper's*. Excerpts of Chapter 4 were published in *Dissent*.

I am deeply indebted to Julia Keydel, who allowed me to use the videotapes and transcripts of interviews with homeless people in New York City.

Fred Siegel was most helpful when I was writing the first draft of this book in Paris. He lent me his own clippings and provided me with informed and sensitive comment on my topics. Herbert Gutman very much helped me to organize my ideas on the black internal migration.

My editor, Dick Seaver, found time in a jammed schedule to go over the details of the manuscript as well as to provide invaluable advice on the structure and themes of the book.

Finally, friends all over the country—most of them members of the Democratic Socialists of America—took this poverty tourist by the hand and helped him to see. They have struggled in Appalachian hollows and Seattle SROs, in union organizing, in minority group activism, in the *barrios* of the Bronx and Los Angeles. They are, so to speak, my co-authors, and if I cannot possibly name them individually because they are so many, they know who they are and they have my eternal gratitude.

THE NEW AMERICAN POVERTY

— 1 —

Impaired Vision

The poor are still there.

Two decades after the President of the United States declared an "unconditional" war on poverty, poverty does not simply continue to exist; worse, we must deal with structures of misery, with a new poverty much more tenacious than the old.

Structures of misery. The idea was a commonplace when one thought of Appalachia a generation ago. An economy controlled by absentee corporations neglected basic investments, which eroded the physical and social infrastructure as well as the tax base. People fled this impossible situation, so there were even fewer human resources, which made further investment unlikely. That in turn further eroded the physical and social infrastructure as well as the tax base. Under such conditions, poverty is not merely an episode or the fault of some heartless Scrooge, but the ongoing product of the organization of disorganization.

Now there are new structures of misery. In the winter of our national discontent in 1982–83, when there were more jobless Americans than at any other time in almost half a century, a young worker walked through the milling, sometimes menacing men on East Third Street in Manhattan and asked the City of New York for a bed at the Municipal Shelter. One of the reasons he was there was that there are steel mills in South Korea. That is, the poor—and the entire American economy—are caught up in a crisis which is literally global. Yet one cannot simply blame changes in the way the world is run for what is happening on East Third Street, or in the *barrios* of Los Angeles, the steel towns of the Monongahela Valley, and the backwoods of Maine.

The great, impersonal forces have indeed created a context in which poverty is much more difficult to abolish than it was twenty years ago. But it is not the South Koreans—or the Japanese, the West Germans, or anyone else—who have decided that the human costs of this wrenching transition should be borne by the most vulnerable Americans. We have done that to ourselves.

One reason is that this economic upheaval did not simply strike at the poor. It had an enormous impact on everyone else and, among many other things, changed the very eyes of the society. In the sixties there was economic growth, political and social movement, hope. What was shocking was that poverty existed at all, and the very fact that it did was an incitement to abolish it. I simplify, of course. Even then, as I pointed out in *The Other America*, suburbanization was removing the middle class from daily contact with the poor. In our geography, as in our social structure, we were becoming two nations.

Moreover, the optimistic sixties often overlooked the systemic nature of its own poverty. I remember a quintessential political cocktail party of those times. It was during the 1964 Presidential campaign at the Dakota, perhaps the most chic apartment building in New York City. A leading trade unionist was talking to some of the intellectual elite. We are going to the moon, he said. Why can't we put an end to the slums? He, and almost everyone else there, knew that our capacities were boundless, that we could deal with ghettos as well as outer space. But there are no people on the moon, no landlords, no silk-stocking districts reluctant to welcome the ex-poor into affluent neighborhoods. Lunar exploration posed technical problems; abolishing poverty raised issues of power and wealth.

Few people realized this in 1964, so there was a social war without a human enemy. The opposing forces were abstractions: hunger, illiteracy, bad housing, inadequate motivation, and the like. It was innocently assumed that ending the outrage of poverty was in everyone's interest. It was not until the seventies, during the debate over Richard Nixon's Family Assistance Plan, that a Southern congressman bluntly stated the more complex truth. If the government provided a minimum income to everyone, "Who," he asked, "will iron my shirts and rake the yard?"

But even if there were more than a few illusions in the sixties, they facilitated some very real gains. There were many of the working poor who, in a decade of falling unemployment, fought their way out of poverty. The aging made dramatic gains through Medicare and increased, indexed social security benefits. Blacks successfully eradicated legal Jim Crow; Chicanos and Filipinos created a union in the fields; even Appalachia registered some gains. If the antipoverty program turned out to be a skirmish rather than an unconditional war, it nonetheless made some significant advances.

In the eighties it is not simply that structural economic change has created new poverties and given old poverties a new lease on life. That very same process has impaired the national vision; misery has simultaneously become more intractable and more difficult to see.

In the seventies and the early eighties, we had both inflation and recession, which subverted the established liberal wisdom; the highest unemployment rates since the Great Depression; and a consequent loss of political and social nerve. Crises, particularly at first, do not make people radical or compassionate. They are frightening, and most people concentrate on saving themselves. Thoughts of "brothers" or "sisters," who are moral kin but not one's blood relatives, are a luxury many cannot afford. It was not an accident that the Economic Opportunity Act of 1964 proclaimed that its goal was "to eliminate the paradox of poverty in the midst of plenty." It is somewhat more problematic to summon the average American to such a struggle in the midst of declining real wages and chronic unemployment.

At the same time, the process of suburbanization, which puts the poor out of sight and mind, has proceeded apace over the past two decades. The central cities have become reservations for the marginalized, as distant from the everyday consciousness as are the Navajos in the empty reaches of the Southwest. In 1982 *The Economist* of London wrote that the security forces in the shopping malls of America were there "to insulate their clientele from the undesirable elements of the real world—and those elements are as likely to be the poor and unwashed as the snow and the sun." "With less physical community," the article went on, "street life in cities will diminish and become less varied, criminals will gain ascendancy, buildings will become like fortresses." That is not, of course, an exercise in futurism; it is a sober description of what is going on in the United States.

So the national vision has been impaired in a number of ways. As men and women turned inward to face their own relative deprivation, it became harder to see anyone else's absolute suffering; and the Balkanization of American social structure only made things worse. More broadly, where the sixties spoke of possibilities, the eighties were forced to become aware of limits, which some assumed, wrongly, were ugly necessities to be imposed on those at the bottom of the society. In the process, America has lost its own generous vision of what it might be.

That is why, among many other things, this book cannot be *The Other America Revisited.*

The Other America was published in 1962 and was struck by lightning in 1963. In January of that year, Dwight Macdonald wrote a long review of the book in *The New Yorker*, which made poverty a topic of conversation in the socially conscious intellectual world of the Northeast. John Kennedy heard of those discussions and, as two members of his administration later told me (Walter Heller and Arthur Schlesinger, Jr.), read *The Other America* and was moved by it. It was, they said, one of many factors in his decision to make poverty a central issue in the forthcoming campaign against Barry Goldwater. Kennedy was assassinated before he could act on that conviction, but Lyndon Johnson followed up on it. When I returned from a year in Europe just before Christmas

1963, I discovered to my amazement that I had played a minor role in a major government shift.

The virtue of *The Other America* was not its complex analysis of the economics of poverty but the fact that it demanded that people look around themselves in a time when society was making it easier to see. The book was implicated in the black movement led by one of the most charismatic Americans of our times, Martin Luther King, Jr.; it was involved in the martyrdom of a young President who had been shocked by the sight of the poor in West Virginia during the 1960 Democratic primary, and in the populist emotions of his successor; it found an audience in the growing ecumenical religious movement that owed so much to Pope John XXIII.

Under those circumstances, people could respond to an informed and impassioned appeal to open their eyes. Society was not conspiring to blind them. But, if I am right in what I have just written, that is not the case today.

There is an ironic illustration of this fact in the excellence, and the profound limitations, of the media coverage of the 1982–83 recession. In the late fifties and early sixties part of the problem was, as I wrote at the time, that the poor were "invisible," that the press and television only rarely covered the ghettos and the backwoods shacks. The contrast with what I found in McKeesport, Pennsylvania, in the winter of 1983 is striking. I had gone to McKeesport to talk to unemployed steelworkers and the activists of the Mon (Monongahela) Valley Unemployed Committee. At one point I interviewed a woman, whom I took to be a local militant, for ten or so minutes before I discovered that she was a reporter. And I was told that when the last of the three commercial networks arrived to shoot their footage, it had been necessary to call a special picket line to give them something to cover. A bank, mistaking this reenactment for a new demonstration, closed early.

This marks a tremendous gain over the years before poverty became an issue in the early sixties. *The Wall Street Journal*, whose editorial page is unimaginatively conservative, has, for instance, provided some of the most moving reportage about the human costs of the current crisis. If there had been such articles and television spots two decades ago, *The Other America* would not have been necessary, or, at least, would never have come to so many people as a revelation. But it is precisely because poverty has become so much more complex and obdurate, because so many Americans cannot afford to respond to what is seen for them by the media, that such journalism, important as it is, is not enough. There must be much more analysis now.

In some of the stories about the recession of 1982–83, it was assumed that the layoffs and the economic decline would go on forever and that the entire industrial working class was on the verge of going to the poorhouse. Jobless steelworkers in Pennsylvania and "shopping-bag ladies" in New York were blithely subsumed under the superficial level of a "new poverty." But many of those steelworkers will not become poor, and saying that they will could divert attention from the truly shocking fact that some, which is too many, will. Indeed, I suspect that the overgeneralizations about the new poverty will inevitably be followed by overgeneralizations about the new prosperity.

The official poverty statistics announced in 1983 were an excellent case in point. They showed that there were as many poor Americans in 1982 as in 1965. The conclusion? That all of the efforts of the past two decades had failed? Not at all. That the other America was going to grow into the indefinite future? Not necessarily. Behind those statistics was a relationship that is practically a cliché for anyone concerned with the issue: When unemployment goes up, which was what happened in the most dramatic way in 1982, poverty increases. But in that same year there was a new, more complex trend that affected the rich and the middle class as well as the poor. Such a tendency, however, exceeds the level of complexity permitted in feature articles or three-minute segments on the evening news.

At the same time, there is a scholarly growth industry that further confuses matters. Not surprisingly, the failure of social nerve and imagination in the seventies was accompanied by an ideological offensive from the right. When that was simply a matter of conservative theories, like "supply side" economics, the damage that could be done was both real and limited, for when government actually acted on the theory, reality had its revenge. But when reactionary "facts" were invented, that was a more serious issue. Statistics, as almost everyone thinks he knows, are not a matter of opinion, but of the numbers generated by the real world itself. If, then, serious thinkers, and even government agencies, began to publish hard figures showing that there were really not as many poor people as we thought, who can argue?

So it was that David Stockman, the director of the Office of Management and Budget, told a House committee in late 1983 that "contrary to press reports . . . poverty is not really as extensive as it was at the outset of the War on Poverty." The figures showing that the percentage of the poor in 1982 was as high as in 1965 were, he said, simply a result of faulty calculations. Moreover, Stockman concluded, the success of Ronald Reagan's economic policies was already even further reducing the real, unexaggerated poverty rate in the United States. This was not just a Presidential assistant scornfully saying that people went to soup lines not because they were hungry, but because they were cheap. This was a serious official, armed with charts and statistics, with hard, unassailable numbers.

Stockman was wrong. As I will show later, his "objective" figures were computed on the basis of highly questionable, very political assumptions. That this was often done honestly and sincerely does not change the perniciousness of the fact. In 1960 the situation was quite different, because there were hardly any statistical studies of poverty at all. So this book, unlike *The Other America*, will have to deal not with an ignorant indifference that makes the poor invisible, but with a sophisticated and "scientific" attempt to define them out of existence.

These are some of the reasons why, after refusing, for some twenty years, various proposals to write another book on poverty, I came to the conclusion that it was necessary not to revisit the other America of the late fifties and early sixties, but to explore the uncharted social landscape of a new poverty. This reality was not, and is not, I must emphasize, the creation of Ronald Reagan. He made the worst of a bad thing, to be sure, scapegoating the poor for imaginary wrongs. But the structures of misery today are not simply the work of the ideological rigidity of a President who can be charming even as he is cruel. They are the results of massive economic and social transformations and they cannot be understood apart from an analysis of them.

I wish that were not so. I wish I could once more evoke poverty, suggest its look, its smell, its often twisted spirit, with just a few rudimentary references to the underlying trends. I am reluctant to do what must be done, because the American people are much more receptive to dramatic moments and vignettes than to accounts of macroeconomic structures. But one must understand why sweatshops, those dinosaurs from the antediluvian age of competitive capitalism, have emerged once again in a time of technological revolution. It is not enough to demand sympathy for women from the Caribbean working a fourteen-hour day for a pittance in the New York City borough of Queens. To open our eyes today, it is also necessary for us to know why those women are there, to see not merely the exploitation they endure, but the structures that cause it as well. For it is precisely those structures that impair our vision in the first place.

I begin, then, with a broad outline of some of the most important national and international forces that can converge on a sweatshop in Queens. And that leads to a basic concept, which owes much to the work of Serge Milano in France: There is no such thing as poverty; there are *poverties*. The difference between the social misery of the eighties and that of the sixties is not a new contrast, but only the last in a long series. In the nineteenth century, during the period of capitalist industrialization, proletarianization was pauperization. A vast mass of former peasants was assembled in huge cities, and wealth was created by the twelve- and fourteen-hour days of a growing pariah class. The radicals, Marx and Engels, saw that, of course; but so did the liberals, Charles Dickens and Victor Hugo. *Oliver Twist*, *Les Miserables*, and *Das Kapital* are about the same reality.

Over time, the determined opposition of those workers educated the educated and transformed the social context. Productivity and technological progress became the mainstream of the system. But if each worker was now going to produce ten or a hundred times the output of his or her parents, where would one find a market for their products? Some French writers, like Milano, call the answer "Fordism," to celebrate the wily American auto manufacturer who introduced the unprecedented five-dollar-a-day wage. Mass production, society learned (and here again it was trade unionists who tutored their college-educated bosses in the new economics), required mass consumption.

It took the Great Depression to drive the lesson home. The poverty of the thirties in the United States was quite capitalist, yet very different from the suffering in the early days of the system. The problem was that the economy had become too productive, given the limits placed on consumption. A quarter of the work force was in the streets; there were desperate needs for food and clothing not being met; there were factories and fields that could have satisfied those needs, but there was "too much" production already. In a paradigmatic moment of the New Deal, the government persuaded farmers to destroy pigs and plow under fields in order to raise farm income by artificial scarcity at a time of widespread hunger.

After World War II, however, it seemed that the nation had stumbled into an answer to that problem. "Fordism" became official policy. The income of the people would still come primarily from the private sector, but now the government took on two new responsibilities: to manipulate fiscal and monetary policy to be sure that there was enough demand to soak up the output of a growing economy, and to provide minimal care for those who fell out of the system. In the years between 1945 and 1970, this worked tolerably well. So it was that if the poverty of the nineteenth century seemed to be an inevitable consequence of the emergence of the system, and that of the Depression a result of its contraction and crisis, the poverty of the sixties seemed to be a deviation from the new norm. The poor existed in the exceptional "pockets" of what was thought to be an "affluent" society.

The poverty of the eighties is different from all those poverties that preceded it.

Around 1970, the United States joined the global economy

for the first time and the American poor began to suffer from the international division of labor in unprecedented ways. Of course, this country had been involved in foreign trade from the earliest days of the Republic. But if America had long been important for the world, the world was not too important for America. We were the technological pioneers, the inventors of the second industrial revolution of steel and mass production, as well as of the third, electronic industrial revolution. After all, we had an internal market so much larger than any other that it was not especially crucial for us to be concerned about foreigners. Even today, after more than a decade of relative decline, the gross national product (GNP) of the United States is six times that of France, four times that of West Germany, three times that of Japan, and twice as big as that of the Soviet Union.

But this country rebuilt the European and Japanese economies after World War II, made a handsome profit in the process, and did the job too well. Our former clients in West Germany and Japan became fierce competitors. At the same time, trade became more important for the United States than ever before. In the seventies, exports almost doubled (from 9 percent to 17 percent) and the imported portion of the internal market more than doubled (from 9 percent to 21 percent). The West Germans and the Japanese, however, proceeded to sell "turnkey" plants—complete factories ready to start up—to South Korea and other Third World countries. With the spread of multinationals—corporations without a country to be loyal to—there was an unprecedented internationalization of the economy.

Suddenly the industrial geography of a good part of the United States—its mass-production heartland—no longer made as much sense as it once had. That did not simply menace the traditional working class with a new poverty, but by beginning to reshape the occupational structure of the United States, it also threatened a new, mainly immigrant working class and undercut the struggle of blacks, Hispanics, and other minorities who suffered from the effects of an institutional economic racism.

Indeed, the international transformation of the American labor market is not a phenomenon peculiar to this country. By an accident of personal life, the first draft of this book was largely written in Paris at a time when I was also visiting Holland, Greece, and Israel. I saw with my own eyes what the European press had turned into a commonplace: the decline of classic industries—especially steel—and the appearance of an international work force in every country. Visually, for instance, one of the most striking changes in Paris over the past two decades has been the enormous increase in the number of Asians and northern and sub-Saharan Africans. Even in Israel, an exceptional society in so many ways, the Oriental—mainly Moroccan—Jews and the Arabs perform the dirty work at the bottom of the economy. The contrast between the electronic engineer and the dishwasher and the disappearance of so many in-between jobs is a fact of life in every advanced country. It is also an important aspect of the new poverty.

And finally, this multifaceted internationalization of poverty occurred at the same time as a technological revolution also restructured America from within. In the auto industry, for instance, it is well known by everyone that a significant portion of the men and women laid off during the 1982–83 recession will never get their jobs back. The companies, like many other corporations, had found a certain utility in the recession. It allowed them to shut down obsolete plants, which also meant destroying living communities, and to plan for more efficient, robotized, automated production. This process is still very much in progress. It has transformed agriculture and the factory, and it is now invading the office.

These massive international and national trends have created the basis for the new structures of misery in the America of the eighties, for a poverty more difficult to defeat than the indignities of twenty years ago. Yet this book will not be primarily concerned with analyzing those changes as they affect the world and domestic markets. Rather I shall concentrate on their impact upon the economic and social underworld of American society, defining the mechanisms that relate the South Korean steel mills to the Municipal Shelter on East Third Street in Manhattan. Sometimes the connections are immediate and obvious—the new poverty within both the traditional working class and the multiracial working class that is in the process of formation—and sometimes the links are tenuous, refracted: The decline in the capacity for compassion, which is a by-product of the economic insecurities of the last decade, deprives the discharged mental patients roaming the hostile streets of the great cities of a sympathy they might otherwise have received.

I shall try to depict these new poverties anecdotally as well as theoretically, not the least because I want to reach out to that basic generosity of the American spirit, which even bad times can never completely destroy. But what is crucial and specific about the poverty of the new "Other America" is that it is so much more systemic and structured than the poverty of twenty years ago. It might be thought that, as a social critic who has long argued that there are inherent and basic problems in America, I take delight in new evidence that I am right. In fact, I deeply wish that my message were not so grim, that I could suggest that if only we would set our hearts and minds to it, it would be easy to end this abomination. That, alas, is no longer true.

Yet the most basic single point in this book is that if the new poverty is so much more intransigent than the old, it is not a fate. The structures of this misery were created by men and women; they can be changed by men and women. That, we shall see, is easier said than done—but it can be done.

I have long thought that perhaps we are all on an arduous pilgrimage which might—only might—lead us to our own humanity. There are times when the pilgrimage halts, when the people are exhausted from wandering in the desert, when the reports of the Promised Land over the Jordan seem preposterous. So it has been for a while in the United States. It is not that men and women have lacked courage and decency. It is that bewildering, distant forces have perplexed them and subverted their capacity for hope. But one day there will be a stirring, and—perhaps hesitantly at first—the long column will begin to move once again.

Where will it go? In 1964, when I went to Washington to work on Lyndon Johnson's task force on poverty, I made a disconcerting discovery. Suddenly I was sitting in a boardroom in the Peace Corps building, and the other people around the table included cabinet members and advisors to the President of the United States who had just told us to come up with a program to end poverty in America. This was, in short, a rendezvous with one of those famous ideas whose time had come. And yet no one there knew what to do. The "poverty warriors," as the press immediately dubbed us, were intellectually impoverished.

It is my modest hope that when the pilgrimage begins again, when the time of the antipoverty idea has returned, this book might point out a path or two. It is my deeper hope that when that day comes, when we join, in solidarity and not in noblesse oblige, with the poor, we will rediscover our own best selves—that we will regain the vision of America.

2

The Future's New Past

In his State of the Union Message of 1964, Lyndon B. Johnson declared an "unconditional war on poverty."

Suddenly, images of Appalachian shacks and black ghettos filled the television screen. Governors and mayors went on pilgrimages to Washington to find out what money could be obtained from this new exercise in federal compassion. Universities organized conferences, and since it was early decreed that there would be "maximum feasible participation" of the poor themselves in the War on Poverty, welfare mothers joined professors and bureaucrats on the stage and, more often than not, scolded the other members of the panel for the hardness of their hearts. The moment was, and is, easy to caricature; it was replete with the breathless, fleeting superficiality of a media event. And yet it was to change the lives of some of the most vulnerable people in the society; it was a portent of the first period of social reform since the New Deal of the thirties.

In 1973, Richard Nixon sent Howard Phillips, a young conservative ideologue, to take over the Office of Economic Opportunity, the major agency that developed out of Johnson's 1964 declaration of war. Phillips thoroughly intended to demolish the OEO, but when a showdown came, the President did not back him. The poverty programs had acquired some political clout, by no means all of it from liberals. What had begun as an adventure in human solidarity had turned, in part at least, into *realpolitik*. But in 1981, when Ronald Reagan launched his savage assault upon the welfare state, there was little effective protest as the poor suffered cuts in government spending two and a half times greater than were received by all the other groups combined.

What had happened in the seventeen years between Johnson's generosity and Reagan's meanness?

That question is far from academic. This area, we have seen, is one in which misinformation has often been more important than fact. Such ignorance, as Gunnar Myrdal has remarked, is never random; it almost always serves the purposes of the powerful. Thus, in trying to outline a brief history of the struggle against poverty during the last two decades, I am trying to rescue not simply the past but the future as well. When American society begins to move again—when a modicum of decency once more becomes possible—it is critical that we not be confused by the memories of events that never happened.

There never was a gigantic program of handouts to the poor, and to the minority poor in particular, called the War on Poverty. The Office of Economic Opportunity, the main new institution that resulted from the President's declaration of social war, made no "handouts" at all. There never was a massive investment of billions of dollars in radical innovations that challenged the very structure of power in the United States. The spending was exceedingly modest, the programs largely unthreatening. There never was a dreary record of failure as the social engineers proved their dreamy incompetence. A majority of the relatively conventional undertakings of this period worked fairly well. If, then, most of the faults of the poverty program never existed, and a good number of its efforts succeeded, why is it that poverty is once again on the march, or, more precisely, has become even more entrenched than when the War on Poverty began?

A good question. But it can only be answered if a non-past is first unwritten.

I

When President Johnson made that declaration of social war, the United States was the most limited welfare state in the Western world.

The welfare state had begun under the conservative Junker, Bismarck, in the 1880s, in part as an act of feudal noblesse oblige, in part as an attempt to steal the thunder from a rising socialist movement. Sickness insurance came to Germany in 1883, to the United Kingdom in 1911; it has not yet come to the United States. Industrial accident insurance became law in Germany in 1884, in the United Kingdom in 1887 and 1906, and in this country in 1930. A pension system was adopted in Germany in 1889, in the United Kingdom in 1908, and in America in 1935. Health insurance was introduced in Germany in 1880, in the United Kingdom in 1948, and in the United States in 1965—but only for people over sixty-five years of age. The War on Poverty, then, was launched in the advanced capitalist nation where the poor—and everyone else, for that matter—had the fewest economic and social rights.

Moreover, even when the United States did finally get around to legislating its most basic welfare-state program, social security, it did so in an extremely limited way. That program originally provided federal matching grants to the states only for assistance to the aged, to the blind, "and to families with dependent children with a deceased, absent, or incapacitated parent." Even that measure was added as an afterthought to the basic pension system. It was only in 1950 that amendments permitted the states to help children with a present, and not incapacitated, parent, and it took until 1961 to get legislation allowing aid to two-parent families (only twenty states and the District of Columbia have availed themselves of this option). Our basic social legislation was, and still is, antifamily.

Many of these limitations, as Harrel Rodgers points out in

The Cost of Human Neglect, were deliberate. The Southern congresspeople in particular "insisted that assistance programs be administered by the states, and that the states be allowed to determine who would get assistance and how much they would receive." So it was—and is—that the United States has fifty-one separate, and quite different, welfare systems (one for each state, plus one for the District of Columbia).

In the early sixties, under John F. Kennedy, there were signs of change. Ironically, they were first visible in the efforts to deal with youthful crime, as community-action programs were legislated in the Youth Offenses Control Act of 1961. "Juvenile delinquency"—more dramatically, the gang wars of slum youth depicted in the musical *West Side Story*—was a central concern of the period. But in the debates over that one issue, themes were debated that were to set the framework for the entire antipoverty effort of the sixties.

Simply put, poverty was coming to be seen not as the fault of the poor but as a condition imposed upon them by the society and the economy.

Saul Alinsky, the gruff, utterly irreverent theorist and practitioner of confrontation politics, who first became known for his success in mobilizing white, working-class ethnics in the "back of the yards" area of Chicago, argued that poverty was not a psychic problem of deviant individuals but a consequence of economic insecurity. Two social scientists, Richard Cloward and Lloyd Ohlin, went a step farther: "Delinquency is not, in the final analysis, a property of individuals or even subcultures; it is a property of social systems in which these individuals are enmeshed." There were others in this debate—experts from the Ford Foundation, for instance—who thought that one could use existing institutions to deal with these problems. But the main thrust of the dialogue was that one would have to take on the power structure itself, that conflict was going to be as necessary as compassion.

Then, in 1962, the focus shifted from delinquency to poverty. The Council of Economic Advisors had decided that the nation faced "structural" unemployment that would not respond to Keynesian fiscal and monetary cures. Robert Lampman, one of the few economists of the fifties concerned with the poor (John Kenneth Galbraith, though the title of *The Affluent Society* was massively misconstrued by people who had not read the book, was another), wrote a memo showing that between 1956 and 1961 there had been a slowing down in the rate of eliminating poverty. That memo was passed on to the young President. So was my book *The Other America*.

The disputes about what to do became, of course, more intense when the subject matter shifted from juvenile delinquency to a major national program to end poverty in the United States. So Lyndon Johnson turned to Sargent Shriver to unite the battling factions and to come up with a program that could be law by the 1964 Presidential election.

I have already written about my brief and modest participation in these events. I do so again because I happened to observe some debates and decisions that had a great deal to do with what took place long after I departed. I had been invited to have lunch with Shriver two days after he was appointed (the call came via Frank Mankiewicz and Paul Jacobs). That lunch turned into a two-week, seven-days-a-week, sixteen-to-eighteen-hours-a-day participation in the original task force that shaped the first concept of the War on Poverty—a concept that was never really put into practice.

First, the mood. The antipoverty program was not a civil rights program, but it was, in good measure, a result of the civil rights movement. Martin Luther King, Jr., focused upon the outrage of statutory segregation, not upon economics, but he knew full well that he led a people who were economic, as well as racial, pariahs. More to the point, his luminous leadership had reached the hearts of many whites as well as blacks, and had made a commitment to morality and simple humanity seem practical. I have always suspected that President Kennedy, and later President Johnson, responded to that mood; but I know, from my own experience, that almost everyone in that first antipoverty mobilization did.

For instance, friends, or even just acquaintances, of mine phoned as soon as it became public that I was working with Shriver, and asked if I could help them get jobs in this new effort, even jobs that would pay significantly less than what they were making. At the Antipoverty Task Force, which was then centered in the Peace Corps of which Shriver was the director, there was a "movement" sense of urgency: "Finish the memo tonight and have the White House send it to me by car so we can talk about it at breakfast." As Paul Jacobs quipped, "Sarge puts benzedrine in the air-conditioning system."

The discussions were not so lighthearted, since serious questions of ideology, money, and power were at stake. There was, as I noted in the last chapter, a good deal of indecision and ignorance and more than a little contradiction. One of the most basic conflicts was between those (the Department of Health, Education and Welfare; the Council of Economic Advisors) who wanted to make community action the centerpiece, and those (the Department of Labor) who saw jobs and full employment as the key. The Shriver task force was created precisely to break the bureaucratic impasse. And, after those first two hectic weeks, we came up with something like a consensus. The government's programs dealing with the poor, everyone agreed, were scattered throughout every department; they were uncoordinated and often contradictory. For instance, there were programs to move people out of the cities—and other programs to move them back in. What was needed, we said, was not another "line" agency charged with some special function. There were already too many of those. Rather, there should be a central coordinating institution with privileged access to the President, which would try to give some kind of coherence to efforts that too often canceled one another out. Shriver was to be Lyndon Johnson's "chief of staff," not his battlefield commander.

The day before Shriver was to make his first presentation to the President, Frank Mankiewicz, Paul Jacobs, and I decided, rather quixotically, to write a proposal setting forth what should be done rather than what seemed politically expedient. So we developed a fairly radical statement of that consensus about the need for coordination, arguing that there would have to be considerable restructuring of the economy and society if poverty was to be abolished. To our amazement, Shriver incorporated about 80 percent of our ideas into the outline he took to Johnson. Even more astonishing, Shriver reported that the President said that if it took such measures to win the fight, he would take them.

But our relatively radical version of the task force's consensus never came to pass—and neither did any version of it. The "war on poverty," James Sundquist (a member of the task force) shrewdly remarks, became "the poverty program." LBJ's soaring phrases—an "unconditional" war on poverty—came to describe a very worthwhile, extremely modest, and, with a few exceptions, conventional reality. The office that was supposed to mobilize all the jostling, partial solutions into a great and concerted campaign soon became in itself a jostling, partial solution. Most of what it did was successful, but not in terms of that original idea.

The problem was that many Americans heard the President's rhetoric and did not notice that reality contradicted it. They thought the nation was doing so much because they had it on the highest authority—only the highest authority was wrong. Daniel Patrick Moynihan commented in the early seventies that the program was "oversold and underfinanced to the point that its failure was almost a matter of design." That is right if one understands that what "failed" was an original plan that was never implemented. But the overselling of a good cause had serious—and bad—consequences. First, when things did not get dramatically better for the poor in the second half of the sixties, there was frustration, rage, and even violence because of broken promises. And, second, when things became problematic for everyone in the seventies, people could say, "If only we had not been so foolishly generous to the poor, this would not have happened." The savior that never was became the scapegoat that is.

II

Why did this happen? Did cynical politicians simply manipulate the issue for their own purposes? Events were, and are, much more complex than that.

The basic reason why Lyndon Johnson's commitment "to eliminate the paradox of poverty in the midst of plenty" failed was the war in Vietnam. Other factors were at work. This, however, was the reason. Even if all the other problems could have been solved, the wrong war in Southeast Asia would have destroyed the right war at home.

There is a rhythm in federal innovations. A new idea is broached—say, social security or food stamps—and a principle is adopted. In the first year or so, not much money is spent as plans are laid, guidelines established. Then there is a steady increase in expenditures as the program goes into effect—the food stamp program cost Washington $577 million in 1970, an estimated $10.9 billion in 1984, even after the Reagan cuts. Put simply but not at all unfairly, the OEO never got much beyond the first stage. In its glory days, it received about $800 million in the first fiscal year, and a total of less than $6 billion between 1965 and 1968.

There are some fascinating figures on how much money it should have been given. If the funding provided for one of the very first experimental community-action programs in New Haven had been generalized for the nation as a whole, it would have meant outlays of between $10 and $13 billion a year. But Mitchell Svirdoff, the administrator of the New Haven effort, has argued that it only got about one-third of what it really needed. Put in national terms, that would have meant expenditures in the $30–40-billion range. One can argue—I would not agree—that the latter figure is much too high; one could even question that there should have been the actual New Haven levels of spending on a nationwide basis. But what is not debatable is the fact that the OEO, even at the time of its greatest popularity, got less than 10 percent of the lower figure. It never cost even one percent of the federal budget and never reached the "takeoff" point that is normal in most federal programs.

Vietnam was why. I had long imagined a conversation between Sargent Shriver and Lyndon Johnson. When I talked to Shriver in the fall of 1982, he confirmed that it had actually taken place. In 1966, Shriver, obviously assuming that the standard federal pattern was going to prevail, drew up an ambitious, long-range budget for the OEO that would allow it to fulfill its promise. He went to see the President in Texas in the early autumn and was told that because of the expenditures for Vietnam, there was not enough money to fulfill his request.

Why not raise taxes? Shriver asked Johnson. That, he was told, can't be done to the Democrats in Congress on the eve of an election. The President then went on to say that Secretary McNamara had assured him that the war would be over by the end of the year. In 1967 there would be no problems.

Of course, when light did finally come at the end of the Vietnam tunnel, it illuminated an American defeat, occurring at a time when the economy was already malfunctioning badly and under the administration of a Republican President who wanted to dismantle, not expand, the OEO. There were other problems with the War on Poverty, but Vietnam, it should never be forgotten, was terminal.

After the theories and visions of the task force, politics took control. The dispute about whether the emphasis should be on job training and community action was settled in Solomonic style: one major title in the law for each. The Job Corps (which was later made a part of CETA, the Comprehensive Employment and Training Act) was hardly a radical departure. In many ways it was modeled on both the New Deal experience of the thirties—the Civilian Conservation Corps—and extremely successful Defense Department programs that taught skills very quickly. It was not a failure, and there are hard numbers to suggest that it was a success.

I do not want to overestimate the results. When the Job Corps was launched, I was among the critics who pointed out that there were people being trained for jobs that didn't exist, that it was critical to have actual jobs targeted for each trainee. Those criticisms were, and still are, valid. But here, as so often in popular evaluations of the War on Poverty, problems are exaggerated into a judgment of total failure.

There are serious analyses—by the Urban Institute and the Congressional Budget Office, by Ken Auletta, and by Blanche Bernstein, the former commissioner of New York's Human Resources Administration and a "hawkish" critic of the liberals in the War on Poverty—which show that, for all its faults, the job-training effort not only helped individuals but saved money for the society as well. That accomplishment, it must be stressed, took place under the worst auspices. The original Job Corps had only a few years of operating in the relatively full employment atmosphere of the sixties. But then, in the recession of 1969–70, the American economy entered into a new period of chronic and rising joblessness. So CETA, the Job Corps' successor, was given an almost impossible charge: to prepare the most disadvantaged workers to go into a labor market that often did not have openings even for those much more skilled than they.

That problem is not simply a matter of objective economics; it also has to do with the psychology of work. Full employment creates a social atmosphere in which it is now natural for everyone to be employed. One thinks of the "unemployables" of the 1930s who toiled to such great effect in the defense factories during World War II. A guaranteed job for trainees is important and can even be created by legislative fiat; but a mass psychology that sees work as the norm is a critically important by-product of full employment. During ten of the fifteen years of the War on Poverty, its training programs confronted the exact opposite situation, an America in which joblessness was rising. And yet even serious critics, such as Blanche Bernstein, admit that it had a positive impact.

"Everyone" knows that the job program failed, just as "everyone" took the first reports of difficulties in the preschool education program, Head Start, as definitive and didn't notice that the later data showed very real gains. Community Action, the second major emphasis of the War on Poverty, was, however, a more complex case. It was not simply ignorance that turned a good part of the white working class against the War on Poverty.

Shrewd analysts, such as Frances Fox Piven and Richard Cloward, have suggested that the antipoverty effort was an attempt to contain the mounting anger at the bottom of the society by making a few modest concessions. They argued, in fact, that it was a response of liberal Democrats to the danger of losing an important black constituency. I disagree. A much more ironic dialectic was at work in which the War on Poverty generated, rather than manipulated, militancy and thus caused one of its own most serious problems. I insist upon this sad history partly because I want to avoid its recurrence in the future.

The black ghettos of 1963–64, when the poverty issue was placed on the agenda, were not in revolt. Between 1965 and 1968, *after* Lyndon Johnson's commitment, they were. One of the unintended consequences of that declaration of social war was to legitimize suffering, to make it honorable rather than shameful and therefore possibly militant. Another result was to excite expectations that, above all after the tragic decision to massively escalate the war in Vietnam, could not be satisfied. Frustrated hope is a potent but not always rational force. It began to pulse in the second half of the sixties.

The first five years of that decade had been characterized by a curious combination of protest and good feelings. The young blacks who began the sit-ins in 1960 were not the dispossessed from the lower depths, but, as all reports emphasized at the time, were well-dressed, unthreatening young women and men who endured the taunts of racists at the lunch counter while reading uplifting books. So, too, were the white student leftists who had made Students for a Democratic Society (SDS) a significant factor by 1964. Their slogan in the Presidential campaign of that year was not exactly revolutionary: "Part of the Way with LBJ." It reflected critical support for the President.

I remember a meeting in Washington in the early sixties. Stokely Carmichael, who was later to become a symbol of black nationalism and intransigence as leader of the Student Nonviolent Coordinating Committee (SNCC), and a white activist were reminiscing. They had been in adjoining cells in the Parchman Prison in Mississippi, had talked constantly and become friends, but had not seen each other, since they were kept under lock and key the whole time. It was only when the blessed day arrived when they were allowed to take showers that they discovered that one of them was black, the other white. They laughed as they retold the story, for the point was—then—that race really didn't make much difference to those carrying on a common struggle against racism.

But then, in the second half of the sixties, the mood changed. As the extravagant promises of an "unconditional" War on Poverty were not kept, as the ugly American intervention in Vietnam escalated, an optimistic, even trusting, generation became bitter. That shift was reflected in some of the community-action organizations.

Community action was, in part, the result of those theories developed in the analysis of juvenile delinquency. The poor, it was said, could not be the mere passive beneficiaries of the noblesse oblige of middle-class people with a conscience, above all because such a patronizing strategy would perpetuate, even with the best intentions in the world, that very sense of powerlessness which was a major part of the problem. That was true, but then some of the advocates of this view went on to suggest that Washington should fund revolutionary action against the power structure, a notion that ignored the fact that Washington was the pinnacle of the power structure.

At the same time, there was a conservative rationale for the idea of "maximum feasible participation of the poor" in the War on Poverty. Sargent Shriver, a man with a deeply religious social conscience, also came from the world of business. There would be, he told us, no "leaf raking," no make-work in the antipoverty campaign. The poor were going to participate in the sense that they would not be allowed to goof off. And at the local level there were more than a few mayors who thought that "maximum feasible participation of the poor" meant that the elected representatives of the people in City Hall were going to control the program.

So there was, as Daniel Patrick Moynihan wrote later, "maximum feasible misunderstanding," and that had very much to do with some Americans turning against the War on Poverty. Not, mind you, that community action was a failure; it *did* empower people all over the country. Cesar Chavez, who has done so much to organize the farm workers, came out of the Alinsky school and practiced both confrontation and alliance-building to great effect. The white college students who went to Mississippi in the "freedom summer" of 1964 did not always act wisely—they sometimes gratuitously offended the local mores and made it all the more difficult to carry on the necessary struggle against racism—but their work, and then the self-organization of the black South in voter-registration campaigns, helped transform America. A conservative social critic like Tom Wolfe can poke fun at guilty liberals who allowed themselves to be "Mau-Maued" into concessions by revolutionary rhetoricians, but there were rent strikes and campaigns against "redlining" (banks refusing to invest in poor neighborhoods, which were defined by a red line on a map) which helped build a community-action movement that survives to this day.

But community action in the sixties also collided head-on with an ugly prejudice that was, however, rooted in a reality of American society.

That reality, the dirty little secret of our country, is that most Americans don't have enough money. Most are not poor—*and* most are not affluent. So when hard-working people *thought*—wrongly—that the government was showering their tax dollars on "lazy welfare cheats," it was infuriating. And when aggressive representatives of those "welfare cheats" lectured the nonpoor, but nonaffluent, people on their obligation to pay even more, that was the last straw. This situation was compounded by what one might call the sociology of rhetoric. Words are highly political.

Poor is a "good" word. It resonates in the United States with values deeply embedded in the Judeo-Christian tradition. In the Jubilee Year of ancient Israel, debts were forgiven, wealth was leveled; in the Sermon on the Mount, Christ, who was born in a stable, made clear his identification with the lowly and downtrodden. In Western, and American, culture, it is a sign of piety and decency to be concerned for the poor. When you feed the hungry, Christ said, you feed me. To be sure, Western civilization honored that conviction in the breach more than in practice, yet it is always there to move one to sympathy and even to action.

Welfare is a "bad" word. It describes people who are lazy and dedicated to cheating society as a whole. It is well known in many country clubs that the typical welfare recipient in the United

States has a freezer filled with steak, or even a shiny car parked right behind the tenement or housing project. These people, the popular wisdom knows, are mainly promiscuous black women with huge families spawned to raise their benefits and to protect them from having to work. These "facts" make Aid for Families of Dependent Children (AFDC) one of the most unpopular federal programs.

Never mind that in 1979 most AFDC recipients were white (51.7 percent as against 43 percent black and 4.4 percent American Indian or other), or that in the same year 70.5 percent of the AFDC families had one or two children and only 13.9 percent had four or more. Forget that the percentage of children born outside of marriage increased much less rapidly among AFDC mothers than it did in the population as a whole in recent years. Disregard the fact that in 1980 the average monthly payment to AFDC families was $280 ($88 a month in Mississippi, $376 in New York), a sum that would not put much steak in the freezer. Ignore the reality that in 1983 the revenue lost by special treatment of capital gains was $28 billion, while AFDC payments from Washington were estimated at $8.2 billion.

There is an even larger irony in all of this. Henry Aaron of the Brookings Institution has documented that between 1961 and 1976, federal spending for the poor increased from $4.6 billion to $34.6 billion—and outlays for the nonpoor went from $29.4 billion to $197.8 billion. The poverty portion of the federal budget moved from 4.7 percent in 1961 to 9.4 percent in 1976, but nonpoverty social spending rose from 30.1 percent to 54 percent. The reason for these trends is simple: truly massive monies were allocated to raising and indexing social security benefits and providing Medicare for the aging. In each case, the nonpoor, who are roughly 85 percent of the people over sixty-five, got much, much more than the poor.

But were the working and middle-class people who railed against those "welfare cheats" simply wrong? Not at all. Middle America did pay more than its proportionate share of the costs of welfare, and there was a significant group of Americans who were freeloading. But the "cheats" were the very rich who received huge but discreet welfare benefits through the tax system, not the poor. There was, then, reality—misperceived reality—at the core of the prejudice against the AFDC mothers.

These intricacies do not, however, make the prejudice any less ugly. If Lyndon Johnson had declared a "war for the welfare recipients" he would have been hooted down. Welfare is, for largely mistaken reasons, "bad"; the poor are "good."

To the degree that public attention shifted from the poor to the welfare recipients, support for federal action declined. AFDC had nothing to do with the Office of Economic Opportunity. Yet when, in the sixties and early seventies, there was a welfare "explosion," all programs for the poor were blamed. There were just under 3 million welfare recipients in 1960 and 10.8 million in 1976, when the trend peaked. Between 1968 and 1972, new cases were added to the rolls at a double-digit rate, with the highest increase—26.2 percent—in 1971.

I refer to the welfare "explosion" in quotes. Why, if the numbers are so large and clear? Because this was an explosion only in terms of the exceedingly low point of departure. In 1960, there were about 3 million AFDC recipients out of (according to the official count) 39.9 million poor people. So only 10 percent of the impoverished were on the rolls in the first place. And in the peak year of 1976, with 10.8 million getting AFDC, there were 25 million Americans officially defined as poor, and less than half of them received AFDC benefits.

Public opinion is not, however, based upon the careful analysis of relative numbers and trends. The average American became aware of a gigantic "welfare mess" in the late sixties and early seventies. And since the general mood of the nation was changing—from the buoyant optimism that accompanied the years of growth in the sixties to the cranky pessimism that came with the economic roller coaster of the seventies—the "War on Poverty" was blamed for developments that were totally beyond its control. The nation had stopped thinking about the "good" poor; it was now concerned with the "bad" welfare chiselers.

But if the OEO had not initiated that tripling of a benefit population, which had been much too low to begin with, what did cause that increase? At least two factors were at work, both of them unintended consequences of the Johnsonian rhetoric. The poor themselves were told in 1964 that they were not to blame for their poverty, that the nation was responsible. As a result, at least some of the stigma that had attached to welfare disappeared. It was no longer dishonorable to claim rights to which one had been entitled all along but had never used out of a sense of shame. At the same time, the social workers who ran the system were profoundly affected by the new cultural mood and began to see themselves—quite rightly, in my opinion—as advocates rather than bureaucrats.

Frances Piven and Richard Cloward saw this new situation as an opportunity for radical organizing. As they described it some years later: "The mood of applicants in the welfare waiting room had changed. They were no longer as humble, as self-effacing, as pleading; they were more indignant, angrier, more demanding." This atmosphere, Piven and Cloward thought, opened up the possibility of disrupting the system itself by making maximum demands upon it, thereby provoking a political crisis. A Democratic Party that had been trying to cap the volcano would no longer be able to hold back a social explosion.

That strategy was spelled out in late 1965. The next year, the National Welfare Rights Organization (NWRO) came into existence under the leadership of George Wiley, an extremely talented and decent scientist who had become a major leader in the Congress of Racial Equality (CORE), one of the most important civil rights organizations of the period. But, Piven and Cloward note, NWRO never really got off the ground; at its peak it only enrolled 22,000 members in 1969 (out of a total potential jurisdiction of around 9 million). The problem, they write, was that as soon as individuals got their benefits, they saw no further need for the organization.

If, however, welfare rights organizing was not the basic reason for the increase in the AFDC rolls, it was very much part of the mood that was to anger the white working class. Most American working people will do almost anything to avoid welfare. They believe with a deep passion in the Protestant work ethic. I discovered this in a vivid way in the mid-seventies when I debated a conservative New York television commentator before an audience of members of District Council 37 of the American Federation of State, County and Municipal Employees. In the first part of the debate I had no trouble winning the audience to my side. After all, I was attacking a man who was a foe of the public sector in which the listeners worked.

But then my opponent started to attack welfare. The audience, the majority of which was black, responded enthusiastically, angrily. It seemed that almost everyone there had some outrageous story about loafing and cheating. The point is, the American work ethic is a matter of social class and has nothing to do with race. But when the believer in the work ethic is white and has some vague racist idea that AFDC is black, "welfare" becomes doubly damned. For that person the sight of a militant AFDC mother on the local evening news as she demands her rights is an incitement to rage.

I remember the tension in Chicago at the meeting of the platform committee of the Democratic National Convention in 1968. I was there to testify on social and economic issues on behalf of the McCarthy campaign, and so was present when a woman from NWRO was given the floor. She lashed out at the committee and the Democratic Party for not having done half enough, and she was quite right. But her stance was confrontational and made me more than uneasy, even though I thought her points were substantial. At the end of her allotted time the chair asked her to conclude, and she launched into a tirade, saying that she was not yet ready to "give the platform back" to them. She finished in her own good time and told the chair that he could have his platform back. The content of her statement, it seemed to me, had been subverted by the way in which it was presented.

It was good that the poor stopped being ashamed of themselves and started demanding their rights. Most of them were not responsible for their plight. The welfare state, as the brilliant British analyst Richard Titmus pointed out some time ago, is in large measure inadequate compensation for the actions of a "diswelfare state." Society in pursuit of its own goals harms entire groups and classes of people; for example, the mechanization of Southern agriculture drives hundreds of thousands of uneducated people out of the fields and into the cities. The nonpoor gain—they benefit from an increase in agricultural productivity—and those who were displaced in order to make that efficiency possible are then given minimal help in dealing with their disrupted, even impossible, lives.

It is simple justice, not arrogance, to denounce this outrage and to demand redress. The community-action programs encouraged people to do precisely that. But very early on, the politicians moved to keep community action from making any serious changes. In 1967 there was a "city hall amendment" which guaranteed that the local elected officials would have control over the "maximum feasible participation of the poor." Indeed, the program was not sufficiently tame to win the support of a majority of Republicans in the House of Representatives and almost half of the OEO's most vociferous critics, the Southern Democrats (who came from the poorest part of the United States!).

But if the hopes that community action would effect a real transfer of political and economic power to the other America were thus disappointed very early on, the radical rhetoric intensified even as the conservative political reality asserted itself. The price was the increased anger of the working-class and middle-class critics of the antipoverty effort. In a very thoughtful critique of the demonstrations at the 1968 Democratic Convention, the radical journalist I. F. Stone remarked that acting in a revolutionary fashion in a nonrevolutionary period is an invitation to counterrevolution. So it was.

III

Vietnam had subverted the War on Poverty almost before it began; Presidential rhetoric that was too hopeful, and militant rhetoric that was ineffectively angry, further compounded the problem; and finally, it was the malfunctioning of the American economy in the seventies that set the stage for Ronald Reagan's war on the poor of 1981–82. It was a most improbable reformer, Richard Nixon, who first blundered into the new reality.

In one sense, Nixon's Family Assistance Plan of 1969 (FAP) was a response to the problem we had defined in the Shriver task force of 1964. Daniel Patrick Moynihan, who was Nixon's chief advisor on social policy in 1969 and 1970, had been on the task force and then became instrumental in convincing the new President that he should become a "Tory Democrat" on the model of Benjamin Disraeli. The core concept of FAP was that of a guaranteed annual income for all citizens, although Nixon often denied that his proposal was that bold for fear of offending his conservative friends with what seemed to be a leftist idea. Yet what was clear from the outset was that this was a way of dealing with the fragmentation of the American welfare system.

Nixon's motives were technocratic, not populist like Johnson's. Welfare was a "mess" because it was fifty different programs, and that, it was said, caused people to move from stingy to generous states. (The data actually make that point questionable.) To be sure, the fact that a good part of the left, including many of the community organizers and the now-radicalized SDS, had made the idea their own was a drawback for the Republican President. But then, hadn't Milton Friedman long ago advocated a "negative income tax" as a substitute for the entire welfare state? And wasn't the negative income tax—in which, at a certain low income level, the government pays the citizen in proportion to his/her lack of income rather than, as in the positive income tax, the citizen paying the government in proportion to his/her income—a technique for providing the guaranteed annual income?

It wasn't that simple. There was, for instance, the problem of the "notch." A basic concept of FAP was to encourage people to work by ending the hallowed American custom of reducing welfare by a dollar for every dollar earned—i.e., of imposing a 100-percent tax on "lazy" beneficiaries. Under the new proposal, the welfare recipient who took a job would only be progressively phased out of public assistance as earnings mounted. But what about Medicaid, food stamps, and other means-tested programs?

By getting a job and increasing cash income, a person could lose eligibility for such noncash programs and could actually reduce real living standards by working hard. Below a certain income "notch," it was rational to refuse a job in order to keep the noncash goods and services.

There was a second, and related, problem. The basic, minimum benefit under FAP had to be high enough to sustain a nonworking poor family (the "dependent" poor). But if one took that level as a base, then a majority of American workers would qualify for at least some benefits because—the dirty little secret again—their actual income was less than the combined income from wages and FAP. But if the FAP benefit were set low enough to deal with this problem, it would not provide an adequate income for the nonworking family.

So there was a conflict of interest between the nonworking welfare poor in states with relatively high benefits—who would not gain at all, since the FAP minimum was less than what they were already receiving—and the working poor, who would get some help for the first time, as well as the welfare poor in states like Mississippi, where Nixon's utterly inadequate minimum amounted to a huge increase. As a result of these contradictions, FAP was not only opposed by the reactionaries but also by the black members of Congress from the most progressive states, where the bill would have little positive effect.

These difficulties were as nothing, however, compared with a problem that first surfaced in a bit of vintage Nixon cynicism.

In an attempt to get conservative support for his proposal, Nixon introduced an "obligation to work" into the bill. Actually, the President was well aware of the fact that this part of the law was unenforceable; you cannot dragoon someone into taking a job that does not exist. "I don't give a damn about the work requirement," Moynihan quotes Nixon as saying. "This is the price of getting the $1,600" (the minimum-income level, which was considered much too generous in some of the conservative Southern Congressional districts). Little did Nixon know that the unemployment levels that allowed him to make his meaningless, manipulative concession were the harbinger of a decade of chronic joblessness that would eventually destroy both the economic and political base for any campaign against poverty, whether liberal or Tory.

Joblessness was at a 4.9-percent rate in 1970 and up to 5.9 percent in 1971. By the standards of the time, that was an outrage. (In 1982–83, a decade later, those levels would seem to be a salvation.) If there had been full employment, a guaranteed annual income might have been both economically and politically feasible; under the circumstances, it was in deep trouble on both counts.

In 1969, Moynihan, refracting the liberal faith in permanent economic growth—the business cycle, it was well and erroneously known, had been tamed—wrote in *Maximum Feasible Misunderstanding* that one of the challenges to government in the future was to devise ways of spending the enormous tax revenues yielded by an ever-expanding GNP. If that had been even remotely the case—if, say, the years from 1969 to 1977 had been as prosperous as those from 1961 to 1968—then even if Moynihan's utopia had not been at hand, there would have been ample funds to finance a decent welfare minimum. And since the workers and everyone else would have been even better off than the welfare poor, anger and resentment would not have become such a force.

But it is not just that full employment would have made higher levels of social spending possible; it would have radically decreased the number of people who needed help, as well. In the sixties, the number of poor families headed by a full-time worker declined dramatically as the falling joblessness rates of the Kennedy-Johnson years made themselves felt. In the seventies, the poverty population was on the same roller coaster as the economy, going up, going down. And in the eighties, the numbers of the poor did not simply increase, which would be bad enough, but since the achievement of full employment had now become much more difficult than anyone had ever dreamed in the sixties, the abolition of poverty became that much more problematic.

As is so often the case, politics lagged behind economics. There was not a direct legislative attack on the poor in the seventies, not the least because the poverty program had acquired some bureaucratic constituents in the city halls of the nation, who were more effective advocates than the unregistered voters in the slums and backwoods. But the economy turned savagely upon the other America long before Ronald Reagan became President. Between 1973 and 1981, the real value of food stamps fell by 12 percent, and AFDC benefits, measured in constant dollars, declined by 28 percent between 1972 and 1981. Indeed, an AFDC family of four, with no earnings and food stamps, had 4 percent less buying power than an AFDC family in 1969, before food stamps became available.

These trends resulted in countless private tragedies, but something more sinister and public was taking place at the same time, preparing a mass audience to accept Reagan's cruel oversimplifications and outright distortions in the 1980s. In the sixties, Kennedy and Johnson had persuaded the people that social justice was smart economics. Johnson, in particular, emphasized how rebuilding the cities and educating the poor would create jobs, profits, and increased productivity. The economy, it was said, was no longer a "zero-sum game" where winners pay losers and someone's gain must be another person's loss. Now America was playing a "positive-sum game" in which, if no one group got too demanding, all would be satisfied from the dividends of endless growth, and a social revolution would take place without the inconvenience of changing any institutions.

All that was the euphoric overgeneralization of a decade of growth, but it was also potent politics. But as the seventies lurched from economic crisis to economic crisis, a contrary and much grander oversimplification took over: It was social spending, all that money lavished on the poor and the minorities, that had caused the drop in productivity and even corrupted the very moral fiber of the society. If only those funds had been invested in machines, if only the rich had been given money to put into factories, all would be better, even for the poor. Where the sixties believed that justice was good economics, the seventies, in a desperate search for a scapegoat for a "stagflation" no one had predicted and few understood, asserted that meanness was good economics.

So it was that there was very little public protest when, in

1981, the new President imposed 60 percent of his budget cuts upon the poor: AFDC was reduced by 11.7 percent, food stamps by 18.8 percent, other food programs by 13.3 percent. There was considerable administration talk about a "safety net," but this really meant that the White House had courageously declared that it would not challenge programs with strong political backing, like social security.

These were some of the reasons why an Urban Institute study discovered that between 1979 and 1984, income inequality grew significantly. The bad times had lowered the incomes of the richest fifth by .5 percent and that of the poorest fifth by 9.4 percent. Most shocking of all, taxes for the bottom quintile went up from 9.7 percent of income in 1979 to 11.9 percent in 1984, while the rates of the richest fifth *declined* by .5 percent.

Thus, America under Ronald Reagan turned savagely against a gigantic antipoverty boondoggle that never took place. And, for a complex series of reasons—their own economic insecurity first and foremost—decent people who had welcomed the War on Poverty now supported the war on the poor.

IV

In June of 1980, there was a wake for the War on Poverty, though it was not billed as such.

It was a celebration of VISTA, the "domestic Peace Corps." In the afternoon there were cookies and punch on the White House lawn as power—diminished, threatened power, to be sure—had a last picnic with social conscience. Mrs. Carter was there, presiding over the Southern mansion the nation provides for its Presidents, escorted by a military aide in dazzling dress whites. There were activists from the sixties, like Sam Brown, the organizer of the great antiwar moratorium of 1969, who had been head of federal volunteer activity under the Carter administration; there was Ray Rogers, the trade unionist who had organized the imaginative and successful campaign to force the J. P. Stevens company to negotiate with the Amalgamated Clothing and Textile Workers; and there were activists of every race and ethnic group, veterans of Appalachian hollows and Southwestern *barrios*.

It was a tableau out of antipoverty history, one last incarnation of that coalition of noblesse oblige from the top and middle of the society, and militancy from its lower depths. Later that evening, at the Kennedy Center, when Peter and Mary (of Peter, Paul, and Mary, the movement group that had performed at so many rallies) sang "Blowin' in the Wind," it was like being in a warm, friendly time machine.

But you can't go home again, above all in the eighties, which, for the poor at least, promise to be a much nastier decade than the sixties. There is no way to go back to the strategies of another, easier time and place. So this history ultimately teaches us that we are back at Square One, or, rather, that we have advanced to a Square One with a much bleaker prospect than in 1964.

If we have learned anything from this past, we now know that the antipoverty movement of the rest of this century must be internationalist. It was the wrong and bloody war in Southeast Asia that undercut the right and nonviolent war in the United States. And it is the international economy that is now one of the main reasons that the plight of the poor is much more problematic than it was when Johnson committed the nation to end poverty. We also know that the next time around it is a matter of life and death to include the organized workers and the middle class in a coalition with the poor. And that is not done by declaring it to be desirable or necessary, but by developing programs that are in the interests of all three constituencies.

Finally, there must be an intellectual offensive against the conservative disinformation campaign around the War on Poverty. We must carefully document the fact that the radical and extravagant past, which is blamed for our present woes, never existed. Instead there was a decent, often timid and underfinanced program that had two or three years of hope and well over a decade of impossible problems. Under the circumstances, it did rather well. But in setting that record straight, one cannot tacitly adopt the value judgment of the right, disputing only the facts but admitting that the alleged boldness would have been a mistake if it had actually happened. The next time we will have to be as innovative in fact as the sixties were in rhetoric. If we are not, when we are faced with a much more difficult battle than that of the sixties, we will fail again. And once more it will be poverty that wins the war.

3
Limbo

There is a small monument on a bluff above the Monongahela River near Pittsburgh. It is located at a nondescript intersection, just behind a workers' bar that has become slightly fashionable. It would be easy to miss it if you didn't know it was there.

This is Homestead, the mill town where the strikers defeated the Pinkertons in a pitched and bloody battle in 1892. This is Homestead, where the steelworkers' Declaration of Independence was proclaimed on July 5, 1936, during the glory days of the legendary Steel Workers Organizing Committee. The monument to these events may be modest, but the militancy it commemorates is still alive here, sometimes to the chagrin of its official heir, the United Steel Workers of America (USW).

Is this history about to be erased? Will the fate of its descendants be like that of the Jones and Laughlin plant, which lies along the river like a beached whale? Who will buy a beached whale from Jones and Laughlin? Who will hire beached people?

It is important to be precise about who the "beached people" are. They are not the working poor, who have always hovered on the brink of poverty, one firing or one illness away from personal catastrophe. In many cases they are not even part of the nation's dirty little secret, the fact that a majority of working Americans, though not poor, don't have enough money to participate in anything that can be remotely called affluence. We are talking now mainly about the "labor aristocracy," the upper stratum of the working class. Indeed, it is precisely because these people have enjoyed a relatively privileged position among workers that what is happening to them now is as much a psychological as an economic shock.

These people are not yet poor, and a good number of them will, after harrowing and humiliating experiences, relocate and once again join the economic mainstream. So it is wrong to say that all the unemployed steelworkers and auto workers and others from the smokestack industries of the industrial heartland are the "new poor" of the eighties. That was a media exaggeration of the winter of 1981–82. But—and this is the unprecedented aspect of the situation—a significant number of them could become poor, particularly the ones who are forty or older. We enter, then, a limbo, a place of in-between, where everyone is suddenly confronted with the frightening, totally unexpected prospect of being pushed down into poverty, and where, for some, that fear will become reality.

This chapter could have not been written twenty or twenty-five years ago, during the rediscovery of poverty in the United States, because its subject matter did not yet exist. That is a measure of how new, how shattering, this phenomenon is.

I

If you ask the unemployed steelworkers in the Mon (Monongahela) Valley about their social class, they do not have a moment's hesitation: the middle class. "We pay the taxes and take care of the kids and go out for beer and pizza," a steelworker's wife—an activist in her own right—insisted. "We're middle class." Or, as Douglas Fraser, the former president of the auto workers' union put it, they are "working people of the middle class," a sociological contradiction and a psychological fact in a country where the working class exists but cannot say its own name.

That is ironic in a physical and social setting which all but shouts that name. The landscape of the place is Appalachian, with ridges and hollows, but the industrial geography is the Ruhr or Wales. Mills hulk along the valley floor in the center of grimy towns, rows of houses ride the crests of the hills. One can see ethnicity with the naked eye: the onionlike spires of a Greek Orthodox church; the Slovak inscription on a school; the basement with a soup kitchen, which Irish-American nuns rent from Hungarian-American Protestants. Everything about the place asserts its working-class character, except the workers.

It is more complicated than that, of course. True enough, there are third-generation steel families. But if the unemployed woman worker volunteering at the Catholic soup kitchen is the daughter of a laid-off father (who has thirty years' seniority but still isn't working) and the granddaughter of a millhand, the seeming continuity masks an enormous shift. In the early years of the century, the unskilled got $1.98 for a twelve-hour day; last year, one unemployed activist told me, he made almost $30,000.

But then it is precisely that gain which makes the current situation such a wrenching experience, for it shatters an identity that was not inherited but forged in the course of many struggles. The lawyer-doctor-managerial middle class did not have to shoot it out with the Pinkertons to get into the country club; but these "working people of the middle class" had to fight, and even die, to win beer and pizza and the possibility that their children could go to college and escape from these valleys. Now that dream is in tatters, and the dreamers are suddenly looking into a social abyss.

But they are not yet poor. This is not a quibble over definitions, but the recognition of the difference between two worlds. With relatively few exceptions, like the movement led by Martin Luther King, Jr., the poor have not been organized. Their fury is often self-destructive (alcoholism, drug addiction, family violence) or criminal, and even their collective action tends to be sporadic, like the riots of the past two decades. But the men and women in these steeltowns are not beaten down—at least not yet—and they are trade unionists, accustomed to a certain discipline and purposiveness. They, like most working people in this country, are contemptuous of welfare. They will consume their savings, double up with relatives, borrow, do almost anything to avoid taking money from the government.

Let me stress again that that attitude is a function of class, not race. Several years before I met the white steelworkers of the Mon Valley, I talked to black auto workers in St. Louis who shared the very same attitudes about welfare recipients. They had, they told me, all known that such people were lazy and irresponsible. Only now they were learning in a most bitter way—more than a year of unemployment—that they had been glib and superficial.

And yet I suspect that the psychological shock of prolonged—seemingly endless—unemployment may be greater among whites than blacks. The latter do share the strong feeling of the "working people of the middle class" that income should be a compensation for labor. But they come from a world where, because of the structured inequality imposed upon blacks and other minorities in the economy, Aid for Families of Dependent Children is a commonplace. So it was that, some years ago, when strikers could still qualify for food stamps in New York, the blacks in one union had to take the whites and show them how to apply for that benefit. Indeed, as one leader of that local remarked to me not too long ago, the white workers may now be victimized by whatever racism infects them. If they now have to contemplate Medicaid and food stamps and even AFDC, that means they are becoming, in their own terms, black.

In the winter of 1983 I talked to the activists at the Mon Valley Unemployed Committee in McKeesport, Pennsylvania. They were not yet at the point of no return, and since then there has been a slight upturn in employment in the area. Yet if these impressions are marked by a particular time and place, they are typical of the problems faced by hundreds of thousands or even millions of workers in the smokestack industries of the American industrial heartland.

McKeesport is a steeltown near Pittsburgh, with a huge mill

at its core. The plant was almost completely shut down in January 1983, and the results were plain to see. Department stores and smaller shops were closed. On the plate-glass doors of what had been a "quad" movie theater, a leaflet announced the opening of a "Depression-style soup kitchen" at the Y.

A few blocks from this scene of municipal decay there is a three-story building, remarkable only for the fact that it is located opposite a railroad tower without a railroad (it is a preserved landmark, like the Jones and Laughlin plant). This is the headquarters of an antipoverty agency on its way, like others of its kind around the country, toward oblivion. But there were still hyperkinetic dropouts attending class, and there was some weatherizing equipment—from a very rational program employing the poor to protect the poor against winter—out in the parking lot. The atmosphere was shabby—there was a hole in a corridor wall, and insulation was hanging out.

The Mon Valley Unemployed Committee had an office on the third floor and it brimmed with energy, like every "movement" headquarters in the first phase of a difficult but exhilarating struggle. The organizers have all worked in the mills, and it soon became clear that most of them were atypical, having been involved in some kind of political work before. They had begun as a committee within the USW, and many of them had been opponents of union concessions to management, but now they had broadened their base to include all of the unemployed. Moreover, even if some of these people were veterans of earlier battles, the mood was not at all that of the sectarian left. As one of the militants without a radical background—an Irish Democrat and proud of it—explained to me, you could have any kind of past and any kind of philosophy, but you had to keep both out of the day-to-day work.

The committee had arranged for me to go to the home of a black woman who had been forced to get AFDC when her husband—a supervisor, not a production worker—had lost his job. She was proof that life is not quite as obvious as the simplistic scenarios about a "new poverty" imply.

At first I thought I had a rendezvous with a stereotype, a

woman forced into AFDC in a house that, for a while, had had all the utilities turned off and even now lacked phone service. But that house turned out to be a neat little structure on a well-kept block with a reassuring church on the corner. The "welfare mother" was not a stereotype but a striking, articulate young woman who had done some modeling. The children were bright and attractive, and when they and their mother posed for a photograph, one thought of a caption about the triumph of the black middle class. The marriage was intact, but the husband didn't want to talk to me, which was likely a reaction arising from wounded pride. The mother freely admitted she had done some hard drinking when the layoff came, but that episode was over now. So far, almost nothing corresponded to my expectations. And yet there was no phone, the furniture came from a charity agency, the bank had almost foreclosed the mortgage, and there had been no presents on Christmas Day. This woman, then, was not a representative of the "new poor," but of the new possibility of poverty. If the economy remains reasonably strong, her family will go back to being "middle class" without any trouble. If not, it could become unambiguously poor.

The contrast in three food lines I visited reinforced these complexities. At Intersection, the center run by the Irish Catholic nuns in the basement of the Hungarian church, the atmosphere was redolent of welfare poverty, of the walking wounded who limp and hurt even during the good times when the mills are hiring. I felt at home, since I had lived with such people for two years at the Catholic Worker when I was a young man. And the nuns who ran the place had the warmth and deeply religious decency that I had found among the best people at the Worker. "We started out being a Catholic center," Sister Peg said, "but then Protestants came to help and we said the project was Christian, and Jews came and we said it was Judeo-Christian, and finally atheists pitched in and we didn't use labels any more."

Most of the men and women waiting in the basement for lunch were, it seemed to me, beaten. Defeated. Even the man who had completed a two-year CETA program that led nowhere struck me as resigned more than angry. And down at the Y, an incongruously modern building for a self-styled "Depression soup kitchen," there were few takers on the first day of the project. Admission was supposed to depend upon a union card, but people with union cards don't want to be told they are at a "Depression-style soup kitchen." The affable young black woman in charge of the kitchen had figured that out and was talking about changing the name. To be poor in America is to be unable to afford your pride, and there is still plenty of pride in these valleys, even if there is little money.

And yet, at the Steel Workers' local down at the Edgar Thompson works in Braddock, Pennsylvania, men and women walked briskly down a line, picking up paper bags of food. That local—and many others as well, and the Mon Valley Committee itself—do this twice a month to supplement, but not provide for, the diet of the unemployed workers. At Christmas there had been turkeys. At first, I was told, two hundred people showed up; then four hundred; recently more than one thousand. I thought that the mood might be depressed and dejected, but it was social and lighthearted. The food line had become a break in the endless routine of waiting for the plants to reopen, even a time for socializing. It was self-help, not charity—the union, not the government or even the Y.

I do not want to romanticize. I was told of people in the area who seemed to be coping but took out their frustration in private drinking and spouse-battering. In December I had talked to Ted Barrett, the director of Region Nine of the UAW, the New England region of the union. They had been hit badly by layoffs, and the union was starting storefront centers to help the jobless make it through the winter. The standard pathologies of unemployment were all there, Barrett told me: the alcoholism, the beaten wives, and—perhaps most important, he thought—the guilty, angry abuse of children.

Still, hope was not dead. At the Braddock union local, I talked to the wife of an unemployed steelworker who was volunteering to help out with the food distribution. She had been a beautician and had just finished an introductory CETA course and was going on to a two-year community college program in data processing.

Her husband, she said, was going to the CETA office the next week.

That, Ronald Reagan would say, is proof of the rightness of his policies. If only the unemployed would go out and look for work, they would find it. And that young woman helping out on the food line, his argument would say, had instinctively made the right decision, relocating herself in a high-tech occupation like data processing. But there are problems with this perspective, and I will be blunt about them.

We encounter questions about the future here, and in a time when the professional forecasters and the econometric models have been wrong more often than they have been right, because the old variables are changing, it would be foolish to pretend to any great precision about what will happen down the road.

Even so, I believe there is compelling evidence that structural changes in the very nature of work and income in the United States are likely to make it impossible for a good number of those steelworkers to find jobs outside their own industry on terms acceptable to them—or to the society. This theme, as we shall see, does not simply apply to the new poverty of the traditional working class; it is a critical factor in the new poverty of the new working class, of blacks and women as well. What follows is a first look at a phenomenon of enormous importance.

We have it on the authority of the conservative economist Rudolph Penner, the man who became director of the Congressional Budget Office under the Reagan Presidency with a Republican majority in the Senate, that between 1978 and 1983 there was a dramatic increase "in the number of poor persons in young two-parent families." This intact and youthful family was once a source of great optimism. Poverty, it was and is still said, is simply the result of family breakdown, and when husband and wife remain together it vanishes rapidly. But in 1982 the intact family constituted the largest poverty group: 40 percent of the poor as against 35 percent for families headed by a non-elderly woman. (The relative decrease of the latter category was accompanied by an absolute increase and thus did not signal an improvement in its status, but only a worsening in the fate of the intact families.)

However, it is true, as Penner testified, that declining unemployment rates will probably better the situation of those young families. But how much? Here one encounters the fact that the recession of 1981–82 coincided with a significant change in the very structure of work and income in the United States. This does not mean that *all* of those families plunged into poverty will remain there. It does suggest that more of them will stay poor than would have done so in the past. It is a sign, then, of the new poverty of the traditional working class.

Barry Bluestone, a brilliant economist at Boston College, has defined the structural change that leads to this pessimistic assessment. A significant number of American workers are "skidding" from job to job in the eighties. That is, they are unemployed and find new work, which is good—but they find new work at a much lower rate of pay, which is not only an individual but a societal problem. Work in the electronic components industry rose by 75.9 percent between 1960 and 1972, and by another 25.6 percent between 1973 and 1980. When a man or a woman shifts from the primary metals industry to the electronic components industry, his or her new salary is only 61 percent of the old.

The same factor operates in jobs for new entrants to the labor force. The greatest number of openings are being created in the service sector (food, health, business services), where wages are low. In late 1983, both *Business Week* and *Fortune* noted that the American class structure was bifurcating, with the upper class and the lower class growing, the middle contracting. But that middle, Bruce Steinberg commented in *Fortune*, was precisely the great mass market of the American economy, the place where one found huge numbers of buyers for consumers' durable goods such as washing machines and coffeemakers. "Skidding," therefore, is not simply a personal tragedy for individual workers. It is a moment in a vicious downward spiral for the society as a whole—some workers drop out of the middle, which contracts the market and therefore causes more workers, who had been producing for that middle, to drop out. And the spiral continues.

Blanche Bernstein, the "hard line" critic of welfare, forgets this tremendous economic factor. The jobs of the eighties, she writes with considerable complacency in *The Politics of Welfare*, will pay about half the wage of factory jobs which are disappearing. In 1983 the Bureau of Labor Statistics confirmed Bernstein's prediction. In the decade of the eighties, the bureau said, there would be half a million new jobs for both nurse's aides and janitors, 400,000 openings for fast-food workers, 377,000 for general office clerks—and only 133,000 places for computer operators and 112,000 for programmers. But what will happen to the United States if it reaches a new employment equilibrium at the cost of half of the income of former workers in smokestack industries, if there is downward social mobility within the traditional American working class?

The established wisdom tells the auto workers to take a permanent cut in wages on the grounds that their income had been too high; similar advice is given to the steelworkers. It is as if the society has developed a collective amnesia with regard to one of the central clichés of the growth years of the fifties and sixties, which states that increases in the buying power of the great mass of the people is a precondition for further expansion and for high profits. So even if the human rejects of basic industry were to find new jobs at lower pay, that would be very bad news, not simply for the individuals involved, but for the American economy as a whole.

Moreover, the theories about "relocating" vast numbers of people is overoptimistic in the extreme.

Between 1960 and 1978, employment in the steel industry declined by about 100,000 jobs, roughly 20 percent of the total. Almost all of that loss was concentrated in production, where the total number of workers went down by 25 percent. That, however, was nothing like the shutdowns which have occurred in the last two or three years. If a young woman who had been a beautician can become a data processor, and if perhaps her steelworker husband can do so too, can a hundred thousand men and women follow in their path? And what about the people in their late forties or early fifties? Will they, in the words of the UAW song, be "too old to work and too young to die"?

The answer to that last question is not completely hypothetical. After I got back from McKeesport, I talked to an Ohio organizer who had been involved in Youngstown, where the disaster hit much earlier than it did in Pennsylvania. After the first wave of layoffs in the seventies, she told me, a fair number of young workers did find new jobs, even within the steel industry. But with the more recently unemployed, the situation is completely different. Some of the mills are being physically dismantled—which is happening in the Pittsburgh area—and it becomes hard to believe that there ever will be work again.

At the same time—and this is one of the many complexities that do not fit under the rubric of the "new poor"—the fact that they are homeowners makes it difficult for them to pull up stakes and look for work elsewhere. Whatever they had been able to save had gone into equity in a modest house, and they are fighting to keep that intact. Moreover, if they did leave and try to sell the house, who would buy it? So people stay and try to hang on. When the unemployment benefits run out, the Youngstown organizer continued, a lot of families manage to survive because the wife is able to find a job in a fast-food place or some other low-wage operation in the service sector. Not too long ago, some of the thinkers at the Brookings Institution discovered that America's unemployment problems were, in large measure, the fault of all those women who rushed into the labor market in the sixties and seventies.

The unstated assumption of that Brookings argument was that frivolous females pursuing "mad money" were displacing serious breadwinners. The fact, among the steelworkers in the Monongahela and Mahoning valleys (Youngstown) and among the auto workers in New England—the fact almost everywhere—is that those women are the reason why the Great Recession of 1981–82 did not turn into the Great Depression. But then, supposing that a family does manage to piece together a strategy for survival with a job at McDonald's, what about medical care?

That is one of the greatest fears one encounters among the steelworkers in McKeesport. When they lose their jobs, they also lose—how quickly depends upon the union contract—their health insurance. That insurance, however, does not simply provide coverage for the worker himself; it is the basis of medical care for his wife (if she is not working) and, above all, for their children. So, as one mother at the Mon Valley office said, one simply postpones a trip to the doctor. That can work as long as there is no medical emergency—although the health cost of decreased routine care will be paid later on, when preventable diseases occur because they were not caught in time. But what do you do in an emergency?

A "catch-22" appears. In order to qualify for Medicaid on the basis of welfare, you have to be officially poor. But precisely because these working people of the middle class have managed to achieve some equity in their house—or because they have a car worth more than a certain (quite low) sum—they are not officially poor. Give us a lien on the house, they are told; sell the car. But sell it to whom, in a city with 25- or 30-percent unemployment located in a declining region? America, Will Rogers said in the thirties, is the only nation in history to drive to the poorhouse in an automobile. To which we may now add, America is the only nation in the world where home ownership disqualifies people for medical care.

The core problem is, of course, that this country is the only advanced Western society without a system of national health. Our substitute for it has been to insure the health of 90 percent of the people through their jobs (for a family, through the job of the breadwinner—or breadwinners). However, in 1983, *The Economist* reported that there were 34 million Americans who would have no medical coverage during all or part of the year. Eleven million were in the families of workers who had lost their health insurance with their jobs. There is already a pattern—dental care is the first to go, followed by checkups and elective surgery. This situation is made all the worse because medical care is one of the few sectors in the American economy with double-digit rates of inflation (12 percent in 1982) in a time of decreasing inflation almost everywhere else.

This crisis is visible in a bitterly ironic way in the United Automobile Workers union. There are UAW members in both the United States and Canada. They work for the same multinational corporations, and in some cases watch the same television shows and root for the same professional sports teams. But the Canadians have a national health system and are spared this particular humiliation. In the fall of 1982, the UAW's magazine, *Solidarity* (the publication of a movement of workers once thought of as a blue-collar upper class—a thought that was always exaggerated, but was shared by some of the unionists themselves), printed an article on how to apply for Medicaid.

The health issue, we have just seen, is complicated by the fact that so many workers own their homes and are therefore ineligible for Medicaid. This in itself leads to further destructive ironies that underline one of the points made by that Youngstown organizer.

The Mon Valley Unemployed Committee first came to public attention because of its defense of home ownership. Laid-off workers who could not meet their mortgage payments found their houses put up on the block at the sheriff's sale. The banks that foreclosed were, in most cases, shooting fish in a barrel. The houses had been purchased with minimal down payments under various federal guarantees (the Veterans Administration, the FHA). This means that the institutional lenders are sure to get their money back even if they can't resell the house in a depressed market. It also means that it is possible to speculate on misery by picking up homes cheaply at the sheriff's sale. Everyone wins except the working people who had labored for some years to get an equity that is then expropriated (with interest charges and court costs).

The Mon Valley committee dubbed the speculators "vultures" and took to showing up at the sheriff's sale to make a great commotion. Eventually, this persuaded the sheriff—who, it is said, might run for higher office in the near future—to refuse to go on with this unpopular process, an action that was supported by a sympathetic judge—who, it is said, might run for higher office in the near future. This successful campaign was not simple self-help, as important as that is. It was a way of fighting back.

By the end of 1983, the committee had successfully lobbied a bill through the Pennsylvania state legislature which provided that the state would, with a lien on the house as security, assist unemployed workers to make the payments on their houses. In the process, the senate heard testimony from an unemployed mother who told how the bank refused a payment of $1,045 on arrears of $1,095. The family had gone without food, and the husband and wife had sold their wedding rings to get that much money, but they were still short fifty dollars. A "love offering" from their church finally made up the difference.

But—and here the second catch-22 surfaces—if these unemployed workers succeed in defending their homes, that is one more tie to their declining community. So, too, are schools, churches, neighborhoods, friends. The house, however, can be measured in dollars and cents. If they leave the community to go to another area to get a job, they face the enormous difficulty of disposing of their home in a depressed market. In effect, they have to liquidate their most important single savings account—their equity in a house—at a loss. And if there is only the promise of work somewhere else—if they leave because there are rumors that there is work in Houston, when, as was the case in the winter of 1982, joblessness was on the rise in that city—they may well give up something for nothing.

All of these difficulties were compounded for workers in Pennsylvania by an extraordinary law passed in 1982. It divided recipients of welfare into two groups: Those over forty-five years of age or under eighteen were deemed chronically needy and could get year-round help; those between eighteen and forty-five were classified as "transitionally needy" and could only qualify for three months' assistance per year. One of the ways that someone in that second category could be "promoted" to the first was by showing that he or she had worked less than four years during the past eight years. There is a great, and vicious, American pattern at work in these rules: The one group that society refuses to help is the long-term unemployed who have lost their jobs through no fault of their own. So even if those workers to whom I talked in 1982 could pass all the humiliating tests and prove that they were poor, they would get only three months of benefits since they belong to a pariah class of people who have worked hard for a living. So much for the Protestant ethic.

In the Mon Valley, the "middle-class people of the middle class" realized that they, too, were involved in these memories, thus understanding the economy better than did the economists who hailed the discipline now being imposed on working people. The lawyers, doctors, and merchants are being dragged down in the whirlpool of layoffs since their clients, patients, and customers have begun to disappear. So it seemed to me that most of the seven hundred or so who assembled at a protest meeting in the First United Methodist Church of McKeesport one January night in 1983 were members of the professional and commercial middle class.

The program opened with four fervent verses of "A Mighty Fortress Is Our God." The fourth verse thunders, "If they take our house,/Goods, fame, child or spouse,/ Wrench our life away/ They cannot win the day/ Thy Kingdom's ours forever!"—a faith that was being sorely tested in these parts. Then ministers from local churches attacked the antifamily consequences of the economic crisis. They alternated between Sunday-school didacticism and the accents of Jeremiah. The corporations and the banks were sharply criticized, but then, in keeping with the middle-class character of the event, it was proposed that government cooperate with business to solve the problem. The specific action items, such as shifting checking accounts out of irresponsible banks—"WHO CONTROLS THE $–??? MON VALLEY FAMILIES DO!!!"—and having the valley declared a disaster area under Pennsylvania state law, were, it seemed to me, unlikely to have any serious impact. Yet what was important was not so much what was being said as that these people—WASPs, not ethnic; white collar, not blue—were saying it.

Still, it is the blue-collar workers who will determine whether or not these efforts have a significant impact. They are the ones with the organizing skills, the militant tradition, and they have already succeeded in winning a victory on the home-foreclosure issue. But will they succeed in halting the ominous but as yet ambivalent trends in the direction of a new poverty?

History is ambiguous on this count. There was an unemployment movement of some twenty thousand workers in Philadelphia as early as 1832, and there have been sporadic bursts of organizing during economic crises ever since, including "Coxey's army" in 1893, which won some soup kitchens and even public works projects. In the thirties, as Frances Fox Piven and Richard Cloward have written, "most of the people who were thrown out of work suffered quietly, especially at the start of the Depression, when the official denials helped to confuse the unemployed and to make them ashamed of their plight. Men and women haunted the unemployment offices, walked the streets, lined up for every job opening, and doubted themselves for not finding work. Families exhausted their savings, borrowed from relatives, sold their belongings, blaming themselves and each other for losing the struggle to remain self-reliant."

That could have been written about the America of 1982–83 rather than about the America of 1930–31. Those who expect widespread layoffs to automatically generate angry protest and organization do not understand that the first psychological effect of massive unemployment is conservative ("How do I save myself and my family?"–not "How do I save my brothers and sisters?") and self-deprecating. But then, as Piven and Cloward document, unemployed groups did form, most of them sparked by Socialist or Communist organizers. By 1936, the Workers' Alliance, which merged all of the various groups of the unemployed, had 1,600 locals and 600,000 members.

After I got back from McKeesport, I talked to Brendan Sexton, an old friend and veteran trade unionist who had organized for the Steel Workers Organizing Committee and later had become educational director of the Auto Workers. As a young man in his twenties, Brendan had been the president of the Workers' Alliance in New York. His reminiscences highlight the similarities—and the differences—between then and now.

The organizing, he remembered, was spotty. A map of the New York locals would reveal that almost all of them were very close to a Socialist or Communist Party branch. They operated out of settlement houses—Greenwich House in the Village, Henry Street on the Lower East Side, the Brownsville Labor Lyceum in Brooklyn, the YMHA in Washington Heights—and they were, among many other things, social centers for frustrated, bored, hurt people. So the almost convivial atmosphere at the Braddock food distribution was not something new. The Alliance also acted as a union for workers on WPA projects. The writers and performing artists were particularly strong, but there was a significant laborers' local, too. And sometimes there was militant, direct action, like the sit-in at the New Jersey State House.

But there are differences. There was no unemployment compensation in those days, and the bottom dropped out the moment a man or woman lost a job. So the Alliance fought to get people on "home relief," to win immediate benefits instead of waiting for an investigation to prove that a family was truly made up of paupers, and to provide support for single men, who were not covered by any of the social programs.

There is another difference between the situations then and now, and it leads to quite sobering thoughts. The unemployment of the Great Depression was not ended by the economic policies of the New Deal. There was a recession within the Depression in 1937–38 as unemployment *rose* from 14.3 percent to 19 percent, and in 1940, the last peacetime year for the economy, the jobless rate was still 14.6 percent, i.e., higher than in 1937. It was World War II, of course, that put America back to work. And the postwar prosperity, it would now seem, was more a matter of a tremendous upturn in the entire world economy than of the brilliance of the Keynesian policies pursued, say, by an Eisenhower. Indeed, during the Kennedy-Johnson years, the triumphant period of the New Economics, American unemployment rates were generally double those in Europe.

So even the good times of recent years hardly demonstrate that the nation has found a way to deal with periodic unemployment crises. But what if, as the first chapter suggested, we have truly entered a new economic environment and the lessons of the past simply do not apply? What if the workers in McKeesport are only the first wave of those who are going to be hurt by a transformation of the world division of labor, a technological revolution, and an unprecedented internationalization of capital? How will that affect poverty in the United States?

II

The Reagan administration itself is hardly sanguine about the prospects for the future. Even as it claimed—quite wrongly—that the upturn in the spring of 1983 was a result of its own policies, it conceded that unemployment would be, at best, around 8 percent for several years to come. This means that ten million Americans will be out of work in "good" times. So Henry F. Myers, a *Wall Street Journal* columnist, was simply reflecting a consensus of left, right, and center when he wrote, in January 1983: "Many heavy industry jobs are being lost forever, and hurt the most will be many unskilled and semi-skilled workers with few chances of finding other satisfying jobs. 'Smokestack' communities are likely to be depressed indefinitely. Hopes for the 'reindustrialization' of America will be frustrated, even if the U.S. keeps its lead in some high-technology fields."

Consider first some of the short-run consequences if such an analysis is correct.

The answer of the Mon Valley Unemployed Committee is militancy, and it is clearly needed. The worst single response would be that of the period between 1929 and 1934, when most workers crawled to the margins of the society and licked their wounds in shame. But one of the differences between the thirties and the eighties, it must be recognized, militates against the effectiveness of that solution. During the Depression, blue-collar workers in the mines and mills and railroads and construction sites were the majority of the labor force and were concentrated in the Northeast and the Middle West. That gave them a "social weight," a disproportionate impact, once they finally got into motion. But what if there is a Depression in McKeesport and a recovery in Houston? What if the low-paid service industries—and the unskilled, non-union, low-paid jobs in high tech—increase, but there are "pockets" of misery with millions of people in them? There could be ghettos for the white working class, enclaves of hopelessness inside a growing GNP, just as in the black inner cities of the fifties and sixties.

Next, these people could be further isolated as the society, following one of its most hallowed rituals, blames the victims for their plight. "In common-sense terms," Henry Myers wrote in that same *Wall Street Journal* column, "many American workers have simply priced themselves out of the market." The steelworkers were, of course, cited as a particularly egregious example. But if this kind of mystification succeeds, then the people trying to fight back in McKeesport will be robbed of something essential to any successful social movement: the sympathy of people outside their own ranks. The CIO in the thirties, and the blacks in the fifties and sixties, were widely and rightly perceived as the representatives of a just cause, and not just a narrow faction. But American workers, and steelworkers in particular, have been blamed for creating their own miseries.

An Office of Technology Assessment study reported two years ago that from 1969 to 1978, "foreign hourly employment costs (in dollars) rose one and one half to three times faster than in the United States. As a result, U.S. unit labor costs moved from the highest to the second lowest. . . ." If one takes into account the social, rather than the individual, wage of foreign workers—the value of their national health care, child allowances, longer paid holidays, etc.—the cost of the American steelworker shrinks still further. And the crisis in steel is not the result of excessive environmentalism, either: From 1971 to 1977, as that same government study shows, Japanese capital costs for environmental compliance were 65 percent higher than American investments against pollution.

Indeed, the analysis of the situation by most of the steelworkers to whom I talked is considerably more sophisticated than that of *The Wall Street Journal*. These men and women were, almost without exception, opposed to the concessions agreed to by the international leadership of the USW and then rejected by the presidents of the steel locals. Were they, then, obdurate, intransigent, shortsighted? In no way. They were willing to make enormous concessions in pay and fringe benefits if, but only if, the companies agreed to invest the money thus saved in the Mon Valley. Why, they said, should they give up hard-earned benefits in order to finance another U.S. Steel multibillion-dollar takeover of an oil company?—a move which followed upon the announcement that it would not build a new steel plant in Ohio.

The fact is, American steel has been a greedy, mismanaged, technologically backward industry paying high dividends and engaging in takeovers while allowing 25 percent of the plant to become obsolete. But the steelworkers have been blamed for the stupidities of the front office; in addition to being unjust, this claim has subverted the moral basis of the movement of the unemployed.

Indeed, shortly after the USW finally did come to an agreement with the steel companies in 1983, the suspicions of the workers about the companies were dramatically confirmed. U.S. Steel announced that it would buy unfinished steel from Britain's nationalized industry and then further process it in this country. The argument was, as always, that this was the only way to save some of the jobs at its Fairless, Pennsylvania, plant. It would be necessary to shut down some of the jobs at Fairless, it was said, to save the others. One irony in all of this was that U.S. Steel had argued for protectionist measures on the grounds that they were needed to protect American producers from state-subsidized foreign competitors. Now U.S. Steel was proposing to import from one of those state-subsidized competitors!

But what is critical here is not the economic argument. It is the fact that, having extracted maximum concessions from the steelworkers, a major steel corporation proceeds, arbitrarily and without any kind of consultation, to make decisions that will profoundly affect the lives of thousands who had just made sacrifices in order to keep their jobs. For instance, in December of 1983, U.S. Steel announced that it was eliminating another 15,400 production jobs by shutting down more mills. In reporting that action, *The New York Times* noted that, in return for the concessions made by the workers earlier that year, the company had promised not to close any mills. That was the only sentence in the *Times*'s story that raised, or rather alluded to, the larger moral implication of Big Steel's action. Thus, investment decisions that may condemn a significant number of Americans to poverty are taken in private boardrooms, and the victims hear of their plight on the evening news.

This consideration becomes particularly important when one considers the longer run—those massive and international trends that are transforming the American economy. Will they take place in such a way as to create new, structural sources of poverty in the United States? Quite possibly.

At the outset, let me warn against exaggeration. The smokestack industries and their blue-collar workers are not going to disappear in the next year, or in the next twenty years. Even if the worst of the present trends prevail, there will be millions of Americans who, in the year 2000, will still be workers in factories. According to a study by the Congressional Budget Office (CBO), 70 percent of current manufacturing jobs will still exist in that year. This, it should be noted, is based on the assumption that the nation does not respond creatively to the present crisis.

If, however, we were to make new departures—and how we might do that will be outlined in Chapter 10—there could be a significant reindustrialization of the heartland. There are tremendous unmet needs within the United States and the world for urban infrastructure investment, agricultural implements, housing, and much else. If we, and the rest of the world, could find a way to channel resources toward meeting those needs—and, among many other things, end the orgy of corporate speculation that has seen billions lavished on nonproductive games in recent years—then many of the contemporary trends could be changed. They are, after all, only trends, not fates; understanding that, and then acting upon the knowledge, is a key to dealing with all of the problems described in this book and not just those of steel or auto workers.

But suppose that the required political mobilization and policy change does not take place. Suppose that the trends do turn into inevitabilities. What does this tell us about our unhappy future?

The CBO computes that, based on present figures, 15 percent of the manufacturing jobs in the United States will be eliminated in the eighties. That would mean that three million workers would be, as they say, "dislocated." By the year 2000, the CBO continues, that number would grow to seven million. We are talking here, it should be emphasized, about individuals. Most of those three or seven million are members of families. Using a crude measure, which, however, is adequate for our present purpose, we are talking about between nine and twenty-one million Americans whose lives will be disrupted in one way or another by these economic and social trends over the next two decades.

This is not to suggest that all of those dislocated workers are going to become poor. They are not. It is to argue that there is now a pool of people who are in danger of becoming poor which is almost as large as the number officially defined as poor. It is therefore important to become a little more precise with regard to those at risk who are most likely to be pushed down into the economic underworld of American society.

In all of these calculations it is possible for honest men and women to disagree with statistical estimates. For example, the CBO figured in 1982 that the number of dislocated workers could be set anywhere between 100,000 and 2.1 million. There are, the CBO said, three main categories of people who face this problem: workers in declining industries; workers in declining areas; workers in declining occupations. If you add all three together, you come up with 2.1 million or more who, in the very near future, are likely to lose their jobs. If you count only those who possess all three characteristics—workers in declining occupations in declining industries in declining areas—you get the lower number. For my purposes, the higher figure is relevant since it focuses upon trends rather than upon individuals in need of immediate help.

But note also that we are not here confronting a typical problem that persisted throughout the seventies. In that decade, every time unemployment went up, so did poverty. This reflected the impact of joblessness upon marginal workers, upon the last hired and first fired, upon blacks, Hispanics, and other minorities, and upon women. What is new now is that the dislocated worker is to be found in industries such as auto and steel, which in past times suffered, at the worst, from temporary layoffs that did not threaten the unemployed with poverty. In the recession of 1974–75, the number of the official poor went up by a million and a half; between 1979 and 1982, the increase was about eight million.

But these trends do not capture the problem defined in this chapter. Most of the people described here, including those who are going to become poor, are not yet poor. They are, remember, working people who have made relatively good wages during the past decade or so. They have unemployment insurance and sometimes even supplementary unemployment compensation from the company, perhaps some savings. For those who are pushed down into poverty, they will represent something new. They are a reserve army of the future poor, and it is thus cold comfort to say that they are not yet poor.

Who among them are the most likely to make the descent into poverty? Our numbers are rather clear about that: the older workers. Even in better times, the older workers remained unemployed longer than anyone else. Ironically, the more seniority a man or woman had, the more wages he or she lost from a layoff (such workers had higher pay and longer joblessness). In a study of plant closings in the meat-packing industry in the late fifties and early sixties, workers over fifty-five years old were out on the street for a year or more at double the rate of those under thirty-five years of age.

Why? Employers want younger workers so that they can benefit for a longer time from the training they give them. Older workers are less educated than younger workers and are therefore somewhat less able to adapt to new skills and conditions. Older workers are, for understandable reasons, more rooted in their communities, more tied down by home ownership and family responsibility than the younger workers. They are therefore less likely to pack up and go in search of an uncertain job. If one takes forty-five years of age as a cutoff point (and it is rather high, so it understates the problem), we are talking about half of the dislocated workers defined by the CBO.

I do not, however, want to allow this chapter to degenerate into an argument about statistical nuances. Let it simply be said that almost any version of the figures shows that there is a huge population, counted in the millions, of men and women who had "good" jobs in the sixties and the seventies, who are now in danger of becoming poor. I have no doubt that some, perhaps many, will avoid that fate. How many does not depend upon individual pluck but upon the performance of an American economy that has been in serious trouble for more than a decade and has by no means conquered its structural problems now.

But, ironically, there is a reason for hope: The same trends that are now attacking the blue-collar workers in the smokestack industries may well afflict white-collar workers, college graduates, even middle-level managers. If this were to happen—and if there were political movements to point out the common problems of different social classes—then it would be possible to talk about a majority movement in the United States to confront these issues. It could avoid the grimmest possibility: new ghettos of poverty, often new white ghettos of poverty, in the midst of a relatively satisfied society.

In the late seventies, one scholar, Stephen Dresch, presented shrewd testimony to the Congress: "In a traumatic reversal of historic experience," Dresch said, "children born to persons achieving adulthood in the 1950s and 1960s will, on average, experience relatively lower status than their parents." Upward social mobility has been, certainly in theory and sometimes even in practice, the American answer to the problem of inequality. We have either created more "good" jobs or else improved existing inequalities with cosmetic touches. Above all, even when there was no change in social position, a growing national product made it possible for almost everyone to make some gains. There were more openings for professionals, and steelworkers could, even though they remained in the mill, make $20,000 or $30,000 a year.

The scenario I am now suggesting is that the professionals are hit by many of the same economic forces that disrupt the lives of the millworkers. That possibility can be glimpsed in a fascinating issue of *Scientific American* in September 1982, devoted to "The Mechanization of Work." In manufacturing, Thomas G. Gunn wrote, the major impact of the new technology will be in "organizing, scheduling, and managing the total manufacturing enterprise, from product design to fabrication, distribution, and field service." Where, for instance, middle-level managers were needed to monitor supplies to be sure that certain parts were available at precisely the right time in the production schedule, but not too early, which would result in costly stockpiling, computers can now "back schedule" every stage of the process with inhuman precision. Computer-aided design already means that at General Motors the redesigning of a single automobile model now takes fourteen months instead of the once standard twenty-four months.

That may well be only the beginning of a more radical change. In computer-assisted design, one still needs draftspeople to turn out the blueprints on the computer, and there are junior colleges now training people for such work. But if, as seems likely, computer-*integrated* design comes to pass, the engineer will design the new part on a computer without the aid of anyone else. As Bob Kuttner put it, then "the 'new' job of CAD/CAM technician goes the way of the buggywhip maker."

This same revolution has the potential of transforming office work; indeed, it has already begun to do so. Between 1972 and 1980, the number of stenographers in the United States declined by almost 50 percent, while the computer and peripheral equipment operators increased by over 150 percent. In banking, almost everyone is now familiar with the twenty-four-hour bank, the simple computer that a person can use to make deposits and withdrawals, shift funds from one account to another, or pay bills, at any time of the night or day. Right now, reporters for *The New York Times* use a portable computer terminal that can store notes, receive data, and be used to write a story that is then transmitted to a central computer, which eventually transmits it for electronic typesetting.

College students have already been forced to understand this problem. By the mid-seventies, most of them realized that a liberal-arts bachelor's degree was worth about as much as a high-school diploma of a generation ago. This does not necessarily lead to poverty—neither the college-educated cabdriver nor the underemployed lawyer is poor—but it certainly creates an enormous amount of social frustration. It may even be that, in the eighties, the "new class" of educated employees will come to understand that the new working-class poverty is not something happening to a distant "them," but is the consequence of trends that affect the entire society, the graduates included. That realization could provide the basis for a majority political movement to deal with these problems.

Are these clouds really, then, lined with silver? I do not know; I only hope so. But what I am certain of, beyond any question of statistical quibbling, is that I have seen with my own eyes the sociological limbo of American working people. It was there in McKeesport, it is there throughout the old industrial heartland. People who, twenty or even ten years ago, were secure in their jobs and communities now live somewhere between poverty and semi-affluence, walking the edge of an economic precipice. Their problems will be ameliorated, but far from ended, by economic recovery, if this really does come. For they, or people like them, are likely to face downward social mobility for twenty or thirty years, unless this country turns around.

These are not, then, the instant "new poor" that the media discovered in that winter of American discontent, 1982–83. There is something much worse: a deep, structural source of a new poverty that could persist into the indefinite future.

— 4 —

The New Gradgrinds

"Now what I want is, Facts. Teach the boys and girls nothing but Facts. Facts alone are wanted in life. Plant nothing else, and root out everything else. . . . Thomas Gradgrind, sir. A man of realities."

So Charles Dickens began his novel *Hard Times*. Thomas Gradgrind is a cruel, distorted, marvelous caricature of a follower of the utilitarian social thinker Jeremy Bentham, and he sees numbers instead of people. Dickens himself was, of course, one of the greatest chroniclers of poverty who ever lived. A liberal, not a radical, he hoped—as the ending of his haunting story of the "hungry forties," *A Christmas Carol*, made clear—that good and decent people would finally wake to their responsibility, that Scrooge and Tiny Tim would sit at the same table together. But if power turned out to be much more hardhearted than he thought, and change more a result of conflict than of the belated decency of the rich, he made the poor and their tormentors come alive in a mob of imagined people.

A little later, in *Hard Times*, there appears this unforgettable evocation of Gradgrind's study, crammed with the "blue books" of the government statisticians: "In that most charmed apartment, the most complicated kind of questions were cast up, got into exact totals, and finally settled—if those concerned could only be brought to know it. As if an astronomical observatory should be made without any windows, and the astronomer should arrange the starry universe solely by pen, ink, and paper, so Mr. Gradgrind in *his* observatory (and there are so many like it), had no need to cast an eye upon the teeming myriads of human beings around him, but he could settle all their destinies on a slate, and wipe out all their tears with one dirty little bit of sponge."

For instance, in January 1984, President Reagan's task force on food assistance refused to recognize the palpable evidence of growing hunger in the United States. Late in 1983, Senator Edward Kennedy had gone to San Francisco, Minneapolis, Detroit, Pittsburgh, and eastern Kentucky. He had talked to the people on the soup kitchen lines and found that many of them were the new poor: the members of intact families, not drifters or welfare mothers.

In addition to these personal impressions, Kennedy gathered data. In Kentucky, various food programs had increased by between 75 and 400 percent; in Minneapolis–St. Paul, the rise was between 150 and 400 percent; in San Francisco, 200 to 400 percent; in Pittsburgh and Detroit, between 300 and 400 percent. The President's Commission on Hunger in America found such reports merely "anecdotal." Indeed, it relied on the new Gradgrind statistics showing a decline in poverty to argue that the problem of hunger had been exaggerated. But those statistics, as we shall see, systematically underestimate the number of the poor. No matter. A computer programmed with reactionary premises was taken as more authoritative than all the evidence assembled by Senator Kennedy or even the testimony of the conservative director of the Congressional Budget Office.

I assume that the commission would find the testimony of one hunger activist even more absurd. In talking with poor people in various parts of the country, she had encountered a uniform strategy in dealing with hunger: to feed the children (and the mother, for that matter) popcorn and water when the money and the food stamps run out. Isn't it obvious that such people are not "hungry," i.e., that their stomachs are full? I have seen similar patterns over the years, only I was more familiar with potatoes as a cheap staple. That, not so incidentally, is why hungry people can be overweight from a bloated, starchy, dangerous diet. However, the Hunger Commission did not want to have any truck with human data; they, after all, had their numbers to tell them the truth.

The policy implications of that naïve trust in biased statistics are frightening. Federal food monies, the commission said, should be given to the states and they should decide how to spend them. But it was, and is, one of the greatest accomplishments of the food stamp program that it establishes uniform national levels of nutritional assistance, that the Mississippi poor got as much as the New York poor, something that never happens when, as in the case of AFDC, there is "state's rights" welfare.

In a sense, I would like very much to ignore all the statistical and definitional complexities, not the least because the serried figures are so distant from the reality of poverty. Yet that cannot be done. In the modern world, where prejudices disguise themselves as impersonal equations and cruelty is rationalized by mathematical arguments, one has to counter misleading numbers with more honest numbers. Otherwise, President Reagan's task force will be able to wrap itself in the mantle of spurious "objectivity."

But then, this undertaking is not merely a matter of defending the poor against the new Gradgrinds. How one defines poverty also has profound policy implications. It might at first seem that it would be in the interests of the poor to show that they are a much more numerous group of people than anyone has ever realized. To a point, that is true. But the irrepressible woman who made the first official American definitions of poverty in the 1960s, Mollie Orshansky—the very opposite of a Gradgrind, indeed the heroine of this chapter in which his descendants are the villain—points out that the higher the poverty line, the more important are the working poor, and the relatively less important are the dependent poor. But such statistics can then imply that normal economic progress will deal with poverty, that full employment, which is an utterly necessary precondition for the abolition of this misery, is also a sufficient condition. So, by enlarging the poverty population, one makes it more difficult to see the most desperate and marginal people concealed within it.

Of course, the problem in recent years has not come from overstating the number of the poor, but from profoundly understating it. That tendency is, in turn, a part of a national trend.

Sometime in the sixties, Senator George Aiken of Vermont came up with the inspired suggestion that the United States simply declare that it had won the war in Vietnam and then, on this note of triumph, bring its troops back home. That excellent advice was not accepted by Lyndon Johnson, but a perverse version of it has animated many government statisticians in recent years. There have been some remarkable statistical victories over social ills, which have left reality totally unchanged. For instance, full employment is defined by a rate of unemployment—the "full employment unemployment rate." In the early sixties, that rate was set at 3 percent, with an interim target for the Kennedy administration of 4 percent. Time passed and the level of acceptable unemployment was regularly and officially increased. To be fair, the experts had the decency to change the name of what they were defining: from "full employment" to "high employment" to—the current euphemism—"the inflation threshold unemployment rate." By 1983, the Council of Economic Advisors had, in effect, raised the old full employment unemployment rate to 7 percent. That made full employment easier to achieve and also left eight million jobless in the streets in "good times."

Another such statistical victory was much less subtle. In the early seventies, a Democratic Congress forced the Nixon and Ford administrations to publish a "tax expenditure" budget. Tax expenditures occur when the government reduces or eliminates the tax of a specified group of citizens—decreeing, for example, that mortgage interest is deductible, but rent is not, as a means of encouraging home construction and ownership—an action which gives that group money that is as real as a welfare check but quite a bit more dignified. Publication of the tax expenditure budget can, however, be an embarrassment, since it documents enormous handouts for the middle class and rich: 84 percent of the $19.6 billion in annual lost revenue from the deductibility of mortgage interest goes to people earning more than $30,000 a year.

In the 1981 tax law, the Reagan administration had carried out a redistribution of income from working people and the middle class to the rich. How, then, to deal with this reality when the time comes for the publication of the tax expenditure budget? Simple. The Secretary of the Treasury omits 13 items from the tax expenditure budget prepared by the Joint Congressional Committee on Taxation. That, the CBO calculated in 1982, reduces tax expenditures by $17.5 billion in 1982 and by a projected $67.2 billion in 1987. In 1983, when the CBO was under more conservative management, it estimated that the administration's definitions would cut a mere $36.3 billion from the tax expenditure budget in 1987. That "saving" is worth about four times the current outlays on Aid for Families of Dependent Children.

However, it is in the case of poverty that the political manipulation of the numbers is most marked. The reason is simple enough. The official government definitions in this area serve to determine eligibility for various entitlement programs. A change of a few tenths of a percent in the population that receives government assistance can mean a reduction in federal outlays of millions and millions of dollars. In the sixties, when it was assumed that an endless, crisis-free process of economic growth would automatically generate huge revenues for Washington, that did not seem too important. But in the seventies and early eighties, with the nation in deep economic trouble, an imaginary statistical victory over poverty became a way of cutting down on real spending.

And yet statistics always have been political, and in recent times that perennial trend has simply become more gross. Back in 1963, Mollie Orshansky worked on what was to become the official definition of the "poverty line" (the "line" is actually the level of poverty for an urban family of four, and there are other lines for larger and smaller units, for those who live in the country, etc.). She decided to use a minimal diet—sufficient to hold body and soul together but not much more—as the base. There were, however, four food plans that had been developed by the U.S. Department of Agriculture. All of them sought to define a nutritionally adequate diet, but they differed in details—and in cost.

Orshansky's strategy was to take the price of a minimal diet and multiply it by three to compute the total income at the poverty line(s). In 1955 the Department of Agriculture had carried out a Survey of Food Consumption which concluded that the average American family spent one-third of its after-tax income on food, two-thirds on everything else. Therefore, Orshansky reasoned, multiplying the food cost by three would yield an approximation of a total budget. But which of the food plans should be used? It came down to a choice between two of them. If one took the "low cost" budget and multiplied it by three, that would result in a poverty line (for that family of four) of $3,995. But if one used the "economy budget" of the USDA, that meant a poverty line of $3,165. The latter was about 80 percent of the former, and making it the base significantly reduced the number of the *statistical* poor. The Council of Economic Advisors then settled this question through a political decision. It opted for the economy food budget, rounded off the numbers, and, in the first official analysis of poverty in its 1964 report, established the poverty line at $3,000.

I do not want to suggest for a moment that there was something sinister in these events. There is no such thing as a "value-free" analysis of a contentious social issue that relates to the spending of large amounts of money. When, for instance, I came up with my own poverty line in *The Other America* (written in 1960 and 1961, published in 1962), I relied on intuition and a sense of fairness as well as on the few hard numbers then available. I can hardly blame others for being as subjective as I was. Moreover, standards change with time. In 1899, Seebohm Rowntree thought it was possible to make an absolute definition of poverty based on minimum physical needs. But what are minimum physical needs? In the 1880s, the reformers thought it all right for several families on a landing to share a water tap and a privy, or for a family with several children to live in one room.

However, the administration's decision to opt for the lower food budget in 1964 was not, I suspect, taken on the basis of such complexities. The bureaucracy simply did not want to establish a figure that could put 25 or 30 percent of the people—fifty or sixty million citizens—under the poverty line(s). But that choice was made at a time of increasing federal aid to those in need. In the seventies, when the political and cultural winds changed, the political dimension in the definition of poverty did in fact become quite sinister. The new Gradgrinds were using statistics to blot out the tears of suffering men, women, and children.

Indeed, I would argue that the control of statistics is one of the critical functions of power in a democratic society. The numbers define the limits of the possible; they confer the awesome mathematical legitimacy of "fact" upon some parts of reality and deny it to others. Just think, for instance, of how different the American debate might be if, in addition to computing the gross national product, we also figured out the gross national waste, and subtracted the latter from the former to arrive at an Ungross Qualitative Product. Wouldn't the discussions of UQP create a policy world utterly unlike the universe of GNP (which itself came from Keynesian concepts, not from God)?

It is, then, necessary to explore the intellectual thicket in which the numbers hide. As difficult and even tedious as this might seem, it must always be kept in mind that the statistical columns are the surrogates for human misery.

— I —

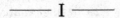

First, it is important to sort out a few basic concepts.

Poverty and inequality are not the same thing, even though they are clearly related to each other. I raise, and stress, this rather intricate point since it is crucial in dealing with one of the conservative critiques of the very idea of an antipoverty effort. The poor, said people like Barry Goldwater in the sixties, are just a statistical artifact and for that matter it is a mathematical impossibility to abolish poverty. There will always be inequality, the senator said (this is, of course, one of the most important components of the conservative faith); there will always be people on the bottom. And since it is impossible to eliminate the lowest fifth, the poor will always exist, albeit with ever-rising living standards.

That is simply not true. The lowest fifth does indeed exist in Sweden, but it is, in both absolute and relative terms, better off than the lowest fifth in the United States. It is less poor. In the early seventies, the Organization for Economic Cooperation and Development estimated, on the basis of the same measure, that 13 percent of Americans were under the poverty line against 3.5 percent of Swedes. Death is a rather absolute fact. In 1975 in Sweden, an infant was much more likely to survive the first year of life than in the United States (there were 8.6 deaths for every thousand births there, 16.1 in this country). More to the present point, the infant mortality rate in the United States for blacks is three times that for Sweden as a whole (24.9 against 8.6 per thousand), and it is clear that one reason for that obscene ratio is the better medical care in Sweden for people at the bottom of the income structure. There are, then, distinctions as objective as death among various lower fifths.

There are also relative differences. In the United States the income of the top quintile is slightly more than eight times that of the bottom quintile; in Japan, which is hardly an egalitarian society, the difference is five to one. The American poor are thus more "unequal" than the Japanese poor. Indeed, America now lags behind ten other advanced nations in terms of its per capita wealth. So the lowest fifth in this country gets a smaller percentage of a smaller economic pie than does the lower fifth in the European welfare states.

For that matter, one can at least imagine a society in which there would be no poverty and considerable inequality. Suppose that the lowest fifth in the United States today had an average income of $30,000—which would obviously mean that it could take care of its own necessities—but that there still was a tiny upper class of billionaires. That is mathematically possible, and

Goldwater's attempt to make a statistical case for that biblical statement so often quoted on the right—that the poor will always be with us, a holy witness to eternal truth—fails.

In saying this, I do not want to fall into the opposite error, i.e., that there is no relationship whatsoever between poverty and inequality. That was, as I have already noted, a central proposition for Lyndon Johnson's antipoverty effort. Growth was going to generate those huge federal surpluses that would have to be spent if they were not to deflate the economy. Therefore, the official sixties thought, it was possible to abolish poverty without any redistribution of income whatsoever. In point of political fact, if there were a major effort to end poverty in a short time—and particularly in the eighties, when the illusion of endless growth has long since vanished—it will have to be redistributionist. Resources are not infinite, and if everyone at the bottom of the society is brought up to a minimal level of decency, those at the top can, and should, pay.

So poverty is not inequality, but it is significantly and intricately related to inequality. There is also a very real sense in which the official definition of the poor has, over the past decade, become both less generous and less exact.

In terms of real buying power, median income—50 percent of the people get more, 50 percent get less—in the seventies went up and down and ultimately nowhere. In 1980 it was, measured in constant dollars, about what it had been in 1970—and 5.5 percent less than it had been in 1979. This is, of course, one more way of saying that the nation has experienced more than a decade of stagnation and crisis, culminating in the absolute decline of 1982. But during this same period, the poverty line, defined as a percentage of median income, went down. It was 54 percent of median income in 1960, 40 percent in 1970, and 38 percent in 1979. Thus it is clear that there was a deterioration of the relative position of the poor even before Ronald Reagan became President.

Indeed, if, according to the computations of HEW in the seventies, one sets poverty equal to one-half the median income, then it has been more or less constant since 1959. Strangely enough, Ronald Reagan's own Presidential Commission on Housing, a zealously conservative group, provided a certain legitimacy for that definition since it defined the "very low income" at precisely 50 percent of median income and even held that "moderately low income" might come up to 80 percent of the median. The Organization for Economic Cooperation and Development has used a similar measure to determine poverty in Europe: two-thirds of average disposable income was its poverty line in the mid-seventies.

Thus, thinkers from the most diverse points on the political spectrum endorse a definition of poverty that would show little or no progress in the United States over the past quarter of a century. Or, rather, there was some significant progress in the sixties, stagnation in the seventies, and decline in the early eighties, the other America thus persisting from Eisenhower to Reagan. Some of the poor have been winners (the aging, the full-time workers, at least until Reagan); some have been losers (the AFDC mothers); but poverty itself has marched serenely onward.

A serious definition of poverty has to be as absolute as death and as relative as changing living standards. One has been told for years that the contemporary American poor are much better off than medieval royalty or present-day Indian beggars. But the contemporary American poor live neither in the Middle Ages nor in India. Because it takes this fact into account, I believe that Peter Townsend's definition of the poor in *Poverty in the United Kingdom* is the most subtle and realistic analysis available. That is why I close this introductory section with a brief account of it.

Townsend writes, with somewhat deceptive simplicity, "Poverty . . . is the lack of resources necessary to permit participation in the activities, customs, and diets commonly approved by society." An interesting example: Tea is without nutritional value, yet, in some countries, it is clearly a "necessity of life." But does this mean that we are back with Barry Goldwater, having defined poverty in such a way as to equate it with the bottom fifth, or tenth, or whatever? Is all this uproar over the "poor" merely a way of saying that some people have more and some less? Not at all.

To begin with, Townsend, a man of the left, anticipated the

central conservative critique of the poverty definition being made from the right today. That critique, as we shall see in the next section, holds that the official poverty line(s), defined in terms of money income, ignores the other sources of income that the alleged poor receive, most notably food stamps, housing subsidies, and medical care. But long before this conservative discovery, Townsend—and the American sociologists S. M. Miller and Pamela Robey—had insisted that poverty be defined in terms of all the major aspects of life, including those famous "in-kind" goods and services.

So when Townsend computed (in the late seventies) the income of the poor and others, he included the cash they received, their capital assets, the value of their employee benefits, public goods and services, and even private in-kind goods and services (gifts, the worth of personal support services). For him, and for Miller and Robey, the reason for this emphasis is contrary to that of the conservatives of recent years: Townsend, Miller, and Robey want to show that the poor are poor in every one of those categories, that it is not simply cash income they lack, but legal services, public amenities, basic human respect, and on and on.*

Using this sophisticated statistical calculus, Townsend made a very important discovery. If one conceives of "deprivation" in terms of the ordinary aspects of daily life—vacations, eating a meal in a restaurant, having a birthday party for a child—then a careful survey of people in the United Kingdom reveals a very important chasm in the society. The evidence from his questionnaire, Townsend writes, shows that there exists a "threshold of deprivation—that is, a point in descending the income scale where deprivation increased disproportionately to the fall in income." Above that point, families and individuals could reasonably participate in the common activities of their society. To be sure, their

*The Social and Economic Committee of the Common Market has adopted a definition of poverty very similar to Townsend's. "Those individuals and families can be considered poor," it has said, "whose resources are so small that they find themselves excluded from the mode of life, the normal patterns and activities, of the countries in which they live. By resources we mean disposable in-kind income as well as private and public goods and services."

income determined exactly how much they could do so, but still they were, so to speak, in the same world as those with more money.

But at the "threshold of deprivation," a quantitative decline in cash (an objective, measurable phenomenon) meant a qualitative decline in social participation (a somewhat less precise notion). This finding was quite parallel to the analysis of mental illness and social class carried on by Hollingshead and Redlich in the United States in the fifties. In that study, it turned out that the mental and emotional problems of all social classes except the poor were in roughly the same statistical range, but that when one crossed a line into the economic underworld of the society, there was suddenly an enormous increase in those difficulties.

Strangely enough, Hegel anticipated Townsend's point by a century and a half. In *The Philosophy of Right* he wrote, "When a great mass falls below a certain level of subsistence, the self-regulating level which is necessary to a member of society—and thereby suffers a loss of the sense of right, of self-respect and honor which arises out of one's own activity and work—this brings forth the mob. . . ." This expressed, of course, a conservative fear, but it was prescient in understanding that there is a point on the income scale which sets the world of the poor against that of everyone else.

Much more recently, Gertrude Himmelfarb's otherwise quite fascinating study of the idea of poverty in the nineteenth century trivializes Townsend's extraordinarily important work. She writes as if his definition were based mainly upon "the lack of hot breakfasts, of birthday parties, of holidays, and of the habit of dining out." In fact, those indicators taken from daily life were merely illustrations of the contrast between the two basic modes of social existence, that of the poor and that of everyone else, and they were cited in a study that is rigorous in its complex statistical analysis. The psyche, the spirit, the very routine of poverty, Townsend is saying, defines a universe of its own.

This takes us quite close to the notion of a "culture of poverty" which was widely debated in the sixties and early seventies, but I don't want to raise that specific point here (it will be treated in its own right in Chapter 8). What is first to be emphasized is that poverty is not an income level but a condition of life, a way of existing. And, second, that insight is not based upon some vague philosophical notion about the nature of poverty. It speaks of a reality that shows up on survey questionnaires and even in the relative frequency of mental illness among the social classes. It is ironic that the conservatives of the seventies and the eighties, to whom I now turn, borrowed just enough of the broader definition of the poor to be able to make a case that poverty had all but vanished. In fact, when one adopts that broader definition in all of its implications, as Townsend did, poverty becomes all the more obdurate.

II

What follows is a statistical detective story.

There are two facts in American society which are as palpable as the nudity of the emperor in the famous legend and just as scrupulously ignored. Between the poor and the nonpoor, who gets the most from social spending? Chapter 2 began to document the answer: The nonpoor get much more than the poor. We will now fill in some of the important details. And there is the second, related issue: Among the poor themselves, who gets the most from Washington? Not the welfare poor, but the aging poor.

The stereotype that is directly contrary to these facts—that the United States devotes the lion's share of its social spending to the lazy, dependent poor—is one of the chief ideological defenses of our complacent callousness. It is an utter falsification, as will be seen when we deal with the most astounding conservative discovery of the 1970s: Poverty has disappeared and no one noticed.

The central thesis in this stunning revelation can be stated simply enough. The official poverty definition only counts cash income. It does not include the money value of the in-kind income received by the poor—food stamps, housing subsidies, and, above all, medical care—and therefore, it is argued, systematically overstates the extent of poverty in the United States. When one does compute the worth of the in-kind income and adds it to the cash income, poverty is either drastically reduced or even abolished. The extent of this statistical triumph depends upon precisely what measure one uses to translate the in-kind goods and services into an equivalent cash sum.

One of the first statements of this theme came from Edgar K. Browning in a 1974 article in *The Public Interest*, the theoretical journal of all those who develop sophisticated arguments for turning the nation's back upon the poor. Browning's article was titled "How Much More Equality Can We Afford?"—which provides a rather obvious clue as to his political bias. By using the argument about uncounted in-kind benefits, Browning concluded that "there is practically no poverty—statistically speaking—in the United States today and indeed there has not been for several years." In 1976, Gerald Ford's Council of Economic Advisors took up this theme, announcing that it had serious doubts about the poverty statistics because they did not calculate the cash value of the in-kind goods and services.

In the mid-seventies, "informed opinion" was ready to take any hypothesis that reduced the number of the poor, and to treat it as a fact. So it was that this highly questionable—indeed, erroneous—theory began to appear in the media as an unvarnished statement about reality. Harry Schwartz of *The New York Times* quoted these speculations and then chided the government for publishing "misleading" figures about poverty. Schwartz and others like him did not notice the extremely fancy statistical footwork required to reach the new conclusions. One analysis, for instance, declared that the nonworking poor—mainly the old and the young, the ill and single parents keeping house—were "voluntarily" unemployed, and went on to count the "potential additional earnings" they would receive for giving up some of their leisure as part of their real income.

Then, in 1977, the Congressional Budget Office, under the direction of a certified liberal, Alice Rivlin, took up the *Public Interest* thesis. By taking the "market value" of the in-kind goods and services, the CBO reduced the poverty population by 47 percent. The next year, Martin Anderson of the Hoover Institution—later to be an advisor to President Reagan—published a book-length statement on the new nonpoverty. In *The Political Economy of Welfare Reform in the United States*, Anderson wrote, "The 'war on poverty' that began in 1964 has been won. The growth of jobs and income in the private economy, combined with an explosive increase in government spending for welfare and income transfer programs, has virtually eliminated poverty in the United States."

To be fair, the political attitudes involved in all of these sweeping redefinitions were complex. Some—the CBO, for instance—argued that the revisions were necessary to show the public that liberal programs had actually worked, which was an interesting rationalization of conservative analysis. Others, like Browning and Anderson, were straightforward in their conservatism. A third conservative tendency took the opposite tack from Browning and Anderson: The federal efforts, it said, had not achieved, but blocked, the elimination of poverty (a notion we will confront in Chapter 6). But whether liberal, optimistically conservative, or pessimistically conservative, all of these thinkers pointed in the same political direction: No more money for antipoverty efforts. The latter had either succeeded too brilliantly or failed too abysmally to justify any further funds.

There were, however, some interesting admissions made along the way. The Congressional Budget Office, for instance, discovered that the normal outcome of the American economy left 25 percent of the people poor. The only reason that appalling percentage did not constitute a menace was that government transfer programs did away with roughly 80 percent of that poverty. Similarly, one of the most determined of the conservative pessimists, Charles Murphy, came up with the concept of "latent poverty": those who were poor before cash and in-kind programs saved them. He concluded that latent poverty had actually increased during the seventies (from 19 percent in 1972 to 22 percent in 1980), and charged, contrary to both the CBO and Anderson, that all that federal spending had been wasted on a treadmill.

By the early eighties, then, the statistical abolition of poverty had turned into an academic cottage industry in the United States. In late 1983, David Stockman testified on behalf of the administration that despite the impression that there had been an enormous increase in poverty—indeed, despite the testimony to that effect by the conservative director of the CBO a month earlier—the numbers of poor were actually declining, with even better days foreseen ahead. Small wonder that *New York Times* thinkers and editorialists around the country had begun to take complex and questionable theories as statements of observed fact. To be sure, they might have taken a tour of the South Bronx in New York, as almost every Presidential candidate did, and the acres of rubble and the milling unemployed people in the middle of the day might have suggested that all was not yet quite well. Most, however, avoided that exertion.

Then, in 1982, the Bureau of the Census published a formidable technical paper on "Alternative Methods for Valuing Selected In-Kind Transfer Benefits and Measuring Their Effect on Poverty." There was a flurry of newspaper reports, but they had to tell of a complexity, not of a stunning simplicity like the secret abolition of poverty. There were, the Census said, serious difficulties in "cashing in" the in-kind benefits. Indeed, one plausible measure reduced the number of the poor by a mere 12.2 percent rather than by 42.3 percent (these are 1979 numbers; i.e., they predate an increase of more than five million people in the officially defined poverty population). Corrections in the United States, particularly intricate statistical corrections, rarely have the media impact of the initial—wrong—revelations. Small wonder, then, that by 1983 so many people had concluded that the poor were either nonexistent or undeserving.

We will attempt to sort out the truth about those in-kind benefits shortly. But there is an important prelude to that task. All of the intellectual effort since 1974 has been devoted to exploring the possibility that we have overestimated the poor. Thus, even the most serious and careful count made by the Bureau of the Census reduces the dimensions of poverty. It should be made clear at this point that I, too, want the figures to be as exact and realistic as possible. After all, I want the most accurate data to guide the formulation of policy in a new war on poverty. So part of my objection to these various revisions has to do with means, not with ends. I think they have done a careless job in carrying out investigations that are quite relevant in themselves. That will be explored in a moment.

But there is a second objection, and it is the subject of my prelude. Why has so much attention been devoted to documenting the overestimation of the poor—and so little to exploring the underestimation of them? In two areas, involving millions of poor people, there is evidence of an undercount. It is a well-kept secret in the United States.

The first area has to do with the definition of poverty in terms of cash income. All of the critics of an overcount take that definition as a starting point, even as they charge that it is utterly inadequate. After they have made their computations about the value of the in-kind benefits, they add them to the official poverty line in order to establish a new poverty (or nonpoverty) line. So, strange as it may seem, they implicitly acknowledge the authority of the very definition they want to replace.

Under the circumstances, one might think it would be a matter of some moment that the person who originally elaborated that cash-income definition of poverty has thought for some time that it underestimates the problem. In 1974 (a year when the official poverty rate went up), Mollie Orshansky argued that the "line" was $3,000 below what it should be and that the poor therefore numbered 55.4 million—not, as in the official count, 23.4 million. In a complex argument presented to the American Statistical Association in 1979, Orshansky (along with C. Fendler) asserted that in 1977—a "good" year for the poor—the official measure understated poverty by a factor of 54 percent, i.e., *it overlooked* 25 *million people.*

The central (but not the only) factor in Orshansky's revisions had to do with the relation between food cost and the total budget of the poor. In 1954, when the definition was first developed, it was assumed that this ratio was 3-to-1, as shown in a 1955 USDA survey of American food consumption patterns. But in 1965, another USDA analysis concluded that the percentage spent on food was actually less than in 1955. Adjusting the definition of poverty to conform to this empirical pattern meant that the multiplier had to be increased from 3 to 3.45. That change, along with some other technical amendments, resulted in Orshansky's conclusion that there had been a significant undercount.

The Bureau of the Census took note of this challenge, though the news did not get through to the media pundits. This procedure, Census said, tended to relativize poverty, and such updating could mask significant reductions in poverty. But, as we have already seen, there is, and must be, a relative component in any definition of the poor. Were 1955 food patterns, which were the base for the original definition of poverty, absolute? If so, in that year there was no poverty at all, compared to diets in Europe in 1755 or in much of India today. And, as Townsend emphasized, one must look at the poor in terms of their participation—in food and everything else—in *their* society, a concept that, as we have seen, has empirical grounding in those careful studies of the poverty threshold in the United Kingdom. Finally, Orshansky's method does not make it as impossible to eliminate poverty as a Barry Goldwater might think; if the seventies had merely been as good as the sixties in this area, her 1977 computation would have been set much lower, even if it were still higher than the official poverty line.

Let me be fair. Decent and serious analysts can reject Orshansky's methodology without being prejudiced against the poor. I am not saying that her measure is the only plausible one. But her case cannot be ignored, because she is one of the most widely recognized and authoritative researchers in the field. But the fact is that those who want to revise the poverty problem downward—who make their 50-percent reductions in the number of the poor—get incomparably more attention than one who presents a very reasonable case for revising upward. It is therefore at least possible that the United States is now undercounting poverty by a factor of much more than 25 million people (I say "much more than" because the poor, by any measure, have significantly increased since 1977).

The second area in which the poor are undercounted is not

a creation of the statistical method used, but a fact. The only question is, how many people does it contain? It is well known that there are many undocumented families in the United States, and it is equally well known that a majority of them are poor. As we will see in Chapter 7, this is the reason why the sweatshop has made a dramatic return to the United States of the seventies and the eighties. The estimates of the size of this undocumented population vary from five to ten million people. Assuming that 80 percent of them are poor, there might be four to eight million impoverished humans in this society who have never achieved the dignity of being a statistic.

In the spring of 1983, the Reagan administration unwittingly lent its authority to my point. The White House said that there were 6.25 million undocumented people in the country and that if the Simpson-Mazzoli immigration bill, which would "legalize" some of them, passed, 1.7 million would become eligible for naturalization. In the Senate version of the bill, the aliens who came to the United States before January 1, 1977, would become permanent residents, while those who entered prior to January 1, 1980, would become temporary residents. That, the Office of Management and Budget said, could mean $9.3 billion in additional welfare costs over a period of four years. Obviously, there is no doubt in the Reagan administration that there are millions of predominantly poor undocumented workers in the United States. No doubt, that is, until it comes to counting the poor, when these people are most conveniently forgotten.

But there are also social realities that point in the other direction. There is an important "underground economy" in the United States, with billions of dollars in unreported income. One of its sectors has nothing to do with the poor: the professionals and skilled workers who barter their services or else provide them, in whole or in part, off the books. Another sector does harbor people who are poor in terms of their reported income, but not in terms of their real income: the world of crime and drugs. But we know, as Chapter 8 will suggest, that class distinctions hold even in the underworld, and that the most successful lawbreakers tend to be white and better educated than the petty criminals.

The latter also spend a disproportionate amount of time in one of the major institutions of American poverty, the prison system.

But even taking into account the probability that there is a certain amount of undeclared income that abolishes the poverty of the underworld poor, still the undocumented workers, and the people counted if one accepts Orshansky's revised definition, are potentially more numerous than *all* those now officially declared to be poor. We are talking about an undercount that could total more than thirty million rather miserable human beings. Even if one were to accept the conservative theories about an overcount in their most extreme version, it is probable that far more people in America are poor than we now recognize officially.

In fact, most of the revisions are sweeping and excessive. Let us now look at how they compute the cash value of in-kind goods and services and see why.

To begin with, the statistical conservatives mix apples and oranges in their calculations. On the one hand, they still use the cash-income definition of poverty; on the other hand, they change it radically. Consider an analogous case. Suppose that the U.S. government were suddenly to announce that it was going to tax the cash value of public schools, including colleges and universities, which would be tacked onto the income of all those with children when they computed their income tax. The insurance value of all employee medical plans would be counted as taxable income, and so would the worth of all business perks, such as food and transportation. It is not, I think, hard to imagine the anguished outcry that would result.

Part of the complaint would be that tax rates which had been decided in terms of cash income, and which were set at a certain level for precisely that reason, were now being applied to noncash income. But that is exactly what the statistical revisionists are doing to the poor. For when the poverty line is adjusted, or when certain in-kind benefits are computed in determining eligibility for a social program, that is not just a matter of theory. It has to do with how much money people get—just as the income tax does.

In two significant areas, then—the technical question of how the poverty line is fixed, and the fact that there is a huge and uncounted population of the undocumented poor—there is evidence of an undercount. As a result, even if the new Gradgrinds were right in their calculations of the overcount, the number of the impoverished is higher than the official statistics indicate, not lower. But—and we return here to our detective story—those new estimates about how we exaggerated poverty are not accurate. Rather they overgeneralize a single, rarely stated fact: The aging poor receive a disproportionate share of the in-kind benefits. To treat their benefits as if they go to the poverty population as a whole is obviously wrong.

This fact about the aging is, we will see later on, a subordinate aspect of a larger truth, i.e., that the welfare state in the United States is primarily for people over sixty-five, most of whom are not now, and for a long time have not been, poor. Obviously I do not say these things because I propose to take benefits away from the aging or to argue that they have been given too much assistance. Quite the opposite. But I do want to point out that there are very special problems in evaluating these benefits—above all in assigning a cash value to nursing home and/or terminal health care—that makes it dubious to attribute them to the poor as a group.

There are three methods that have been devised for computing the cash value of in-kind benefits. The market-method estimates the dollar worth of the benefit in terms of its purchase price in a private market. This is the approach that yields the highest estimates of an overcount and accomplishes the greatest reduction in the number of the poor. It is, as one might guess, favored by conservatives, and was also used by the Congressional Budget Office. When it is employed by conservatives, a considerable irony surfaces. These normally implacable critics of government waste assume that all in-kind goods and services are provided to the poor with 100-percent efficiency, that the public sector is every bit as good as the private sector. Needless to say, such assumptions, so convenient in the argument against any further poverty expenditures, are quickly forgotten when it comes to other areas of social policy.

The second method values the goods and services in terms of their worth to the recipient. What is the cash amount for which the recipients would be willing to trade their right to the in-kind transfer, given their current incomes? Perhaps a poor person does not share that extraordinary conservative assumption that every good and service is provided in just the right proportion and with total efficiency. He or she might want less, or more, of certain benefits than the omniscient bureaucracy posited by trusting the conservatives' decrees. One way of figuring the cash value for the recipient is to look at how much other people, similar in most respects but not getting the in-kind benefit, actually do pay for it.

The third method is called the "poverty budget share value" approach. It deals, among other things, with a central problem in this whole exercise: How does one evaluate the worth of medical care that goes mainly to the aging poor? The Bureau of the Census gives an excellent case in point. In 1979, the market value of Medicaid coverage for an elderly person in New York State was estimated at $4,430. But this was almost $1,000 more than the poverty line for that person ($3,472). Clearly this $4,430 is "income" in a very special sense, since it cannot be spent on food, housing, or any other need (and is indeed most unwelcome "income" since one has to be ill to get it). If one were to take that $4,430 at face value, then a person could enter the middle class, or even the upper middle class, by virtue of having a long, expensive, subsidized terminal illness. So the "poverty share" method limits the value of medical care (or any other in-kind benefit) to its share in the definition of the poverty budget. Anything over that sum is not really additional disposable income but, more often than not, too much of a good thing.

There are many complications in each of these methods, but they need not concern us here. Taking the extreme case—the one in which each approach yields the highest "reduction" in poverty—the differences are striking. In 1979 terms, market value eliminates almost 13 million people, or 42.3 percent of the total; recipient value cuts out a mere 9,305,000 human beings, or 26.7 percent; and poverty budget shares drop out 7,757,000 of the poor, or "only" 20.1 percent. Remember, once again, that the highest computation of the overcount—13 million—is not even equal to one-half of the possible undercount already documented (30 million or more).

Moreover, the bulk of the downward revisions mainly comes from looking at the in-kind benefits of one group among the poor—the 15 percent who are over sixty-five years of age—and then equating them with benefits received by the entire population. This point requires us to focus on the fact that antipoverty measures in the United States are primarily for the aging. It also utterly subverts Martin Anderson's assertion that "an explosive increase in government spending for welfare and income transfer programs" was a major reason for the famous disappearance of poverty in America.

Between 1975 and 1980, according to census figures, the real buying power of cash public assistance transfers ("welfare") did not explode but declined. There was one area that might have seemed to be an exception: Washington increased its outlays for medical care from $28 billion in 1975 to $58.545 billion in 1980. That more than 100-percent increase was, however, fictitious to a considerable degree, since it primarily represented an inflation of medical costs of around 75 percent, not an increase in medical services. Moreover, slightly more than half of that rise is attributable to Medicare, a program for the aging only, 85 percent of whose recipients are not poor. Even if one adds in the 15 percent of the people over sixty-five who might have been poor were it not for Medicare, it is hardly a poverty program.

That leaves Medicaid, which is indeed a means-tested program for the poor alone. Not so incidentally, it accounts for about two-thirds of the in-kind benefits so critical to the statistical triumph over poverty. But then, when one looks a little more closely, it turns out that 46 percent of all Medicaid funds go for nursing homes and other forms of institutional care. To qualify for that, the elderly, blind, or disabled have to forfeit their social security or supplemental social security income. In short, the largest single portion of in-kind income goes to people waiting to die or utterly unable to care for themselves and without any cash income. Whether this constitutes the advance in well-being predicted by the conservatives and the Congressional Budget Office is, I think, at least open to question.

Let us look at the *reductio ad absurdum* of all these figures. In 1979, the medical care benefits for a single aging person were equal to 85.9 percent of the poverty line; for two persons they were 136.7 percent of the line. This latter family, it will be noted, turned a handsome profit on being sick. I do not, let me repeat, begrudge the elderly their benefits, and I opposed their reduction in the social security reform of 1983. But I most strenuously object to assigning those benefits—which are a very special kind of income for a very particular group of the poor—to the poverty population as a whole.

In short, a great deal, but not all, of the reduction of poverty by giving cash value to in-kind benefits is the result of statistical smoke and mirrors. Moreover, even the critique I have made of these tricky numbers somewhat understates the dimensions of poverty. Almost all of the figures used come from the late seventies or from 1980. That is because our calculations obviously always lag somewhat behind the reality they quantify. In this case, that is of great significance, because 1981-1983 was a period in which poverty was on the increase, first of all among those working people described in the last chapter, and, second, among those aging poor whose "one-time" loss of the indexing of their social security benefits in 1983 will affect the base of their payments for the rest of their lives.

How many poor people are there? Honest analysts can sincerely differ on the definition, but the reasons given for the alleged great decrease in the number of the poor in recent years are simply not persuasive. I would suggest that there are in the range of forty to fifty million Americans who live in poverty. That is roughly the same number I suggested more than twenty years ago, but, since the population has increased during those decades, it represents an exceedingly modest decline in the percentage of the poor.

It is also, if I may take off my stifling statistical mask and speak in a human voice, an unambiguous outrage.

III

As we toured the mathematical maze it became apparent that, relatively speaking, the aging poor get better care than anyone else under the poverty line. But that is only one point in a larger case, which may be stated as follows: The entire welfare state in the United States is primarily for people over sixty-five, most of whom are not poor; and this welfare state is the cheapest in the Western world.

Non-defense spending in the 1981 budget was $497.4 billion. Of that, interest payments—which benefited the rich disproportionately, but also helped the federal retirees—accounted for $82.5 billion. Indeed, as we shall see in a moment, more was paid to the recipients of interest than to the poor, which says something about our values. Payments to individuals (mainly social security checks) amounted to $316.6 billion, and roughly $60 billion of that total went to Medicare and Medicaid. As we have seen, 85 percent of the former and at least half of the latter went to people over sixty-five. Various retirement funds (social security, federal employee, railroad retirement, etc.) came to about $256 billion. Most of those monies went to people who were not poor. Indeed, if one looks at the funds directly assigned to the income security of those at the bottom of the society in 1981, they amount to a little less than $43 billion.

Anything that can be remotely called "welfare," then, is about 13 percent of the total federal payments to individuals. Put a little more dramatically, approximately 87 percent of the checks that Washington sends out goes to people who are not poor, not a few of whom spend a good deal of time complaining about welfare cheats. This truth was discovered by Peter Peterson, the former Secretary of Commerce, in a *New York Times* article in early 1982 and presented to the public as something of a revelation. We cannot, Peterson said, balance the budget by taking the poor off welfare, because we don't pay the welfare poor that much in the first place. Therefore, he concluded, we have to turn to social security, which is where the real money is. Peterson's proportions were correct; his policy proposals were, of course, reactionary.

James R. Storey, in a scholarly analysis of the same basic fact for the Urban Institute, concluded that the percentage of public money devoted to need-related programs (the poor) "has actually been less since 1965 than before. About 25 percent of total benefits was spent on aid to the needy before 1965, but this proportion has since ranged between 15 and 20 percent." The aging nonpoor, then, were the ones who made the greatest gains in recent years. They deserved them, and more, but this does not mean that the poor made similar progress.

But isn't this point a statistical trick of my own? It may well be, someone could argue, that the share of the public pie going to the impoverished has gone down, but hasn't the pie itself become much, much larger? If so, the relative decline in the poverty share of social spending disguises an absolute increase.

There are a number of problems with this thesis. We have already seen how a nominal doubling of outlays for health care between 1975 and 1980 amounted to a three-quarters inflation in costs and only a one-quarter increase in actual service. Ronald Reagan delights in citing soaring increases in spending, and almost always uses figures uncorrected for inflation to make his charge more compelling (needless to say, he always corrects for inflation when talking about defense spending), and quite often uses infinitesimal baselines in order to get huge percentage increases. If, however, we are serious about understanding the trends in federal spending, we obviously have to deal with constant dollars. This is particularly important, since many of the things the government buys—medical care, above all—have rates of inflation much higher than the Consumer Price Index.

Second, interest payments have been a growing factor in the budget, not the least because of the power of monetarist ideas in the White House and at the Federal Reserve Bank. Moreover, the interest cost does not represent current outlays on new goods and services, but rather reflects payments for past outlays. So it makes sense, if we want to compute what federal policy is doing in the present, to prescind from the latest component of the budget, which pays for the priorities of the past.

Third, a portion of federal expenditures is the result not of policy choices, but of the business cycle. For instance, Reagan's Council of Economic Advisors conceded in its 1983 report that a one-percent increase in unemployment results in lost revenues and increased costs (unemployment compensation, food stamps, welfare) of $25 billion. I agree with trade-union economists and others that the figure is more likely $30 billion, but there is no need to dispute a mere $5 billion here. The unemployment rate was 7.5 percent when Ronald Reagan took office in January 1981, and 10.8 percent in December 1982. That 3.3-percent increase meant, if one uses the Reagan figure, more than $80 billion in additional expenditures, and about $100 billion if the higher estimate is used. In short, increased unemployment accounted for about half of the federal deficit in 1982. In 1983, when the deficit remained at stratospheric levels even though joblessness was coming down, that factor was clearly not as important. Still, in any given year, one has to differentiate between the spending imposed upon an administration in Washington by the business cycle and the spending (or cuts) decided as a matter of policy. In 1982, for instance, if the unemployment rate had simply been at the official "target" of the early sixties, the budget would have been in surplus.

If we make all of these quite realistic corrections (adjusting for inflation and unemployment, subtracting interest), there is a rather startling result. Total federal outlays as a percentage of the GNP in 1956 under Eisenhower were 17.6 percent and—after all of those presumed "explosions" of the sixties and seventies—were 18.9 percent in 1981. The vast increase in the size of the public economic pie, in terms of GNP, was then 1.3 percent. And two-thirds of that quite modest rise occurred *after* Kennedy and Johnson, under the Presidencies of Richard Nixon and Gerald Ford. So the liberals were responsible for a 0.4-percent increase in real federal spending relative to gross national product. This is not to deny that there was a significant internal shift in the composition of that spending, as the defense portion went down and the social sector increased in the decade 1969–1979. But that shift, as we have seen, channeled money primarily to the nonpoor.

In all of this, the poor made some modest, and absolute, gains in their living standards during the sixties when gross national product was on the rise, and at least some of the new programs helped those who were impoverished but not aging. In the seventies and early eighties, GNP rose and fell, social meanness was up, and social programs were down. There was a relative and absolute decline in the conditions of life in the other America. For the fact is that, contrary to our stereotypes, the welfare state in this country is only incidentally for the poor and is primarily oriented toward people over sixty-five years of age, not toward people living under the poverty line.

That welfare state is also the cheapest in the advanced capitalist world.

If one looks at the percentage of the GNP spent on social programs in the mid- to late seventies, as Robert Reich and Ira Magaziner did in their book, *Minding America's Business*, there is a marked contrast between this country and all the other (relatively) rich nations. The United States spent around 14 percent of GNP on such functions, the West Germans more than twice that, and even the Japanese spent 17 percent. I say "even" the Japanese, because many programs that are in the public sector in the West are carried out privately there; e.g., male workers in major corporations are not laid off and given unemployment compensation, but are kept on by their employers even though there is no work for them. Still, the official Japanese outlays as a percentage of GNP are higher than in the United States.

The low percentage of GNP spent on social programs in the United States is reflected in the fact that this country is one of the least taxed in the Western world. In 1980, according to the OECD, American tax receipts were 30.7 percent of the gross domestic product, which meant that we lagged behind thirteen European nations. In that year, Sweden, under a conservative government, collected 49.9 percent of GDP in taxes; the Netherlands, 46.2 percent; West Germany, 37.2 percent; and Canada, 32.8 percent. Indeed, the United States's relative position actually declined in the years between 1955 and 1980. We ranked eleventh in 1955 and sixteenth in 1980. Thus, in international comparative terms, the American feeling that this is a highly taxed country with an elaborate welfare state contradicts the facts.

I do not want to suggest that all is well with the European welfare state. They, too, devote more funds to the nonpoor than to the poor in their social programs (by a ratio of three to one in the mid-seventies, according to *Le Monde*). And they are in deep trouble because of the economic crisis of the eighties. Indeed, their problems are in some ways even more formidable than those in this country, because they all have national health systems that cover the entire population, and medical costs in Europe are also soaring. I do not wish, then, to contrast a European utopia with an American social slum.

I do, however, want to attack one conservative argument on the basis of the contrast between the European and American welfare states. People like Ronald Reagan and William Simon say that this country fell behind in productivity and competitiveness in the 1970s because it lavished so much money on the unproductive poor and thereby starved private investment. Leave aside the fact that the data of the seventies simply do not support that thesis. The fact is that the Europeans in the postwar period spent much more on social programs *and* had lower rates of unemployment and inflation *and* high levels of investment. West Germany, whose economic performance significantly outclassed that of the United States in every one of these areas, spent twice as high a percentage of its GNP on social programs.

If, in short, social meanness were the key to productivity, America would, on the record of the past twenty years, be the most productive nation on the face of the earth.

But when will we recognize these truths? There are, as this chapter asserts, many more people who are poor than we recognize, not fewer; there is a welfare state that is stingy to those most in need, and second-class by comparison with Europe. When will America open its eyes?

I doubt that Marley's ghost will come to this nation as it sleeps on Christmas eve. Our social blindness will not be cured by a sudden rush of individual conscience on the part of our statistical Scrooges and Gradgrinds. For Thomas Gradgrind was saved. He drove his daughter into a disastrous marriage with a wealthy fraud who pretended to have risen from the lower depths, and he also looked the other way while his son became an embezzler. But he eventually recognized the unintended misery that his heartless, "factual" approach created, in part because he was touched by the decency of the daughter of a circus performer (the ultimate in un-Benthamite occupations).

Dickens's Manchester—"Coketown" in the novel—was incredibly real, an unforgettable rendering of "dark Satanic mills"; his solution, in *Hard Times* as in *A Christmas Carol*, was most sentimental. The eyes of a society are not opened by moralizing ghosts or lovable circus dogs; their field of vision is defined by the social movements of the age. In conservative periods, we become honestly, sincerely myopic; we literally cannot see the poor. Those of us who labor over the numbers, or even talk to people in a dying mill town in Maine, may be able to convince a few of our neighbors, but not much more. And yet, when this time of retreat comes to an end, when vision returns to this society, perhaps this brief excursion into the statistical maze, where the poor have been so carefully hidden, will help us see again.

5

Uprooted

On a gray December day in 1982, I went back to the Catholic Worker, on the Lower East Side of New York. A block away, the Bowery was almost deserted; on the corner of Houston Street and Second Avenue, a group of black men flapped their arms to keep warm; when I got to the Worker House of Hospitality on Third Street, the door was locked.

These simple details define an enormous shift that has taken place in the thirty years since I left the Catholic Worker, in December 1952. They are the clues of a new poverty.

The Worker was founded by Dorothy Day and Peter Maurin in 1933. When I came there at the beginning of 1951, Maurin was dead, but Dorothy was very much alive. A Midwesterner, and then a member of the socialist-communist bohemia in New York before and after World War I, Dorothy had learned Frances Thompson's poem "The Hound of Heaven" from Eugene O'Neill in a Greenwich Village speakeasy during Prohibition. That was one of the moments on a journey to the Catholic Church—"from Union Square [where the radicals used to soapbox] to Rome" she called it—and she was formally converted in the twenties. But she did not lose her leftist values. Rather, she brought her feminism, pacifism, and anarchism (she came to think of socialism as an excessively moderate philosophy) into the Catholic Church, where they were not always welcomed with unconstrained joy.

When she founded the Worker in 1933, she opened its first "house of hospitality." That was during the crisis of the Great Depression when millions were without food or lodging, and taking the traditional Christian injunction to feed the hungry, clothe the naked, and shelter the homeless was a radical program. But then, after World War II, many from that "one-third of the nation" found, if not affluence, at least a place in the postwar economy and society. Most of the houses of hospitality around the country closed, and the New York house, named for St. Joseph, the first worker-saint (Mary's husband was, of course, a carpenter, a building tradesman), ministered to the alcoholics from the Bowery rather than to the unemployed.

The Bowery was a "skid row" (the term comes from the Seattle docks, where the logs came down on skids from their river journey) where people wound up after a sickening descent to the bottom of the society. At the Worker in 1951–52, we ran a breadline in the early morning and a soup kitchen at noon, gave out clothes that were donated to us, and allotted about fifty beds in the house on a first-come, first-served basis. The "staff" lived in voluntary poverty, shared rooms with the people who came in off the street, ate the same food, and wore the same hand-me-down clothes. We were not professionals and, for the most part, did not pretend to be. We ministered to people's immediate necessities—the "corporal works of mercy" of Catholic tradition—and, rather than trying to cure their psychic and spiritual wounds, simply lived with them on a basis of equality (or as near equality as we could get).

The Bowery then was not at all the way it was when I returned thirty years later.

During the two years I had lived at Saint Joseph's House, the blocks along the Bowery from Canal to Fourteenth Street were teeming with people. Indeed, on a summer's day it might have seemed that one had blundered into some kind of urban picnic—but only if you did not notice the ravaged, sometimes haunted faces of the men and occasional women drinking together in desperate conviviality. Most of those people were white males in their forties and fifties, a high proportion Irish and Polish, a few Italians, and practically no Jews or blacks. They came from almost every walk of life. At various times I roomed with a dentist and a former staff writer for the Associated Press. Alcoholism is one of the most brutal forms of downward social mobility, and the trajectory from a profession to drinking muscatel in the streets was not all that uncommon.

Most of these people were not technically "homeless" in that they did not literally wander the streets of the city without a roof over their heads. That did happen—a man would pass out on the sidewalk and a passerby, looking for something to pawn so he could get a drink, might steal his shoes—but the majority lived in the seedy flophouses that lined the Bowery. And the place was not violent—or, rather, when it became violent, the fighters were usually so drunk that they could only do harm to themselves by slipping and falling. At the Worker, where people were sober and sometimes drying out with jangling nerves, there were occasional violent episodes, but not too many.

That Bowery is gone now; my casual impressions in December 1982 actually recorded a trend. This is not, however, cause for jubilation, but rather the sign of a new skid row. It is, as Kim Hopper and Ellen Baxter, two of the finest analysts of the phenomenon, have written, "no longer confined to well-demarcated 'tenderloin' areas of large cities. In most places, the homeless have ceased to observe the old geographical rounds." For more than ten years, a witness told a Congressional committee in 1982, a woman named Mary had been sleeping on the sidewalk by the guard house at the Pennsylvania entrance to the White House, a "modern Lazarus at Caesar's gate. . . ." In short, there were fewer aimless people on the Bowery that December day in 1982 because there were more of them everywhere in the city.

Who are they? Why have they appeared in our midst instead of staying in urban reservations like the Bowery of thirty years ago? Why, indeed, are they at Caesar's gate?

I

The phrase most people used to describe them during the winter of 1982–83 was "the homeless." That, I think, is too narrow a concept, particularly if one takes it literally. I think "the uprooted" is a broader, better term. Let me explain why, first in terms of a brief historical survey.

At the beginning of the capitalist era, in the sixteenth century, the dissolution of feudalism wrenched large numbers of people out of the traditional society that had, in its fashion, cared for them. With the enclosure of common lands, the commercialization of agriculture, and the growth of the wool trade, the old order was collapsing. Sheep, Thomas More said in his *Utopia*, were eating men. Suddenly, England was faced with the problem of "vagrancy." It was not, one should note, a matter of a great many individuals suddenly coming to the conclusion that they would wander the land. It was a social product, the consequence of one of the most gigantic upheavals civilization has ever known. "Vagrancy" almost always is. People do not choose it; it is chosen for them.

Society reacted with stick and carrot. Under Edward VI, for instance, it was decreed that anyone who refused to work "shall be branded by a red-hot iron on the breast with the letter *V*—and shall be adjudged the slave for two years of the person who should inform against such an idler." A century later, paupers were required to wear the letter *P* on their coats. These were some of the ways of handling the paradox defined then and persisting to this very day: "dearth in the midst of plenty." At almost the same time there were the first "poor laws," statutes that first made the famous distinction between the deserving poor (the aged, the helpless) who were given relief, and the undeserving poor (the young and able-bodied) who were to be made apprentices. After all, St. Paul's injunction—he who does not work shall not eat—is the basis of the political economy of the West.

This is a historical illustration of the point borrowed from Richard Titmus, i.e., that the welfare state is almost always inadequate compensation for a *dis*welfare state that hurts the poor and benefits the rich. So it was in the beginning and is now. Over the intervening centuries, every great economic transformation tore people out of their established ways and created a floating population. There was also, particularly in America, a migratory labor market. In the period before and after World War I, there were vagabonds, hoboes, gandy dancers, mainly men who drifted from casual occupation to casual occupation.

The most radical union that ever existed in America organized some of those "knights of the road." It was the Industrial Workers of the World, the "Wobblies," or, in somewhat less charitable slang, the "I Won't Work" movement. In some of the hobo jungles of the period, a membership card in the "One Big Union" was a ticket to a crude meal. But then, this is hardly ancient history. In 1982, Billie Jean Young of Rural America told a Congressional committee about the modern-day equivalents, the blacks driven off the land in the South who "wander from state to state in search of crops, living in cars, buses, trucks, under plastic, and in ditches along the way. . . ." That same year, in a small Nebraska town, I saw a 1930s-style "tourist court"—the tiny little wooden houses that were the precursors of our glossy motels—in which each shack had become a home for a Chicano migrant family who had settled in the area.

And in the thirties, when the connection between economics and migration was so obvious, there were treks like the one immortalized by John Steinbeck in *The Grapes of Wrath.* In 1949, when I first came into contact with the poor as a young, temporary social worker for the St. Louis Board of Education, there was still a "Hooverville" along the Mississippi River, a community of "houses" built of cardboard and discarded crates named in ironic honor of the President who led the nation into the Depression. This was the kind of poverty that Dorothy Day initially confronted.

But when I talked to Peggy Scherer, Frank Donovan, and Arthur Lacey at the Worker on that December day in 1982, the problems we discussed were not those of the thirties, or even of the fifties when I was at the Worker. The door to the house, as I said, was locked. That is the symbol of an enormous change. In my time the door was always open during the day, and anyone could walk in. But now the drifting population is much younger and much angrier. There have been fights in the food line, tensions between blacks, Hispanics, and Anglos. There are many more violence-prone and mentally ill people. Even the followers of Francis of Assisi must bolt the door.

I don't think "homeless" is the proper word for these new poor, since the word implies that their problem is a lack of physical shelter. It is much more profound than that. Some of them have roofs over their heads: adult homes, single-room-occupancy hotels (SROs), city shelters, or psychiatric emergency rooms and wards. And there are distinct, quite different groups of the uprooted: the famous "bag ladies" who huddle in the entranceways to stores at night or ride the subways; young workers, particularly from the minorities, who cannot find a place in the economy of the eighties; and ex–mental patients who have been, in theory, "deinstitutionalized," but in fact have been simply dumped onto the streets of the city or else "reinstitutionalized" in profit-making warehouses for discarded human beings.

What all of them have in common is that they, like those English peasants of the sixteenth century, have been uprooted and sent out, totally unprepared, into a world in bewildering transition. Indeed, they are a particularly dramatic illustration of an aspect of poverty emphasized by the French analyst Eliane Mosse, in her excellent study *The Rich and the Poor*. The poor, she writes, live lives of "precariousness." And, she adds, it is this phenomenon that has intensified in recent years. What follows, then, is an account of some precarious people.

Gregory is sitting in a park at Seventy-second Street and Broadway in New York City. He has been contacted by an outreach worker named Frank, who made his first contact with him by leaving a sandwich in a paper bag with a flier telling of the help that could be given him. Gregory had been scavenging garbage cans; he has the bad teeth that are the badge of his way of life. When Frank finally did meet him, it turned out that Gregory had been qualified for Supplemental Security Income (SSI) all along, but he wasn't getting any money. The reason was that he had lost his identity.

That is, Gregory didn't have a place to live, so there was nowhere he could receive a check. He had been mugged and had lost all of his papers. As Frank tells it, "His physical appearance and condition deteriorated. It was very difficult for him because it was embarrassing to go to the bank [to cash an SSI check, if he had one] the way he looked." So the first thing his newfound friend had to do was to restore his identity—to call SSI, help him apply for Medicaid, get him shaved and showered and deloused—i.e., to return him to some minimal contact with himself and society. He was no longer homeless—at least he was not homeless in 1982—but living at the Times Square Hotel. But he was still uprooted, a man suffering from social shell shock.

The Reverend Richard Virgil is a Lutheran minister in New York, active with a tenants' rights coalition that organizes the people in SROs. He talks of a case like Gregory's that ended in tragedy. When these people are forced out of their (often miserable) SROs, they often lose their bearings. The Reverend Virgil: "I had a situation of a guy that lived over on Riverside Drive who was fighting, struggling to keep his place. . . . Eventually he was forced out and moved to another place five or six blocks away, which for many tenants would be a lucky move. He was still in the neighborhood. But this man was subject to fits, seizures, and the people where he had been living knew that. And if they didn't see him for half a day, or a day, they would check and see what was going on.

"He was only at the new place for about three weeks when I got a phone call after worship one Sunday morning from the police, saying, 'Do you know this particular individual?' and I said yes. And they said, 'Well, we just found him dead in his room and we found your phone number in his pocket, so we are calling to ask you to come and make an identification.' " A "home" is not simply a roof over one's head. It is the center of a web of human relationships. When the web is shredded as a result of social and economic trends, a person is homeless even if he or she has an anonymous room somewhere.

We deal, then, with the uprooted—the lonely, fragile human victims of the massive economic and social trends of the last thirty years.

II

In 1955 there were 559,000 patients in public mental hospitals; in 1979 there were 146,000. The result of this "deinstitutionalization" has been either to reinstitutionalize these people or else to dump them on the streets. Mayor Edward Koch of New York City talked about the latter variant in bitter but accurate words in 1980. "The city can no longer afford," Koch said, "to have its neighborhoods used as mental wards and its police officers used as orderlies." But what is, from New York City's fiscal point of view, an intolerable financial burden is, for the individuals drifting in those urban mental wards, a personal catastrophe that makes their precarious mental and emotional life even worse.

It began with the best will in the world. In the nineteenth century it was conventional wisdom that mental illness could only be dealt with in the controlled environment of a public hospital (an "insane asylum"). Huge centers were built, almost always in rural areas, where the patients could be kept totally out of sight and mind. In the late fifties, hospital wards in New York State designed to hold twenty-five to forty patients contained twice that number, and it was common to have one or two attendants and one nurse in charge of seventy or eighty people. I went through such a ward in St. Louis in the mid-fifties, and the experience was unforgettable: people in white hospital gowns, often almost completely exposed, staring blankly; a woman trailing after the official who was my guide, cursing and threatening. A widely read book of the period provided a name for such places: snakepits.

In 1955, Congress, alarmed by reports of such intolerable situations, set up a Joint Commission on Mental Illness and Health. In 1961 it proposed a program of "deinstitutionalization" and community mental health centers. President Kennedy adopted its recommendations in 1963. The state hospitals, he said, "have been shamefully understaffed, overcrowded, unpleasant institutions from which death is the only hope of release." To deal with that miserable reality, the country would be divided into "catchment areas" and there would be a national network of community mental health centers, originally to be set up with federal "seed money," eventually to be locally financed. The ill in spirit were to be rescued from their hidden and often hideous asylums and brought back into the mainstream of society. That vision would also be facilitated by the march of science. New drugs had been discovered, powerful tranquilizers that would allow upset and bewildered people to cope with the world around them.

Once these plans were carried out, President Kennedy said, "Reliance on the cold mercy of custodial isolation will be supplanted by the open warmth of community concern and capability." Events were to mock that dream.

In fairly short order it became clear that a whole continuum of support institutions would be necessary if this bold concept was going to work. Time and again, responsible groups made that obvious point, and Congress listened. The excellent intentions of American society were clearly stated in the 1975 Amendment to the Community Mental Health Centers Act, the 1977 Comptroller General's Report to Congress, the 1978 President's Commission on Mental Health, the Mental Health Systems Act of 1979, and on and on. Moreover, there was a growing literature that documented how the deinstitutionalized could, in fact, live meaningful lives in well-organized community settings.

But the plans were either not implemented or else were implemented in a way that made the problem, and the individual agony, worse. The failure was not simply a matter of malevolence. In part, it was one more by-product of the economic crisis of the seventies and eighties, and of the fiscal crisis that it provoked. The cities and the states were delighted to approve a program that saved them money, and in the optimistic atmosphere of the sixties when the effort began, they did not bother too much about the theoretical commitment to the local financing of community centers at some time in an undefined future. But when it became necessary to act upon the critical aspect of deinstitutionalization—providing a decent alternative to a system that everyone agreed was inhumane—the city, state, and federal governments were under financial constraints they had not even imagined when the program started. By the end of the seventies, only 725 community health centers had been built and there were eight hundred catchment areas around the country without any coverage at all. Manhattan, where the problem of the discharged patients is patently visible on the streets, only had two centers. The mentally and emotionally ill as well as the retarded were volunteered by the hale and healthy to help balance the budget.

But money was not the only problem. Fear was another. People and neighborhoods became extremely anxious when they learned that a center was going to be built nearby. The "open warmth" anticipated by Kennedy was ice-cold, angry. Karen Kinsel is a woman who works with the mentally disturbed in New York. A self-styled "Republican and atheist" who says that she never has been in a demonstration, she was appalled one day when an elderly man came up and asked her for money for food. She was particularly shocked because the incident took place on the Upper East Side, one of the most affluent areas of New York City. Frightened and upset, she began to do volunteer work for the homeless and eventually became a full-time staff member at a hotel for the homeless, where she deals with emotionally and mentally disturbed people on a daily basis.

Her friends, she feels, have been disdainful toward her commitment. "Most of them," she says, "know very little about the program. . . . People seem to be afraid of it because they begin to realize how easily it can happen to you if you don't have some kind of social support for when crises occur in your life. When they see people who have really broken through this, they see themselves too closely and are very put off by it. . . . Some of my liberal friends find it, you know, quote, 'very touching,' and they offer to do things—generally not direct care. Many people want to do something but will not do direct care. They will not sit and talk with a woman and comfort her, take her to welfare. That is just too much for them."

Perhaps the most paradoxical expression of this fear is the

one I encountered in the winter of 1983 at the Dorothy Day Soup Kitchen at St. John's Church in Bangor, Maine. The people eating there were distinctly unthreatening, and there were even some hippies, refugees in a New England time warp. There is no problem getting volunteers to help, the cheerful priest in charge of the place told me; the problem is to fit them all into the schedule. But, he went on, the same people who will come and work in the kitchen and serve the poor at the tables will tell you that they would be afraid if such a facility were opened in their neighborhood.

If John Kennedy's original program had actually been carried out, if effective and well-funded centers had been put in place right away, I suspect that there might have been some resistance, but that it would have been manageable. What people in a city like New York fear today, however, is not a community center on a small, human scale with a professional staff, but the reality of spaced-out—sometimes acting-out—men and women who often do, indeed, seem to turn the street into a mental ward.

There is even a cruel sort of politics played with this issue. In New York, for instance, neighborhoods vie with one another to keep these strange and bizarre people off their particular turf, and it has not been unknown for politicians to punish enemies and recalcitrant wards by assigning them more of the human rejects. And housing policy may have had a part in this tragedy. In the sixties and seventies, more and more people (and real-estate speculators) took advantage of the tax breaks given to owners of cooperatives and condominiums. So a fair number were transformed from renters into owners. But that, as a woman who works with the homeless on New York's Upper West Side notes, made them more worried about property values, particularly since the area was being "gentrified." Their property was threatened along with their sensibilities.

The "hardness" of middle-class hearts is not simply some kind of moral flaw, a natural callousness toward human suffering. That is the effect, not the cause. It was the utter failure of public policy to do what it rightly proclaimed was absolutely necessary—the fact that deinstitutionalization came to mean, in a significant part, dumping bewildered human beings into environments they did not understand and could not deal with—that gave those hearts some rational basis for becoming hard. Perhaps society's inability to seize the precious moment when things might have turned out otherwise is irreversible. If it is not, the opportunity will only come again when society is actually willing to make it possible for people to be decent.

So far I have told only part of the story—the nice part. Now it is necessary to speak of those who made money out of this agony.

In 1935, Henry Saintestivan points out, Congress inadvertently laid the basis of a profit-making nursing-home industry. The social security law of that year would not permit payments to be made to the inmates of public institutions. This was because of widespread criticism of the "poorhouses" run by the states. However, the new statute did permit money to go to "boarding houses" where social security recipients lived with other "unrelated individuals." (Washington's statistical categories are sometimes unintentionally revealing; "unrelated individuals" could be a metaphor for the uprooted.) In time, the "boarding houses" became nursing homes and the nursing homes turned into a thriving, profit-making industry whose major source of income was the public purse.

There were two ways in which tax dollars supported the industry. First, the 14,048 private nursing homes in existence in 1981 received a great amount of money directly from federal, state, and local government. The total governmental contribution in that year was $13.559 billion, considerably more than all the funds spent on AFDC, Washington's most important "welfare" program. Second, a significant portion of that money came from individuals who used their social security checks to pay for it (or, in the case of incompetence, had their social security checks assigned by others to pay for it).

Almost all of the federal payments for nursing-home care come from Medicaid. But then, in 1972, Supplemental Security Income (SSI) was created for the aged, blind, and disabled poor not covered, or not covered adequately, under other programs. By 1981, well over half of its $4.019 billion went to people under sixty-five. They are the non-aging, walking wounded of American society. Just as in the social security law, SSI money cannot be sent to "inmates of public institutions," but can go to the residents of boarding houses. The result: a new, profit-making industry. "Adult homes" are intermediate-care facilities originally intended for the "frail elderly" who are medically healthy but need some care, such as having meals prepared or linen changed. But then, with deinstitutionalization, the underpopulated adult homes spotted a new market: the SSI funds and other government monies. In units housing as few as five people and as many as 375, *The New York Times* reported, they "welcomed the tide of formerly hospitalized mental patients and their Supplemental Security Income checks."

In 1980, Dr. Jack Weinberg, the administrator of the Illinois Mental Health Institute, testified before the Senate Special Committee on Aging. Senator Charles Percy asked, "Don't you imagine that there is the possibility that the operators of nursing homes . . . put pressure on the state and other government officials to release patients because they want to fill beds? They have got stockholders' reports to show. They have got empty beds and they are going to fill them with bodies. . . . Don't you think that sets the pressure up to fill these beds?" Weinberg answered: "It certainly does. . . . Someone in my family was approached by a nursing home operator asking [that he] approach me to direct patients into his home and that he would offer me a stipend of $100 per head."

So it was that Kim Hopper and Ellen Baxter concluded in 1982 that the "deinstitutionalization policy is more accurately described as one of *re*institutionalization." Of the estimated 1.7 million to 2.4 million chronically mentally ill adults in the United States, 750,000 are in nursing homes, 300,000 to 400,000 are "in unsafe or substandard board and care homes." Still others are in SROs, which, like nursing and adult homes, are private institutions paid with public funds, but without many of the nominal safeguards required in the former. This vast population is not living in the streets. There is a roof over every head—but the people are no less homeless, no less uprooted, for that fact.

They are also often the victims of bureaucratic rules and of the unintended consequences of federal laws. Gregory, the man in the park who lost his identity, is not an isolated or atypical case. Carol Bellamy, the president of the New York City Council, told Congress in 1982 that many of the mentally disabled cannot negotiate the complex review and appeals procedure of the Social Security Administration. And even when they do surmount that hurdle, they are often simply turned down by a government that is economizing on costs and human care. Of the people who turned to the New York City shelter program in 1982 and were found to have severe mental disabilities, only 26 percent, Bellamy testified, were accepted. At the same time, the city's efforts to help are subverted by the rule that says SSI payments can't go to inmates of public institutions (during the homelessness "crisis" of the winter of 1982–83, that restriction was relaxed, but only relaxed).

Meanwhile, the bureaucracies play complicated games to see what jurisdiction will pick up the check for the mentally ill. When they are in state hospitals, the state pays. But when they are sent out to local communities and come under Medicaid, New York City and other localities have to pick up 25 percent of the cost. From 1977 to 1980, 40,000 patients were sent from state institutions to New York City, and when Mayor Koch made his bitter comment about turning the streets into public wards for mental patients, he was, among other things, maneuvering to get the state to put up more of the money for the care of the city's disabled.

We are a long way from "the open warmth of community concern" envisioned by John Kennedy in 1963. Some of the mentally ill are simply dumped on the streets; others are reinstitutionalized in facilities that may or may not represent an advance over the snakepits of old; the public grows frightened and callous; private speculators in mental and emotional anguish profiteer from government funds; politicians play elaborate games to shift the cost to some other jurisdiction.

The ultimate irony is that deinstitutionalization has itself become a cause of more mental illness. The world of the shelters and the SROs is a violent, frightening place, filled with stress; so is life on the streets. And many of the observers believe that people who are uprooted in these various ways have all of their problems made worse. Stress, it was suggested back in the fifties by analysts at Yale, can be a source of mental illness. The reason for the mental health chasm between the poor and everyone else, they suggested, is that life at the bottom of the society is simply more nerve-wracking than life anywhere else in the society.

If that was true for the old poverty—for those who have never been institutionalized, who had managed to stay this side of chronic psychosis and only suffered from episodes in which they lost contact with reality—think of what it is for the mentally ill of the new poverty, for people who have been officially diagnosed as precarious and fragile, when they are dumped into a kind of social jungle. They haunt the America of the eighties, tortured men and women, the ghosts of our good intentions.

III

"Wassail," a traditional English Christmas song, could have been written about one group of the new poor in the America of the eighties:

> *We aren't the daily beggars who beg from*
> *door to door*
> *We are your neighbors' children, and we've*
> *been here before . . .*

The deinstitutionalized mental patients, the bag ladies on the New York subway, are "them," aliens from a world most Americans have never known. But recently, in Europe as well as in this country, our neighbors' children have suddenly appeared among the ranks of the uprooted. They are frightening not because they are bizarre and strange, but because they are "us."

Actually, there are three somewhat distinct groups within this category. All of them share in common the fact that they either work or desperately want to do so, and are uprooted because the economy has no place for them. Some of them suffer from a type of poverty that is not new but has become more problematic; they are the working poor. Then there is one of the most disturbing subcultures of our times, the young people who have been rejected by the world of work almost before they could enter it. Finally, there are those who have held jobs that paid well above the poverty line, but have been laid off and have already fallen through the tattered "safety net" in the America of Ronald Reagan.

Contrary to the stereotype, the poor are not lazy. If one leaves aside the poverty families headed by a woman (a special case that will be discussed in Chapter 8), about two-thirds of the heads of poor families worked at least part time in 1980—and 43.1 percent were full-time workers. If one subtracts those too ill to work from the total, and adds in the unemployed who simply could not find jobs, well over half of the employable householders among the poor in 1980 were either working full time or trying to do so. In America as a whole, 55.7 percent of the people held full-time jobs in that year—i.e., those in the other America who could work did so at almost the same rate as those who often called them lazy freeloaders.

But the minimum wage in the United States is so low that men and women can work full time and not be able to provide minimum necessities for their families. Indeed, it was precisely this group that suffered most from Ronald Reagan's budget cuts in 1981. The President made it harder to qualify for food stamps and Medicaid, and thus struck a severe blow at the working poor (who are the popular "deserving" poor in our culture). These are the people who teeter on the brink of poverty, and the minimal food and medical care they had received helped let them keep their heads above water. Ironically, this policy does not take any benefits away from the welfare poor (the "undeserving" poor, as far as many Americans are concerned), because they get the benefits automatically.

The President's priorities should not come as a surprise, however, since it is cherished conservative dogma that the minimum wage is too high, that what is needed is the competitive stimulus that lower incomes would bring. This argument holds that by setting the cost of marginal labor above the actual market rate, well-meaning liberals have priced the poor, and the minority poor in particular, out of the labor force. Only if the nation allows the law of supply and demand to further depress the incomes of those at the bottom will the excluded get a chance to work. In fact, even the data presented by proponents of this theory, such as the black economist Walter Williams, do not prove it. In the fifties and early sixties, when the minimum wage was raised, black teenagers increased their labor-force participation; in the late sixties and the seventies, when the minimum wage was raised, that participation declined. This suggests that it was not the minimum wage that caused the decline—if that were the case, the rate would have dropped in the fifties and early sixties, too—but some new economic factors in the later period. And that is precisely what is analyzed in this book.

Indeed, the numbers point not at the "evil" of the minimum wage, but in another, most unconservative direction; they show that poverty is better conceived of as a magnetic field than as a "line." At any given point, there is a large "at risk" population in the United States. It is composed of unskilled, low-paid workers who are one recession, one illness, one accident away from being poor. For instance, a University of Michigan study that tracked five thousand families over a period of ten years found that 25.2 percent received welfare at one point or another in the decade, but less than one-fifth of that number were regularly receiving public assistance. In other words, only about 5 percent of the total sample were, in any sense of the term, "welfare dependent," permanent wards of the state.

Even as David Stockman was testifying that poverty was much less of a problem than most people thought, he documented the existence of this magnetic field of misery. Almost half of the poor, he showed, were impoverished for a year or less—and 15 percent were poor for eight or more years. What is particularly significant in the present context is that, for men, 73.5 percent became poor because their earnings decreased—and 92.2 percent escaped from poverty because their wages increased. In this context, New York City reported in late 1983 that a ten-year decline in the number of people receiving welfare had come to an end with 900,000 new additions to the rolls. A significant part of this increase, the city said, was due to young, unemployed single people who had been forced to ask for public assistance.

This point ramifies in many directions, but the one that is relevant here is that there is, and has been for years, a huge group of people who go in and out of poverty, who live on the edge but try as best they can to survive on their own. What is new in the eighties, then, is not the existence of this category but the fact that it now suffers cruelly from soaring unemployment rates. For this is an area where conservative free-market theory actually does work—to cruel effect. As Rone Tempest of the *Los Angeles Times* documented in an excellent survey of homelessness in 1982, "Jobs that were once the reserve of the lowest classes now seem attractive to members of the class immediately above, who quite naturally make more attractive applicants for employment."

Here, for example, is Delia, a black woman from New York City. "I worked awhile in a factory, as a salesgirl in stores, counter girl in restaurants, waitress in restaurants. I worked at a machine in a factory, an operator. . . ." What happens when she gets laid off? "They don't give you so much notice and all that. They say, 'Don't come in tomorrow, come in later 'cause we ain't got much work to do.' " Her experience was repeated millions of times in recent years. And it also helped create a new group of the homeless poor: the young who are rejected by the labor market before they get a chance to join it.

A survey at San Francisco's Trinity Episcopal Church, reported by Tempest, reflects this development. The church is in the Tenderloin, but now, the rector says, "the standard derelict type comprises no more than 30 percent of the people we serve." A questionnaire of the homeless single men who came for help in December 1982 showed that 40 percent were between 16 and 29 years of age. Another 32 percent were between 30 and 39. There were 70 percent with work skills, 92 percent with high-school diplomas, 30 percent with college degrees.

New York had much the same experience. Carol Bellamy, the city council president, told Congress that the men who came to the city to get shelter had an average age of 36 years in 1981, and 63 percent were under 40. Half were high-school graduates, one-fifth had attended college, and 40 percent said they were looking for a place to sleep because they had lost a job. More than one-third were veterans. These are truly our neighbors' children.

What is particularly disturbing about the phenomenon is the number of young people in their late teens and early twenties who are finding it difficult to get into the labor force at all. Obviously, if unemployment declines and work opens up, the percentage who are permanently disabled by the experience will be smaller. But even the official definitions now assume that a pool of at least seven million unemployed—Karl Marx would have called it a reserve army of labor—is a necessity even in good times. And all the evidence today points to the probability that the "surplus" population will be younger than the rest of the society and disproportionately black and Hispanic—i.e., that it will reinforce the structures of poverty and institutional racism. Not so incidentally, it is this younger age group that is the source of most of the violent crime that has ravaged the United States in recent years.

And finally, there are the new migrants—not the young, not the mentally ill, but the American working men and women who have been forced onto the road in search of a job. They are the Okies of the 1980s, and they were particularly visible in that winter of the national discontent, 1981–82.

The *Los Angeles Times* reports that in Houston, so many of the cars parked outside of day-labor offices, with families sleeping in them, are from Michigan, a state with a black license plate, that they are called the "black tag people." In Denver, an eight-month-old infant girl living in a Toyota with her parents died of the cold even though she was wrapped in blankets. Her father had run out of a string of fast-food jobs. "Homeless America," Rone Tempest wrote, "is a world in motion. All across the land cars prowl the interstates and urban boulevards with license plates from distant places and belongings stuffed in the trunk and stacked on the roof. Michigan heading south, Arizona going north, Ohio west and California east."

Part of the problem, which few Americans understand, is that the majority of the jobless do not collect unemployment benefits. In June 1982 there were 10.4 million people officially out of work. That figure, it must be stressed, particularly understates the dimensions of the misery being analyzed here. To be a statistic, one must either be on temporary layoff or actively looking for work. The 10.4-million figure does not take into account the "discouraged" workers, the people who are not looking for a job because they know they will not find one, and thus have deprived themselves of even the chance of being counted. Yet it is precisely among this group that one is likely to find the most desperate and demoralized people without any benefits at all.

But all was not well with the 10.4 million jobless people in the summer of 1982 who were a part of the government's statistics. Only 42 percent of them were collecting unemployment benefits, and those payments averaged only 46 percent of their before-tax earnings, with the unemployed manufacturing workers getting only 36 percent of what they had been making. For a good number of these people, even the rumor of work was enough to put them on the highway.

But this phenomenon also exists in Europe, where the jobless benefits are much more generous and, in countries such as Belgium and Holland, effectively last as long as the unemployment. VICTIMS OF RECESSION LIVE IN CHEAP HOTELS, DORMS, EVEN TENTS AND BOXES, the European edition of *The Wall Street Journal* reported in a headline in the spring of 1983. In West Germany it is estimated that there are 260,000 people without proper shelter. In Britain the number of people getting a "supplementary benefit" after they exhaust their one year of unemployment compensation has almost doubled since 1979. And, the Europeans note, there seems to be a marked increase in the number of women who have joined the ranks of the uprooted. On the Continent, too, the *Journal* said, "the derelicts have been joined by thousands of young people who have never held jobs; by people who have worked too little to qualify for unemployment benefits; by self-employed workers who have gone bankrupt; by released prisoners and mental patients; and by people who, even with government benefits, haven't enough income to hang on to their homes."

In some cases, as I learned from meeting with trade unionists in Louisville in the fall of 1983, a lifetime of work can be wiped away. A UAW leader told how the farm-implement factory that his local had organized had not simply shut down but gone bankrupt. This meant that pensions accumulated through years of labor had become precarious. Here, too, the catastrophe was particularly acute for the older worker who had been robbed of his or her retirement. This case was part of a pattern: management using bankruptcy, or the threat of bankruptcy, as a means to force concessions from workers or to unilaterally abolish existing legal rights that the workers had won long ago.

The crisis of the uprooted, then, is not a function of the stinginess of the American welfare state—although that most certainly makes matters worse in this country—but of the crisis of the Western economy in the late seventies and eighties. If the analysis outlined in Chapter 1 is accurate, then all of the advanced capitalist societies are facing problems analogous to those that emerged at the very dawn of the capitalist revolution, when "sheep ate men" in an England going through a wrenching economic transition, and "vagrancy" spread across the land.

IV

It is fairly easy to show that unemployed workers are the victims of massive economic trends in the society. But it is also true, though much less obvious, that the seemingly private agonies of drifters on the street, of people who are sometimes totally absorbed in their own dream world, are related to social structures and public policy. There is a sociology and a political science of uprootedness. Two vividly contrasted men constitute a first case in point.

Gregory, the man who lost his identity as well as his SSI check, is talking: "Well . . . I was residing in the subway. My home was the RR train. That's the Fourth Avenue local. It goes from Astoria [Queens] to Bay Ridge in Brooklyn. And the weather, it got a bit nice or more pleasant and I started to take in a bit of sun in Central Park." Why, he was asked, that specific train?

Why the RR? "Well, I was more familiar with that since I come from Brooklyn, and that's the train that goes through Bay Ridge. . . . I had a studio apartment in Bay Ridge."

People who take false names, it is often said, usually keep something of their real names in the pseudonyms. The initials are the same, some syllables repeat. So with Gregory. He was homeless, living on a subway, but he chose the subway that served his old neighborhood. He, and almost everyone else in the society, was clinging to the last fragment of community available to him, and even though he had no money, no papers, no real human contact, he still thought of himself as part of the Bay Ridge section of Brooklyn.

Barney seems, at first, a totally different case from Gregory; he is together, confident, a relatively happy man who inhabits the physical world of the homeless in the Times Square area, but seems to have been emotionally untouched by its ravages. He tells how he saves money from his social security check and is able to take winter vacations. "Yeah, I get the standard allowance, which is $444 . . . which is over $100 a week, and I can cover my expenses very easily and save money on $100 a week. Largely by taking advantage of the government programs. Like I eat at the senior citizens' center for thirty-five-cent meals. My clothes is all thrift shop. . . . And I live in a subsidized apartment where I save money on that."

Why is he so different? "I'm a mechanical engineer. All my life I have worked on budgets and efficiencies and saving money and so I am very careful. I have a budget. I know what my expenses are; I know what I get and what I spend and the difference shows up in the bank." Which is to say that Barney might have been invented by some conservative critic of the welfare state. For he is what all of their imagined poor people are: organized, a calculating, careful *Homo economicus* who maximizes every single benefit, who does indeed turn those in-kind programs into a form of cash income. Uprootedness, then, is not simply a physical problem—it *is* that, as we shall see in a minute—or even a question of personal psychological qualities. It is also a function of social class and social class habits; it is one thing for a Gregory, who never really held a job, or for a former mental patient dumped onto the cruel streets, and another for a mechanical engineer. The problem is, the latter type is a rarity at the bottom of the society.

I romanticize just a bit. Barney's life is not quite so idyllic as it might at first seem: "Like Tuesday evenings, there is something called the treasure hunt where you walk up Lexington Avenue around Fiftieth Street and the wealthy people put out their used clothing. . . . You get that completely for nothing. Well, you find out what night the people put their garbage out on the East Side and you go over there. And you look around. And I've picked up some very nice items over there for nothing." So *Homo economicus* is also reduced to going through other people's garbage.

But then, even when those drifters seem to make demented decisions, they are often acting upon a logic that correctly responds to perverse social reality. For instance, for some of the people who ride the subways or huddle in doorways, their action is a rational choice from among impossible alternatives. Should they live in one of the New York City shelters? These places are bureaucratically organized, sometimes in the worst sense of the word. At one point (the practice was changed later on), all of the homeless were being collected at one center on the Lower East Side of Manhattan, were then bused to locations where they sometimes arrived late at night, and were awakened very early in the morning so that they could be bused back to the intake station. That was neat and well organized, from an official point of view. At the same time, the shelters can also be fearful places, a consequence of the presence of all those young people and of disturbed men and women as well as of racial and ethnic tensions in this new form of poverty.

What about an SRO? There are few of them available. Between 1970 and 1982, New York City lost more than 111,000 such units, representing 87 percent of the total. Kim Hopper and Ellen Baxter report: "Only 17,200 units remain today. Some were abandoned and left to deteriorate; others fell victim to arson; still others were priced out of the range of public assistance recipients;

and a good proportion (as many as 40 percent) fell prey to conversion efforts. Nor is this phenomenon restricted to New York City: nationwide, in the same decade 1,116,000 units—or 47 percent of the total supply—disappeared."

Why ride a subway all night in New York City? For the same reason that Jesus was born in a stable; there are no rooms in the inn. What is more, this is a result of public policy, sometimes of deliberate governmental actions to provide welfare for the middle class at the expense of the poor.

You can glimpse this reality in the 1982 report of Ronald Reagan's Commission on Housing. The quality of America's housing, the commission proudly noted, has "vastly improved" since World War II. Overcrowding (more than one person to a room) is down from 20 percent in 1940 to 4 percent; only 4 percent of the units in 1980 lacked complete plumbing facilities; and the stock of dilapidated housing is now less than 10 percent of the available units. In part, this statistical triumph represents exceedingly simple physical notions about decent housing which ignore the social quality of a deteriorating neighborhood. Still, there is no question that there has been significant progress for the mass of Americans over the postwar period. Only the poor are, as the commission itself shows, an exception to the trend.

Inadequate housing is far more common among renters than among owners—and the poor are disproportionately renters. So 18.6 percent of the "very low income renters" (50 percent of the median income or less) live in inadequate housing, which is almost three times the rate for the society as a whole. Almost 20 percent of black households suffer from that plight, and 12.3 percent of Hispanic households. In current theory, people spending more than 25 to 30 percent of their incomes on housing are paying "too much." But that category has increased since 1950, from 32 percent of all renters to 51 percent. The commission hastened to explain this anomaly. It is, the commission said, simply the expression of the fact that the middle class and the rich became owners at a very rapid rate, the poor remained renters, and the numbers simply reflect the new proportions. True enough. Another way of putting the same analysis is to say, "The better-off got better off; the worse-off got worse off." Ronald Reagan's commissions do not, of course, speak such language.

But then, the point at issue is not simply a bit of moralizing about the well-known misery of the poor. It is rather the substantial question of how government policy contributes to this antisocial outcome.

Gentrification is the ungainly word that has been coined to describe the process whereby the middle class and the rich take over the physically sound and architecturally charming housing of the poor. This is an area in which "trickle down" is supposed to operate. That is, with the exception of public housing, the construction industry does not build homes or apartments for the poor. Its market is found among the middle class and the rich, and their cast-off dwellings, like the clothes Barney found in the garbage on the East Side of Manhattan, are eventually supposed to filter down and satisfy the needs of those at the bottom of the society. The problem is that some of that aging, once wealthy housing can be very attractive. And so the gentrifiers—the "new pioneers," as they have been called—return to the central city and restore the gracious old buildings. Not so incidentally, this action dispossesses the poor.

The most famous single case in point is, of course, the very fashionable Georgetown area of Washington, D.C., which was a slum not too long ago. Greenwich Village in New York City was the center of America's bohemia for more than half a century, in part because it contained cheap apartments on twisting quaint streets. Indeed, bohemia was, and is, the only place in this country where poverty is happy because it is voluntary and lived in the service of the ideal of art. But bohemians, unfortunately for them, have excellent taste, which they eventually pass on to the bourgeoisie from which they fled. Greenwich Village gradually became a most chic place, and today it is one of the most expensive neighborhoods in New York City. Garrets have become high-rent property.

As the artists were pushed out of the Village, they turned to the loft area south of Houston Street (SoHo). But that place then acquired a cachet in ten or fifteen years that it took fifty years for the Village to achieve. And it was not simply that the artists were displaced from the now fashionable lofts; so were the small industrial enterprises that had often provided entry-level jobs for the working poor. During the same period, some of the bohemians had migrated over to the Lower East Side, but there were tensions between them and the poor people there, for they tended to drive up the rents. (Under New York City law, the landlord can increase the basic rate every time an apartment turns over, which happened often among the hippies of the sixties and seventies.)

Now, the people at the Catholic Worker told me, the whole Lower East Side, a point of departure for generations of the poor, is being gentrified. But then, this problem is not simply urban. In January 1983 I went to rural Maine to visit the headquarters of an organization called HOME (Homeowners Organized for More Employment). It is an organization, Catholic in inspiration, that works with the country poor and tries through various forms of cooperative activity to help them help themselves. In the old days, they tell me, there was a kind of self-sufficient poverty, not to be romanticized, but possessing a certain independence and dignity. There was berry-picking, clamming, subsistence farming. But now middle-class people, from Maine and out of state, have been buying up houses and farms. Some of the displaced have found jobs in the mill towns, such as nearby Bucksport, while others drift. There is more alcoholism in an area that has long known that problem, and there is family breakdown. (The description of the latter reminded me of a popular song: "She had a ring on her finger / And time on her hands.")

In short, the middle-class passion for the quaint affects people in rural Maine as well as on the Lower East Side of Manhattan. And, more often than not, there are government subsidies to help the well-off push the poor aside.

Even President Reagan's commission recognized the point. During the 1960s and 1970s, the enormous tax savings from the deductibility of mortgage interest provided much more welfare for the middle class and the rich than it did federal housing programs for the poor. This, the commission admitted, led to a wave of condominium and cooperative conversions, reduced the level of demand for rental housing, and eventually caused a decline in the construction of rental housing. Indeed, as early as 1971, the Census documented a trend in which the traditional pattern—whites move out, blacks move in—shifted in the Northeast as whites began to replace blacks.

In New York City, where the homelessness crisis is most acute, this federally subsidized process was further accelerated by a municipal tax-abatement program that effectively subsidized the conversion of SROs into higher-priced apartments. So much money was involved that many SRO owners took to eviction tactics—sometimes within the law, sometimes not—to force the lower-income, often poor, people out and to make way for the middle class and the rich. After all, the latter had much higher welfare payments, in the form of those tax deductions, than the former with their AFDC and SSI checks. So it was that Father Donald Sakano of the Catholic Charities of the Archdiocese of New York testified in 1981: "Feverish real-estate speculation in strong market areas, such as the West Side, East Midtown, and more recently the Bowery, has caused mass displacement—most often by illegal means—of SRO tenants. . . . The growing number of homeless people coincides with the diminishing number of SRO units. . . . With the number of units vastly reduced, and the vacancy rate in existing units close to zero, there is an absurd gap in available, affordable housing for the single low-income person."

In short, not only is there no room in the inn, but the national and local governments have devoted a fair amount of money to see that there will be none. After all, a lonely, drifting SSI recipient pays no taxes; an upper-middle-class condominium owner does. Again, I do not want to be moralistic. New York City, after it was effectively prodded by a variety of community agencies, has actually devoted time and money to trying to deal with the problem of the uprooted, which New York City helped to create. Moreover, the urban fiscal crisis of the seventies and eighties, in New York and everywhere else, is hardly a product of the evil imagination of callous mayors. It is quite real.

And yet an ancient and cruel logic asserts itself. In the absence of a truly effective political movement mobilized behind serious and humane alternatives, such crises are resolved at the expense of the most vulnerable. They can't fight back; they are without influence. So polite, middle-class society copes by pushing uprooted people out onto the street. The latter then offend the sensibilities of the affluent residents of subsidized apartments, who wonder how people could have ever come to be like that.

—6—

Superfluous People

There were, Disraeli said in the nineteenth century, two nations in Britain, the rich and the poor. There were, I wrote some twenty years ago, two Americas, the semiaffluent America of the majority, and the other America of poverty. Does one now have to add that there are two *black* Americas, one inhabited by those who made significant progress in the past generation, the other peopled by those who are not simply poor—that is hardly new—but who are in danger of becoming completely superfluous?

That possibility can be glimpsed in the very ambivalence of both the data and my own impressions.

In 1959, before the War on Poverty began, there were 1.9 million black families below the poverty line. In 1969, after ten years of extraordinary economic growth, that number had dropped to 1.4 million. But in 1980, after the stagflation seventies, there were 1.8 million black poor families. Over two decades, then, the facts are clear enough, aren't they? A decrease of 500,000 poor families, followed by an increase of 400,000, which means that hardly anything has changed at all.

It is not quite that simple. For the very same years were, to quote Dickens, the best of times and the worst of times. Between 1969 and 1979, nonwhite family income, as a percentage of the income of white families, declined from 65 percent to 63 percent—but the income of nonwhite families headed by a regularly employed man went from 64 percent to 73 percent; that of a family headed by a regularly employed woman rose from 82 percent to 95 percent of the white level. A black woman with a college degree in 1969 received 108 percent of the income of her white sister; if she was West Indian, 132 percent. If, then, black America had been primarily composed of intact families headed by college graduates, everything would have been fine. In fact, it was during this same period that there was a sharp rise in those families headed by a woman who did not work regularly in the paid labor market, if at all. These women and their children were not participating in the gains, but were in danger of falling off the edge of the society.

My own casual impressions were, and are, as contradictory as the official figures. Between 1954 and 1964, I spent a great deal of time in Harlem as a civil rights activist. We worked out of the office of A. Philip Randolph's Brotherhood of Sleeping Car Porters, or else at the Harlem Labor Center, both on 125th Street. That avenue was one of the central axes of vibrant street life: there was the Apollo Theater with its legendary concerts; the Hotel Theresa, which became internationally famous when Fidel Castro stayed there in 1959; and black integrationists, nationalists, and Muslims who carried on excited debates on the corners. There were larger-than-life black leaders, too: Randolph himself; Adam Clayton Powell, part militant and part rogue and always challenging; Malcolm X, the intense Muslim ex-convict who, in the period immediately before his assassination, was moving in the direction of an integrationist vision of a united movement of the poor.

Let there be no mistake—there was tremendous misery, too. Still, the mood was not one of defeat and despair. Around 1964 or 1965, the atmosphere began to change, and as my black co-workers explained to me, it was now not wise for a white—even a civil-rights-activist white whose personal convictions were not, after all, immediately visible to people on the street—to roam the streets of Harlem. But even that development, painful as it was for me, had its positive aspect. In part, it reflected a new sense of pride and dignity, a refusal to be a place where whites "slummed" in jazz joints or patronized the streetwalkers—or even came with noblesse oblige to help out the less fortunate. In the years since, I have simply passed through Harlem from time to time.

One day not too long ago, a silver-haired black cabdriver with a deep, sonorous voice—he reminded me a bit of A. Philip Randolph, who was one of nature's noblemen—drove me across 125th Street. Harlem, it seemed to me, was grim and dilapidated, without that coursing vitality I had known earlier. The Theresa was no longer a hotel; there was a boulevard named for Adam Clayton Powell, but there was no Adam Clayton Powell; the Apollo was closed. I knew from my research that the population had declined, but so, it seemed to me, had the spirit. I talked to the cabdriver and he agreed. He told me he thought a line from a song now applies: "Where do you go from nowhere?"

Not too long afterward, I chatted with one of the most decent black political leaders in the United States, David Dinkins, the City Clerk of New York, a man with whom I had worked in many campaigns. He was optimistic, positive about black New York. He sensed real political stirring. And indeed, if you take political participation as a sign of the morale of a community—and it certainly is an important index—Dinkins's hopes were fulfilled in a very short time. Black involvement in Mario Cuomo's campaign for governor was a major factor in his victory over Ed Koch, and was a departure from previous patterns. The triumph of Harold Washington in Chicago in 1983 was evidence of the same trend; so was the victory of Wilson Goode in Philadelphia the same year, and Mel King's remarkable showing in the Boston mayoral elections.

The ambiguity of the statistics and impressions express, I think, two divergent trends. The stable black working class and a growing black middle class made real gains in the sixties, and even in the seventies. At the same time, a great mass of poor blacks was denied the chance that had come to all of the traditional (pre–World War I) immigrant groups. That is, at that point at which they arrived in the urban labor market ready to climb up the ladder of social mobility, the bottom rungs were being hacked off the ladder. So many blacks are in danger of disappearing down a hole in the American occupational structure.

These divergent trends have many ramifications, and we will explore some of them. One of the most ironic, however, deserves to be noted at the outset. Poor blacks have long suffered the psychological deprivation that went along with the material misery of living in the tenements and shacks of a semiaffluent white society. At the same time, the black middle class was itself impoverished because racism blocked the road to the mainstream of business and the professions. Black lawyers, doctors, insurance agents, and funeral directors—death was one of the few industries that white America let blacks run—were hemmed in by poverty, even if they did not share it themselves. Indeed, as Cayton and Drake showed in their analysis of Chicago during the Depression, *Black Metropolis*, the black "middle class" was, more often than not, a working class in terms of its income. A sleeping-car porter was an exceedingly solid and established citizen, which was one of the reasons for the enormous importance of their union, headed by A. Philip Randolph.

To be sure, there were always tensions even within that rough democracy of misery—between have-littles and have-nots, between descendants of American slaves and those with roots in the West Indies, and so on. There were even those who used to talk bitterly of the National Association for the Advancement of Colored People as the National Association for the Advancement of Certain People. Now, however, there is a black middle class that *is* middle class. But the very same forces that helped create that happy result may well have turned a significant portion of the black population into an underclass, or at least into candidates for that role.

This concept is tentative; the trends are still at work, and in any case they are only trends, not fates, and could be reversed by a political mobilization.

I

Why don't "they" act like "we" did? This has long been the cry of well-meaning white Americans who simply can't understand why blacks don't repeat the classic immigrant experience. Our parents, or grandparents, so the argument goes, came here desperately poor, with nothing more than strong arms and high hopes. They worked their way out of poverty. They didn't go whimpering to the federal government, asking for special privileges. Why don't blacks do as we did? Indeed, there are even some black thinkers who accept this theory. It is, for example, the core of Thomas Sowell's utterly optimistic analysis of black ethnicity. The business economy, Sowell says, has abolished more racism than have all of the federal programs put together. Instead of looking for affirmative action, blacks should turn toward free enterprise, away from government and toward market forces.

Sowell's statement of this case has been subjected to a number of telling scholarly criticisms, but that does not concern me here. Even if one accepts his idyllic account of American ethnic history (which I do not), his thesis works only if one makes the huge assumption that the ethnic and racial future is going to be pretty much like the ethnic and racial past. But that is not the case.

Immigration flows, as Sowell himself acknowledges, change over time. Indeed, one can observe a certain pattern in the progress, or lack of it, within white immigrant groups. Their fate was closely linked to where they came from (a peasant society, an economy that had gone through the capitalist cultural revolution) and when they arrived (before the industrial takeoff in America, at its beginning, or much later). The Italians from northern (developed, capitalist) Italy who went to Argentina prospered much more rapidly than the Italians from southern (backward, semi-feudal, peasant) Italy who came to the United States. The German Jews with backgrounds in business who arrived before the Civil War had a totally different history from the Eastern European Jews who came from the rural *shtetls* to the industrializing America of the late nineteenth and early twentieth centuries.

The Irish were, as Sowell rightly points out, the first American minority group. They were driven from their native land by hunger; they were uneducated, disenfranchised peasants trying to cope with the cruel cities of the mid-century; and for historic reasons they had a taste for both whisky and politics. In some cases in the South, they were used for dangerous work where one did not want to risk a slave (who had cash value). And their resentment toward the affluent draft-dodgers who bought their way out of conscription during the Civil War led them to riot in the streets of New York.

Irish immigration in the middle of the nineteenth century was regarded by polite society with all of the affection that Southern racist sheriffs were later to lavish upon blacks. That is, the Irish were widely regarded as a drunken, brawling, lazy, irresponsible people, and the slang term for a police van—"paddy wagon"—came from all the Irishmen named Patrick (Paddy) who were carted away in them. They were the first minority group, in the sense that, in a previously egalitarian society, they were the first in a long line of nationalities to be thought of as ethnically inferior. For a while they were, to borrow a phrase that has been used to explain anti-Semitism, a "people-class," a menial nation within the United States.

There are obvious similarities between the black poor in America today and the Irish poor of a hundred years ago. But there are enormous differences too, not just between the Irish and the blacks, but between the blacks and all of the European groups of our ethnic legend. Blacks were subjected to the institution of slavery, something that happened to no other group. They were brought here in chains from Africa, and, as far as it was possible, slavery tried to deprive them of their tribal memories. For every other ethnic group, a language, a religion, and a cuisine were rallying points and opportunities for small businesses to develop (restaurants, groceries selling special foods, wineries, breweries). But the ethnic identity of black America was the target of cultural genocide.

The tremendous impact of the television movie *Roots* testifies to the importance of this fact. It depicted the enormous difficulty an American black encountered in trying to find out where in Africa he came from. It was as if a black had to be a detective to find out who he or she was.

There is a danger of romanticizing here, and it has led to a tangle of scholarly interpretations that I will only note. The first generation of antiracist scholars in America dates from the period right before World War II. (That incredibly late date is, in itself, a sign of how deeply racism is embedded in the culture.) For analysts like Gunnar Myrdal and the black historian Franklin Frazier, slavery had destroyed many of the social structures that existed in white society. The matriarchal pattern sometimes observed in contemporary black life was to be explained as a heritage of slavery's assault on family life. In the sixties, Stanley Elkins, a white scholar, interpreted slavery as a "totalitarian" society that had destroyed every vestige of organized resistance.

Strangely enough, the critique of this thesis was to emerge on the left. At first glance, one might think that radicals would embrace theories that emphasized the enormity of the white crime against blacks. But those same theories, often unwittingly, implied that the blacks had indeed been unable to salvage any vestige of their culture and dignity. So there were those (Herbert Aptheker) who stressed slave revolts. The black historian Vincent Harding and the white scholar Eugene Genovese tried to develop more complex models of domination and resistance. I do not want to go into these matters, which lead far, far afield. I simply want to signal that the issues raised here in simplified and summary form are quite contentious when taken up in any kind of detail.

But whatever interpretation one adopts, the fact remains that blacks were subjected to an economic and cultural repression qualitatively greater than that of any other Western immigrant group. One consequence of this history was that, as late as 1940, 80 percent of the blacks in America lived in the South, mainly in the countryside. Their legal slavery had been abolished by Lincoln; their economic peonage as farm laborers or sharecroppers was almost as humiliating as slavery had been. When a vast internal migration did take place, from the rural South to the cities of the South, North, and West, the people who moved had been in America, but not of it, for more than a century. They were, in some ways, quite like the peasant immigrants from southern and eastern Europe, the groups that had the greatest difficulty in integrating into the society. Indeed, if one dates black "immigration" not from the moment of their arrival in this country as slaves, but from the time of their urbanization within it, there are some striking similarities with the Europeans, and one huge difference from them: The blacks entered the economy one generation later than the last of the Western immigrant groups.

To be sure, there had been black migration from the South before the 1940s. Sowell and others argue that at the end of the nineteenth century and in the first decade of the twentieth there were areas where black professionals served white patients and clients. But, as was the case with the German and Eastern European Jews, when larger numbers came, the mood changed. The blacks who arrived in New York City and Chicago before the First World War found a de facto racism and a caste economy, even though they had moved from the Confederacy to the Union. Their anger created the first great mass protest movement, the black nationalism of Marcus Garvey. The entire country was hopeless, many said. A return to Africa was the only solution. The project was a fantasy doomed from the start; the disenchantment that inspired it was quite real.

Agricultural crisis in the twenties and then in the Great Depression of the thirties slowed down the migration. But then A. Philip Randolph's March on Washington Movement pushed President Roosevelt into signing a Fair Employment Practices order for the war industries. As a result, a black industrial working class began to take shape during World War II, a process that continued even after the war ended. In 1981, when blacks were officially 11.6 percent of the population (the figure is an undercount, but that is not too relevant here), they were 13 percent of the heavy-equipment mechanics, 13.8 percent of the checkers and inspectors, 13.2 percent of the welders, 17.1 percent of the assemblers, 21.1 percent of the meat packers and wrappers.

For Franklin Frazier, the scholar, it was precisely this transition from the rural South to the modernity and discipline of working-class life which would finally put an end to the slave heritage. This experience, and not the noblesse oblige of the whites, was ironically going to make blacks more like whites. For A. Philip Randolph, the trade unionist and socialist, the black movement could not be separatist; it had to become a constituent element in a class movement of black and white workers. To be sure, there were problems with that perspective, not so much in the industrial unions (where there was no tradition of union control over who was hired), but in the old craft unions (where there was), some of which had explicitly racist clauses in their constitutions.

Randolph and Frazier were right as far as those blacks who could make the transition into the working class were concerned. I have earlier noted the hostility of black auto workers and public employee unionists toward "welfare chiselers"; blacks shared the class attitudes that, in their white co-workers, were sometimes suffused with racism. Two other experiences reinforce the point. In the late seventies a Puerto Rican leader, José Rivera, asked me to talk to a group of Puerto Rican and black workers at the United Tremont Trades in the South Bronx. The UTT used militant tactics to get jobs on construction projects in the area, and Rivera was a political leader as well as a union leader (he was elected to the New York State Legislature in 1982).

I was asked to speak about socialism to a group of about two dozen workers who had come to the meeting in work clothes after a hard day on the job. What struck me was that all of their objections to socialism—won't people goof off, won't productivity go down, and so on—were exactly what I normally hear from white college students or middle-class professionals. These working people, who live in a depressed area and are members of minority groups still suffering from discrimination, like those UAW and AFSCME members, had internalized the Protestant ethic, which is so pervasive in the American working class. The shabby storefront in the South Bronx was in the American mainstream.

Over the years, I have had much the same experience in talking to Detroit locals and regions of the UAW. One of the most powerful men in the union, a vice-president, is Mark Stepp, a black. And there are black regional directors and staff members in considerable numbers. (Detroit, for a number of reasons, has the highest proportion of black workers in the industry.) These union men and women—these trade-union politicals—are very much like their predecessors of the white working class. So Frazier and Randolph were vindicated.

But not, as so often happens, in exactly the way they had anticipated. They had foreseen a continuation of the basic economic trends of the pre– and post–World War II years into the indefinite future. Had that taken place—had smokestack America expanded in the second half of the century as it had in the first—blacks would indeed have climbed that classic immigrant ladder out of poverty. It would have been more difficult for them than it had been for the immigrants because of racism; and the ladder was not quite as magical as is often remembered (there are still, numerically but not proportionately, more white poor than black poor). But things would not have been as they are now. They would, all other things being equal, be much better for blacks.

The "external" immigrants from Europe arrived mainly before World War I (the decade 1900–1910 was the last time the percentage of the foreign-born increased in this country until 1970–1980). They came in time for the industrial takeoff, and if they suffered terribly during the Great Depression, they had made their way into an expanding blue-collar working class. The "internal" immigrants from the rural South were lucky during World War II, for there was a tremendous expansion of the economy based on a kind of military Keynesianism. But then the white veterans returned to take their jobs back and, even more important, the low-paying, unorganized service sector began to grow, while the better-paying, unionized basic industries entered upon a relative decline. The old pattern of ethnic progress was breaking down.

Complicating all of these matters was the extraordinary character of the black migration in the forties and fifties. It was not a "selective" immigration on the European model, that is, one in which the most ambitious and adventurous struck out for America. Rather, it was more like the Irish immigration of the mid–nineteenth century, in which a massive portion of the population, adventurous or not, was pushed out of the old country because of hunger. First, the jobs drew the blacks north; then the mechanization of agriculture and the destruction of many of the structures of black rural life forced them out of the fields. The state of Mississippi, for instance, experienced a net out-migration (black and white) of 435,000 in the forties and 434,000 in the fifties. So it was that by 1970, nearly half of the 1,440,064 blacks born in Mississippi lived outside of Mississippi. In the sixties there was still further black migration out of that state: 268,000 left.

Black America was, in short, driven to migration by the second American agricultural revolution: the transition from animal to mechanical power on the farm. It had been made possible by the rural electrification programs of the New Deal and then turned into a necessity when the war required increased production with fewer hands. In the postwar period, government subsidized this huge transformation—but without much thought for its social cost and consequences. Money from Washington went to the big farms for withdrawing land from production as part of a policy of creating artificial scarcity to maintain high prices; those billions of government dollars financed further mechanization, which caused more migration—and more social problems. The land-grant universities pioneered in new agricultural technologies and new seeds, such as those tasteless tomatoes that could be harvested by machine, which allowed the portion of the crop that was mechanically picked in California to go from 1.5 percent in 1963 to 95 percent in 1968! Only 10 percent of the cotton crop was harvested by machine in 1949; by 1969 the portion was 96 percent! In the 1840s, a famine drove the Irish from the fields; in the 1940s and 1950s, it was a publicly subsidized abundance that forced so many blacks into the cities. They were, most often, more like refugees than immigrants.

All of this had a profound impact upon both statistics and reality. One of the reasons for the tremendous social mobility in American society was the assumption that a transition from the farm to the city amounted to upward social mobility. That was at least plausible in the period up until 1950. The fall in agricultural employment provided part of the basis for the rise in industrial employment; the former farm laborers became factory workers, more often than not with higher money incomes and fewer hours. But that migration before World War II had been primarily white. When the blacks were driven out of the Southern fields, there was no growing industrial sector to absorb them.

By the seventies, the black leadership had understood that jobs were central to any struggle against economic racism. It was no accident that the Full Employment and Balanced Growth Act of 1978 was originally sponsored by Representative Augustus Hawkins, a black congressman from Watts, the Los Angeles ghetto that had been the scene of the first major urban riot, in 1965. The measure was originally called the Equal Opportunity and Full Employment Act. In the first version, drafted in 1974, the "Humphrey-Hawkins" bill (Senator Hubert Humphrey became a cosponsor) provided a guaranteed legal right to work, which entitled an unemployed person to sue in court if the society would not create a job for him or her. In the version that became law, all enforcement procedures had been eliminated, the goals had been radically reduced, and the President had, in effect, been given the power to suspend the law itself. President Carter did so at the first opportunity.

Some black Americans took advantage of the wartime full employment, the relative good times of the fifties and sixties, and the government antipoverty programs of the sixties. But that huge migration from the rural South to the urban South, North, and West was much too great for a society that was switching from smokestacks to service—from high wages to low—and eventually to chronic high rates of unemployment that penalized the young, the less educated, and the latest arrivals. That is, it penalized blacks most of all.

It was in this postwar period that blacks began to take control of city halls across the nation. That was both a significant political victory and a cruel irony. They achieved power at precisely that historic moment when every major city was in crisis because of the flight of jobs and of the white middle and working classes. By 1980, 70.8 percent of Gary, Indiana, was black; 70.3 percent of Washington, D.C.; 66.6 percent of Atlanta; 63.1 percent of Detroit; 58.2 percent of Newark. Every one of those cities had a black mayor *and* a huge population of the poor. The white, external immigrants had acquired urban political power in an expanding economy; the black, internal migrants, more often than not, won the right to allocate poverty, not wealth. Ironically, in the seventies, Southern black poverty declined, but life in the Northern cities hardly changed at all—until it became much worse in the eighties.

Why weren't the blacks like the classic immigrants? They were, when they had half a chance, even though the disabilities imposed upon them were much greater. But millions of them never had half a chance. Thus, if the two black Americas do indeed exist, they are the product of some of the most powerful forces in the society, not of moral fiber or the lack of it.

II

Drive through Newark, New Jersey, toward East Orange, and you can see a good part of the problem of black poverty with the naked eye. It is the middle of the afternoon and the streets are filled with milling, aimless men and youths. They are superfluous. In what follows, I shall detail some of the statistics that are derived from that enormous social fact of black unemployment. The point, of course, is not the recital of the numbers but the way in which they show how that Newark street is part of a vast and intricate structure that weighs like a destiny upon most, but not all, blacks in the United States and threatens to make some of them economic exiles in their own land.

To begin with, all unemployment figures for blacks understate the problem. Between 1954 and 1976, the rate of male nonparticipation in the labor force—the percentage of men who had withdrawn from the labor market altogether—increased from 3.7 percent to 9.4 percent for blacks between twenty-five and thirty-four years of age, and from 2.5 percent to 4.1 percent for whites. For the 45–54 age group, the trend was even more striking. Blacks dropped out of the labor force at a 6.8-percent rate in 1954, and at a 16.6-percent rate in 1976, while whites went from 3.2 percent to 7.5 percent. These percentages, as we shall see in the next section, are used by conservatives to attack the War on Poverty (it is accused of having encouraged and financed the withdrawal from the work force). What is relevant here is that unemployment rates are computed as a percentage of those holding jobs, or looking for them; it excludes those who have been driven out of the labor market, whatever the reason. The numbers I cite are optimistic, even in all their ugliness. Many of those men standing around on that Newark street do not even function as statistics.

Even with that undercount, in the thirty-five years between 1948 and 1982, black joblessness was, on the average, twice as high as white. From 1965 to 1982, the figures were worse; there were only four years out of twenty-eight in which the black-white ratio fell below two-to-one. In "good times," in 1971 and 1975, black unemployment was "only" 1.8 times as great as white; in 1978, it was 2.3 times greater.

The most startling figure, however, is the one that defines black teenage unemployment. In July 1982, when the general unemployment rate for full-time workers was 9.5 percent, 21 percent of white teenagers were without jobs—and 49.7 percent of black teenagers. That last percentage is 5.07 times higher than the overall rate. It defines, one must remember, a group that is being denied that crucial first contact with the world of work. It is an index of economic and social pathology, of poverty's future in black America.

Does this, then, mean that there has been no black economic progress? Not at all. There were very real gains, particularly in the sixties but even in the seventies. The percentage of black accountants doubled between 1972 and 1981, from 4.3 percent to 9.9 percent; computer specialists went from 5.5 percent to 9.4 percent; chemists from 8.4 percent to 15.2 percent; medical doctors from 6.3 percent to 11 percent. So the proportion of black doctors (11 percent) was almost equal to the official black percentage of the population as a whole (11.6 percent), and the chemists were well above it. All of these gains took place in the best-paid sector of American society, among professional and technical workers.

Of course, things were not quite that good, even when progress was being made. The most striking black advances—they were 12.7 percent of the nurses in 1981, 14.9 percent of the health technicians, 20.2 percent of the social and recreational workers, 11.4 percent of the elementary-school teachers, 15.5 percent of the kindergarten teachers—were in the lowest-paid reaches of the highest-paid category. In this, the situation of blacks and of women is strikingly similar. When either group gets into the professions, it tends to get the lesser roles (nurses rather than surgeons, dental technicians rather than dentists, and so on).

The similarity between the occupational plight of blacks and of women explains a very strange fact, i.e., that black men who worked full time got only 75 percent of the white male full-time wage, while black women got 92 percent of what white women received. The reason is that white women also have inferior jobs. Black women, in short, are almost equal to white women in their common inequality with white men. Moreover—and this is contrary to the hopes of Thomas Sowell—the black gains were made primarily in public- or quasi-public-sector jobs, not in the private labor market. The health technicians, teachers, and social workers advanced primarily because public employment grew in the sixties and seventies even as the blue-collar portion of the work force declined. In part, this was because affirmative action was much easier to enforce in the government sector than in private industry. But here, again, joy must be muted: in the eighties, it is precisely those previous growth areas of black employment that are being cut back. The fiscal crisis of the cities and states could well undo some of the progress that has been made against economic racism.

Let us turn now from the professional and technical workers, who made some progress, to the rest of the labor force, where the situation becomes somewhat more grim. Blacks are a significant portion of file clerks, office machine operators, and receptionists; they are, and have been, a major factor in the post office. Many of these jobs are relatively low-paying, and, with the exception of the post office, most of them are not unionized. In the industrial economy, there are a tremendous number of blacks—mainly women—in the clothing business (15.9 percent of the dressmakers, 21.6 percent of the sewers and stitchers), but these are among the lowest-paid blue-collar jobs in the nation.

Finally—and this is a clear reflection of major economic trends—blacks are "overrepresented" in the service industry, where they make up 18.4 percent of the total work force (compared to 8.5 percent in the skilled category of the crafts). Services are, of course, the lowest-paid sector of the American economy, the domain of the fast-food restaurant worker, the hotel and motel chambermaid, the cook and the dishwasher, the nonprofessionals in the hospitals and schools.

So there was progress in the sixties, but it slowed in the seventies when the number of black professional and craft workers increased only about half as fast as it had during the 1960s. The result was that, if one looked at the income of blacks rather than at the earnings of those who worked—that is, if one took a measure that reflected the higher unemployment rates, the people driven out of the labor force altogether, etc.—the black percentage of white income declined in the seventies, from 61 percent to 57 percent. There are much more optimistic figures if you only compare full-time working blacks with whites. One government agency almost sang a *Te Deum* when it announced that intact black couples with two incomes were on a par with similar white couples. All that figure did was to ignore the reality of black family and occupational life.

Andrew Brimmer, the first black member of the board of governors of the Federal Reserve Bank, understood the basic trend as far back as 1970. In a speech at Tuskegee Institute he talked of the schism in the black community between those making gains at the top and the growing misery at the bottom. A Pangloss in the federal bureaucracy could show that things were getting better every day if he or she merely concentrated on one-half of that massive social shift. To do so was to miss the fact that there were now two black Americas.

But even that notion may be too hopeful. The stratum of blacks who have progressed is, to a greater degree than whites, very much at risk. As we have seen, a good many of the gains were made by auto workers and steelworkers who became part of a stable working class—and who are found in precisely those industries with the highest unemployment rates and the greatest potential for permanent job loss. There is, then, a racist aspect to what is happening in the steel valleys and auto cities. Also, there are all those blacks who got relatively good jobs in a public sector that is now firing rather than hiring.

In any case, at the end of the seventies, to be black in America was to suffer from poverty at a rate more than three times higher than the rest of the people. In 1980, the official count found that 10.2 percent of whites, and 32.5 percent of blacks, were poor. Why this differential? After all, the Jim Crow laws were all finally abolished in the sixties as Martin Luther King, Jr., led the most effective mass movement in America since the unionization surge of the thirties. And by the seventies, most of the differential hiring lines within industry (where there were, in effect, "black" jobs and "white" jobs) had been abolished. Why, then, even after some significant progress had been made in the professions and in manufacture, were blacks still in such an inferior position?

Part of the answer has just been suggested. For a variety of historic reasons—and independent of any willful racism—the very economic structure of the United States operates to maintain racist differentials that have been abolished in the legal structure. The Civil War ended slavery—but left most blacks as de facto peons in a segregated Southern society. The movements of the fifties and sixties abolished formal segregation—but left many blacks disproportionately poor. They received low pay when they worked, and they were out of work, or out of the labor market altogether, more than any other group. They had more children than white society, and about half of the teenagers were out of work.

Indeed, one could even perceive the bitterness of this trend in the difference between the riots of the sixties and those of the seventies and eighties. The urban risings of the sixties were, I thought then and think now, counterproductive even if they were understandable. But there was a political dimension in that the looters distinguished between black-run and white-run stores. But in the 1977 riots in New York City, in the wake of a power failure, there was no such political subtlety at work. The looting was indiscriminate. The explosions of the sixties were the expression of angry hope; those of the seventies and eighties have been violent outbursts of a despair that eventually cost the rioters more than it cost their enemies. For instance, two years after the Liberty City riots in Miami in 1980, only 20 percent of the damaged businesses had been repaired, insurance rates had gone up, and life had become even more grim.

The President's Commission on Civil Disorders said in 1968 that the cause of the riots in that decade was to be found in "racism," a conclusion that was widely applauded. That was, I think, too easy an explanation. It implied that the social and economic disorganization faced by black Americans was the result of the psychological state of mind of white America, a kind of deliberate—and racist—ill will. That exists, no question about it, and it has to be fought at every turn. But it is a relatively simple part of the problem. For there is an economic structure of racism that will persist even if every white who hates blacks goes through a total conversion. It will not respond to sermons or books or excellent television documentaries, because it is not a state of mind but an occupational hierarchy rooted in history and institutionalized in the labor market.

Moreover, if the analysis of the first chapter is correct, that economic structure of racism is likely to become all the more oppressive, all the more effective, during the 1980s. Those massive trends—the internalization of capital, the transformation of the world division of labor, technological revolution—all tend to imperil significant areas in which black gains have been made. There could be, then, retrogression, a deepening of systemic black economic inferiority in the years ahead, as a large number of people become irrelevant in the labor market through no fault of their own.

Nonsense, the conservatives would reply. The facts are much

as they have just been presented. All that has been omitted is the essential fact that blacks were forced into this position by well-meaning white liberals and radicals who, out of mistaken sympathy, drove them out of the economy. Yes, there is an underclass, and Michael Harrington and his friends helped create it.

III

Ronald Reagan made a typically sweeping statement of the basic thesis in a speech in May 1983. The rise of government in the last half-century, the President said, was like the "abuse of power" by George III of England that led to the American Revolution. Food stamps, the minimum wage, urban renewal, and the array of Great Society programs, he charged, had actually made Americans poorer than they were fifteen years ago.

Typically, Reagan mixed apples and oranges in reckless fashion. The minimum wage was a New Deal reform, and if it is responsible for recent poverty, as conservatives repeat over and over, how does one explain that there were forty years of relative prosperity after its passage, before its evil effect became evident? The urban-renewal programs did indeed often contribute to making the housing situation of the poor worse, but that was because they were dominated by businessmen, usually Republicans, a fact that was regularly denounced by the very liberals whom Reagan makes responsible for all our troubles. Food stamps did more to abolish hunger in America than any other program, and how that contributed to increasing poverty is, at best, unclear. That leaves the theory that the Great Society caused an increase in poverty.

In all likelihood, the Reagan speech was a crude and agitational version of a serious conservative theory that bears particularly on the position of black Americans in the economy and society. One of the most sophisticated statements of the idea can be found in a series of articles in the neoconservative journal *The Public Interest* in 1982 and 1983. The most striking summary of the argument was made by Charles Murray in "The Two Wars

Against Poverty: Economic Growth and the Great Society." I take it up in considerable detail because it is a subtle—if very wrong—articulation of themes that pervade the society and find their way into Presidential simplifications. I should say at the outset that I do not think there is any racist intention behind this analysis, even though it could have a pernicious impact upon the black struggle in America.

"If the War on Poverty is considered as having begun in 1950 instead of 1964," Murray writes, "it may be fairly said that we were winning the war until Lyndon Johnson decided to wage it." Behind that paradox is an underlying theory: Economic growth ends poverty, and social programs promote it, most dramatically among blacks. Therefore the transition from the fifties and Eisenhower laissez-faire to the sixties and Kennedy-Johnson interventionism actually increased the number of the poor.

It is interesting that conservatives would agree with a basic proposition of this book—that poverty has been on the increase. Murray, who wants to blame the Great Society, dates the new vitality of poverty from 1967–68; I, with a totally different explanation, would locate the turning point a little later on. But we agree on the fact. Indeed, I have already credited Murray with having invented a quite useful category, "latent poverty," i.e., the number of Americans who would be poor were it not for transfer programs. In his reading, latent poverty decreased during the fifties and up until 1968, dropping from 32 percent of the people to 18.2 percent. But then it rose to 21 percent in 1976 and to 22 percent in 1980.

This meant, Murray argues, that the "extremely large increases in social welfare spending during the 1970s were papering over the increase in latent poverty." (Leave aside for the moment that, as Chapter 4 showed, there were no "extremely large increases in social spending in the 1970s.") Why this pattern? Welfare expenditures, he says, shot up in 1967 and 1968 (in fact, there was a modest increase, caused mainly by people who had always been qualified for benefits finally taking advantage of them), and that was when the poor, above all the black poor, began to withdraw from the labor market in order to live off the new, and generous, benefits. It was this phenomenon, an unintended consequence of liberal policy, that resulted in the growth of latent poverty. A significant number of people had now immunized themselves against the truly successful antipoverty program of economic growth by simply retiring to the comfortable sidelines provided by the Great Society.

Before I turn to the centerpiece of this theory, the decline in black labor-force participation, I should at least note one curious conceptual error in Murray's case. Poverty went down, he triumphantly points out, as GNP went up. Therefore—and this is stated as against an imaginary liberal opponent—"trickle down" really worked. Murray is confused. All liberals and radicals in the sixties were in favor of full employment (and the Humphrey-Hawkins bill was a central focus of those groups, particularly the blacks, in the seventies). They understood that economic growth, which would benefit the top and the middle of the society, would also aid those at the bottom. That, of course, has nothing to do with the economics of "trickle down," which state that the way to stimulate growth is by giving money to the rich, who will then invest it in ways that benefit the poor.

That was the basic approach of Reagan's 1981 tax cut, and we know from reality that not only did it redistribute tax burdens from the rich to the middle class and working people; it also financed speculation and corporate takeovers, and produced practically no real-world investments in job-generating enterprises. It is a great error to think, as Murray does, that opposition to welfare for the rich as a means of promoting economic growth is to be equated with opposition to economic growth. Indeed, the ideal of almost every serious person on the left would be the abolition of welfare through the creation of a full-employment society that would not need it.

But all this is prelude to Murray's central thesis about the link between black poverty and the Great Society. I take it quite seriously because it has inspired the White House, the editorialists, and thousands of complacent conversations in the country clubs of America, even though the people repeating the idea don't know where it comes from and almost always mangle it in the process. As the President did.

Murray's basic argument has a precedent that is almost two

hundred years old. In 1798, Malthus published his *Essay on Population*, asserting that population would grow geometrically while the means of subsistence would only increase arithmetically. Therefore, he said—and on this point he was, in effect, arguing against Adam Smith—the poor laws were a cause of poverty, for they encouraged the superfluous people of the society to breed and ameliorated the misery that was necessary to force the essentially lazy lower orders to work. Things are no longer put so bluntly, and just because Malthus turned out to be wrong, at least as far as England was concerned, does not prove that his twentieth-century counterparts are also wrong. It is, however, food for thought. Murray is a latter-day Malthusian who holds that helping the poor often promotes poverty. In the late sixties, when the new social programs took hold, he argues, blacks began to leave the labor market at a much greater rate than whites. In the early sixties, he says, black and white participation in the work force was roughly equivalent. That is not true, since every age group of black males in 1963 was twice as likely to have withdrawn from the working population as were white males (e.g., in the 45–54 age group, 8.9 percent of blacks had withdrawn, against 3.8 percent of whites). This is not a statistical quibble, for it bears on a central point in Murray's case, i.e., that it was precisely in 1967–69, when the Great Society programs came into effect, that this differential began to widen.

Murray writes: "Whether unemployment was high or low until 1967, black males behaved the same as whites; after 1967 they did not." This was not, Murray notes, a racial phenomenon, since poor whites were also dropping out. But it was a consequence of the liberal programs, and it was most visible among blacks since so many of them were, and are, poor. The conclusion: "*Something* happened in the mid-1960s that changed the incentives for low-income workers to stay in the job market. The Great Society reforms constitute the biggest, most visible, most plausible candidate."

I noted earlier, in analyzing the definition of poverty, that the conservatives believe deeply in *Homo economicus*. Increase the welfare benefits and, by lightning calculation and utterly rational action, the poor, the blacks, will drop out of the labor market. *Homo economicus* is, of course, an Adam Smith invention, so this prejudice should not come as a surprise. But another way of putting it is that the conservatives are vulgar Marxists. That is, they believe in a one-to-one relationship between the economic and the political or the psychological. In this case there is presumed to be an instantaneous and massive social impact, the result of a single cause (welfare benefits increase), which occurs immediately after that cause is put into place.

Still, how does one deal with the basic data showing that all those blacks dropped out of the labor force right around the time of the Great Society? By showing that the data are wrong, something that was done by Donald O. Parsons in the *American Economic Review* about two years before Murray published his article. In a very careful analysis, Parsons demonstrated that the pattern of both blacks and whites dropping out of the labor force, but blacks at a much higher rate, dates back to the Eisenhower fifties, not to the Great Society sixties. Parsons relates this development to a change in the social security law in 1957 which opened up new possibilities for disability benefits.

But if that were the case, why would blacks drop out at a faster rate? By 1976 the dropout rate for blacks between twenty-five and thirty-four was 9.4 percent compared to 4.1 percent for whites, 16.6 percent for blacks between forty-five and fifty-four compared to 7.5 percent for whites in the same age group. Why? Parsons's answer, developed with great sophistication, has a certain stunning simplicity. In order to qualify for disability benefits, one has to withdraw from the work force and run the risk of being turned down (60 percent of all initial requests were refused in 1975). Therefore, the lower-paid worker would have less to lose and more to gain. A part of the explanation, then, is not the excessive generosity of the federal government but the excessive poverty of the black labor force. Indeed, there was a ceiling on the benefits that made them attractive only to those at the bottom of the occupational structure.

The second factor cited by Parsons is perhaps even more striking: Blacks are more likely to be disabled, and are therefore more likely to qualify for those benefits. In establishing this, he analyzed a national longitudinal survey (that is, a survey that tracks a single large group of people over a number of years rather than one that uses periodic samples of different people) of males between forty-five and fifty-nine. He discovered that those people who died within seven to nine years had a significantly higher rate of withdrawal than those who survived beyond that period. In doing this, Parsons ingeniously offset any possibility that the dropouts were faking illness. The early deaths were a rather dramatic confirmation that this group—which is disproportionately black—was really sick.

The conclusion? If one "controls" (discounts) the special circumstances of black workers—that they are lower paid than whites and are more likely to be disabled—then there is no difference between the blacks and the whites. In short, the real cause of the high rate of black withdrawal from the labor market is not to be found in the welfare programs of the sixties, or even in the social security disability regulations of the fifties, but in the economic and medical misery of black life, which makes such withdrawal rational and even necessary.

Long before Parsons made his careful statistical analysis, an extremely sensitive anthropological observer, Elliot Liebow, had arrived at many of the same conclusions by talking to and observing black "streetcorner men" in Washington, D.C., in the early sixties. *Tally's Corner*—Liebow named it after one of the men hanging out around the New Deal Carry-Out Shop—describes a world that is classically representative of one of the most important structures of poverty (for whites and blacks). People spend much of their time on the street, the jukeboxes and phonographs fill the air with sound, men mill about in the middle of the afternoon, couples mate for a while and then part in the standard pattern of "serial monogamy." The streetcorner males take jobs for a while, but then drop out. They drift.

Why don't they get regular jobs? Liebow quotes Richard, one of the regulars at the Carry-Out: "I graduated from high school but I don't know anything. I'm dumb. Most of the time I don't even say I graduated 'cause then somebody asks me a question and I can't answer it, and they think I was lying about graduating. . . . They graduated me but I didn't know anything. I had lousy grades but I guess they wanted to get rid of me." Richard, who had been doing plastering and minor repairs on a piecework basis, was offered a regular job doing the same thing. He turned it down. Liebow comments: "Convinced that 'I'm dumb . . . I don't know anything,' he 'knew right away' he couldn't do it, despite the fact that he had been doing just this sort of work all along."

There are, Liebow generalizes later on, both constant failure and the constant fear of failure among these men. It is not, as some social scientists suggest, that they are "present-oriented," lacking the "future-orientation" of the stable worker who internalizes the Protestant ethic. The difference has to do not with their different future orientations, but with their different futures. It can be argued that it is precisely because these black men accept the values of the larger society but are not given a serious opportunity to achieve them that they live as they do. For someone who has a real chance to work at decent wages, simply hanging out would be neurotic, irrational conduct. For one who does not—who lacks a future to which he or she can orient—it can be a way, if not of coping, then of disguising one's fate as a freely chosen, purposely irresponsible life-style. In the debate over whether there is a "culture" of poverty, Liebow holds that these ways of acting out are not patterns transmitted from father to son but adaptations to a similarly perverse reality made independently by each successive generation.

Liebow's skilled anthropological interpretation of his conversations with the men at Tally's Corner was corroborated by a more traditional method used by Leonard Goodwin in 1972. The question he asked, and the title of his book, was *Do the Poor Want to Work?* Goodwin surveyed a wide variety of people, probing their attitudes toward work. Everyone, from the welfare mother to the suburban white woman, had the same deep commitment to the work ethic. Where they differed was not in wanting to work but in their estimation of the chances for success in doing so. The welfare mothers, the sons from fatherless families, genuflected before the Protestant ethic but had little confidence that they could act upon it. Perhaps the most striking finding was that the white poor were more confident than the nonpoor blacks that they could succeed.

"The low work activity of welfare women," Goodwin concluded, "is a result not of their rejecting the significance of work, but of their continually experiencing failure in work and thus finding welfare an acceptable alternative."

The conservatives will have none of this. In following an ancient American tradition, they prefer to blame the victim. Much as the policeman who hit a man would then charge him with assaulting an officer, the Reagan administration responded to the reaction of the working poor who had various minimal social benefits taken away from them. Many people—myself included—had assumed that when their income was lowered and brought closer to the poverty line, many workers would quit their jobs and apply for welfare. Most, it turned out, did not. Why? Linda McMahon, the head of the Health and Human Services Department's Office of Family Assistance has an answer: "The people taken off the welfare were people with other resources." This is a comforting theory for conservatives, for it defines the central problem as one of welfare cheats.

The evidence of this chapter suggests a radically different interpretation. Those poor people with jobs are so attached to the work ethic that they will keep working even when the government takes part of their desperately low income away from them. The poverty and low income of black America are neither a choice nor a trick to get welfare payments. They are the result of a long and bitter history that, even after all the juridical discrimination was defeated in the course of bitter and sometimes bloody struggles, left blacks in a systemically inferior position in the economy.

That was true twenty years ago, and it is true today. It hardly defines a "new" poverty, but simply states that the old poverty has been much more difficult to eliminate than people once thought it would be. There is, however, a much more sinister trend in all of this, and it is quite new. On the one hand there are very real gains—too modest and made by too few, but real nevertheless. And on the other hand there is an even greater deterioration in the position of the black people at the bottom. It is not so much a matter of whether their objective living standard is higher or lower, as important as that is. Rather, it is now quite possible that they have been turned into a superfluous people.

Until recently, blacks were penalized in the urban labor market in comparison with whites. But what if, as I think is quite possible, quantity has now turned into quality? What if there are *no* foreseeable jobs—not good jobs, well-paid jobs, but jobs—in the mainstream economy for a significant portion of the huge generation of the black young? What if there is a new generation of useless human beings?

I do not believe in fates. Trends that are the consequences of society's activity can be ultimately transformed by society. There are ways in which these grim tendencies can be reversed. But the irony that is central to this chapter makes that task all the more difficult: The very process of social differentiation that, coupled with political struggle, made it possible for some black people to fight their way out of poverty and into the middle class may well have broken the few and fragile links that bound an even larger portion of the black population to the economy and society.

Let us go back for a moment to the trends tormenting the steelworkers described earlier. The middle of American society—using a rough measure, the stratum with annual incomes of between $17,000 and $41,000—is contracting. A minority are moving upward, the vast majority are being pushed down. According to one typical count, it will be remembered, eight million families dropped out of the middle between 1978 and 1983. For once, blacks are participating in the same trend as whites—only it is a disastrous trend, so what has been won is an equal right to misery. In black America as well as in white, things are better for the fortunate few, and worse—or at least much more precarious—for the people in the middle. They have, of course, always been intolerable for those at the bottom.

But this means that economic discrimination has acquired a new lease on life and that the American dilemma defined by Myrdal—equality in theory and racism in practice—may have invaded the black world itself, which has been becoming more separate and unequal.

7

The Poor Against the Poor

Most Americans know the Okies—the farmers forced to flee the Dust Bowl of the 1930s, who came to California—from John Steinbeck's moving novel *The Grapes of Wrath.* Or rather, the majority know them from the magnificent movie based on that novel, starring Henry Fonda. In one of the last scenes there is an unforgettable moment in which Fonda, fleeing the police, commits himself to a lifetime struggle for justice. He presents an unforgettable image of the victim ready to challenge his tormentors.

Fewer people know that Woody Guthrie's song "This Land Is Your Land" is not a simple, sentimental love song for the United States of America but a bitter expression of that same Okie battle. They don't ask themselves why the narrator of the song tells how he "walked that ribbon of highway," nor do they understand that the line "this land is my land" is the refrain of a migrant who has been stopped at the California border by the police who are guarding Paradise against the encroachment of the Depression "vagrants."

Fewest of all are those who realize that when the Okies came, they displaced Chicanos and Mexicanos (the former being American citizens or permanent residents of Mexican descent, the latter being Mexican citizens working in the United States). There were even cases where Okies were used as strikebreakers against Hispanics who had organized into unions. In the twenties, only about 20 percent of the farm workers were Anglos (non-Hispanic whites); by 1936, 85 to 90 percent were, as jobless Anglos drove the Chicanos from the fields. The big growers and business people of California have always treated the Chicanos and Mexicanos in orthodox Marxist fashion, as a reserve army of labor to be manipulated at will for their own purposes. In the 1930s, the Okies were sometimes the tools of that manipulation.

I recount these events for a reason. When one looks at the tremendous increase in immigration into the United States in recent years, one confronts a part of our forgotten past and our all-too-actual present: the war of the poor against the poor.

Between the mid-twenties and the fifties, there were a number of reasons why Americans could become nostalgic about the immigrant experience. The percentage of the foreign-born in the population dropped from 14.6 in 1910 to 5.4 in 1960. That was largely the work of the Depression and World War II, sometimes with an assist from the United States government, e.g., the deportation of a million Mexicans during "Operation Wetback" in 1954. Meanwhile, the children of the pre–World War I immigrants were, all things being equal, making progress in an expanding economy. They remembered their parents' experience in the light of their own present success and homes; the edges were rounded off our history.

But then the times began to change once again. In the seventies, a sober estimate said that the United States was experiencing an annual inflow of one million foreigners (500,000 "legal," 500,000 "undocumented"). In the previous peak decade, between 1901 and 1910, the average was 880,000 a year. True, the American population is much larger now than it was then, the proportion of the whole being therefore smaller. But the native-born American population is growing even more slowly than it did during the Great Depression, and that one-million figure could well equal between 40 and 50 percent of the annual population change in the United States. This happened, of course, at a time when the economic crisis was shattering much of the conventional wisdom and many of the traditional patterns. Suddenly confusion was everywhere.

What, for instance, is the left or liberal attitude on the issue? At first the answer seems obvious: the right is racist, nativist, xenophobic; the left, internationalist. So the right is against immigration, the left for it. That, as we shall see, was never quite true. Before World War I, there were both racists and antiracists on the left who wanted to limit immigration. And in the present, how does one deal with the fact that the United Farm Workers, led by Cesar Chavez, an organization composed predominantly of Chicanos and Filipinos, has often opposed programs to bring in temporary Mexican workers, while Ronald Reagan campaigned for them in 1980 with the explicit backing of the National Council of Agricultural Employers?

There are further complications. The notion of the Third World is useful as a very broad definition of countries and peoples in Asia, Africa, and Latin America, all of whom have suffered in one way or another from the same Western domination of the planet. But it must always be carefully remembered that the Third World contains enormous differences as well as similarities. Asia, it can be argued, is overpopulated and sub-Saharan Africa underpopulated. And the Third World within the borders of the United States is even more diversified. One-third of the Asian adults in this country have college degrees (for whites, the figure is 17.2 percent); the median Asian income in 1980 was $22,075, compared with $20,840 for whites, $14,711 for Hispanics, $12,618 for blacks. At the top, 8.6 percent of Asians had incomes of more than $50,000 a year (whites 6.2 percent, Hispanics 2.4 percent, blacks 1.9 percent).

Conclusion: Asians are well off? Not at all. I talked to Bill Hing in San Francisco, an articulate and very knowledgeable lawyer who has worked with the poor among his people. The "Taiwan" Chinese do, indeed, often arrive with considerable resources and become property owners of substance. But the "Hong Kong" Chinese are often impoverished. They live in the old Chinatown in the North Beach section (which has crossed Broadway and is expanding into what had been an Italian district, a pattern that also can be seen in Manhattan). The poor Chinese, Hing says, are mainly legal, but their housing is often substandard and many work in garment shops at low wages, only half of which are unionized. In the Mission District one can find sweatshops, an old-fashioned component of American misery that has returned to "postindustrial" America.

To complicate matters, Hing continues, there is a Korean area with a fairly large middle class and not a few tensions with black neighborhoods on its periphery. And there is a stable Vietnamese community, very much focused on the church, which is ironically found in San Francisco's Tenderloin district. The new immigration is a new kind of immigration. So is its poverty.

Starting with the Irish in the 1840s and 1850s, the immigrants of the nineteenth and early twentieth centuries were mainly poor. They had problems with other ethnic groups and with the established power structure, but not so much within themselves. In this they resembled the blacks up until about 1960. But now there are differences, and even class differences, within the new immigrations. I got a sense of what that can mean when I spoke with Delfino Zarela at his law office in East Los Angeles, the Chicano *barrio* of that city.

The poverty was palpable around Zarela's office. The streets on the way there were shabby and rundown, the walls covered with Spanish graffiti. A nearby Southern California slum—that is to say, a slum with individual houses rather than teeming tenements, a not-so-obvious slum—which had been black over twenty years ago when I worked there as a civil rights organizer, is now Hispanic. It has been poor for generations.

Zarela is an advocate for the Chicanos, a man bitterly critical of government policy. He is opposed to the Simpson-Mazzoli bill, a change in the immigration statutes which would, among other things, establish a national identity card based on a social security number, in order to see to it that business people do not hire the undocumented workers. Zarela, and many others, are fearful not simply of the anti-civil-liberties aspect of the measure, but of the way in which it could be used to discriminate against Chicanos and Chicanas. And yet he conceded that there were a fair number of people in the community, including undocumented immigrants who would get amnesty under the new law, whose attitude was "the hell with the others." They were here; they saw the closed border as being in their economic interests. There is even a home-owning middle class, part of which shares these sentiments.

Beyond the conflicts within the immigrant groups, which are somewhat new, there are the hostilities between them that are, alas, classic. At times they can be literally murderous, as when blacks in the Miami ghetto riots of 1968 were as violent toward the Cubans as toward the Anglo whites. At times they are more muted, yet unmistakable, like the black businessmen in Harlem who tried to organize a boycott of the growing number of Korean stores on 125th Street. Moreover, the poor who are here, legally or illegally, are often pitted against the poor at the gate of the society. In those legendary and somewhat romanticized days before World War II, the United States did indeed welcome the huddled masses of the world. To be sure, no Chinese could apply after 1884. But the Europeans did come in a great flood.

Now, however, the immigration issue raises the whole question of world poverty. In 1980, President Carter announced that all Cubans who wanted to leave their country would be welcome to the United States (a move that was to cost him in political popularity). The great rush of the "Mariel" refugees was widely reported as evidence of people voting against Communist dictatorship with their feet (or, in this case, with boats). That was certainly part of what happened. However, a Cuban friend of mine who had supported Castro during the fight against Batista, but broke with him on left-wing grounds not too long thereafter, had a different interpretation. Go to any country in Latin America, he said, and announce that the United States will give a visa to anyone who wants one. Whatever the social or political system of that nation, the American embassy will be swamped by applicants.

It is not simply that there is a huge, impoverished population to the south of the United States, in Latin America and the Caribbean. It is also that these peoples have had their lives disrupted by economic, social, and sometimes military change, and know from radio and movies and television about the United States in a way that the classical immigrants never did. But it is, as Delfino Zarela sadly documented, at least thought to be in the interests of some of the immigrant poor already here to keep the external poor out. At every point, then, in the social reality of the new immigrant poverty—national and international—one constantly meets tragedies in Hegel's rather profound sense of the word: not the conflict of right against wrong, but of right against right.

How else could one describe a war of the poor against the poor?

— I —

America's attitude toward immigrants has always been composed of three elements: (1) the need to get certain jobs, often dirty jobs, done, (2) racism, and (3) genuine democratic idealism. The last component is real but overly well known, and if I stress the grosser and uglier motives, it is not to deny the decency of the national spirit but only to put it into context.

In my outline of this history, Hispanics will loom quite large, and that requires a few words of introduction. According to the official Immigration and Naturalization Service (INS) figures, 35 percent of the legal inflow in the years 1968–1977 was Hispanic. If one takes moderate estimates of the undocumented population, which, for obvious reasons of proximity, is much more Hispanic than Asian or African, it is likely that about half of the one million immigrants a year in the seventies were Hispanic. Writing in *Foreign Affairs*, Michael Teitelbaum comments: "Such linguistic concentration is quite unprecedented in the long history of U. S. immigration. While there were substantial concentrations of a particular language group in past decades (e.g., 28 percent German-speaking in 1881–90 and 23 percent Italian-speaking in 1901–10), previous immigration flows generally were characterized by a broad diversity of linguistic flows. . . ."

But does a common language make a common nationality? Prescinding from all the weighty theoretical questions and simply looking at the current Hispanic reality, the answer is no. In the Los Angeles *barrio*, for instance, there are neighborhoods dominated by people from Guatemala, El Salvador, and Colombia in the midst of a predominantly Chicano population. In Brooklyn, a friend of mine discovered, there is a "little Peru." Dominicans, who are often black as well as Spanish-speaking, are obviously in a different social and ethnic position from the upper-class Cubans who fled Castro and established themselves in Miami.

Indeed, that Cuban population is radically different from the Puerto Ricans and the Chicanos. In the "Little Havana" section of Miami, you can walk for blocks and blocks without hearing a word of English spoken, and the area is rundown and tacky, even though the Cuban exiles are significantly better off than the blacks. But one also encounters Cubans in expensive restaurants; there is an upper class here, part of it wealthy through the Batista dictatorship. So it was that while the Puerto Ricans and Chicanos voted for Jimmy Carter in 1980 (and for Ted Kennedy in the primaries), the Cubans were, for foreign policy reasons, staunch supporters of Ronald Reagan.

In short, the very notion of a Hispanic identity may be something of an oversimplification on the part of outsiders who think that everyone who speaks Spanish must be as similar as everyone who speaks Italian or Yiddish. That is of some political importance, since there could well be an anti-Hispanic prejudice, even though there is not a unified Hispanic consciousness. Here, as in every other aspect of the new immigration, there is a complexity that is foreign to the nostalgic concepts derived from the old immigration.

Having noted that, we can go back to the beginning. It was an act of official racism against the Chinese.

The Chinese had been brought to the United States when there was hard work to be done building the railroads of the West right after the Civil War. There was still a frontier then, and the country had no immigration policy to speak of, but welcomed anyone and everyone to help conquer a continent (and kill Indians). But—and the history of the war of the poor against the poor begins here, at least as far as immigrants are concerned—the white workers of the West Coast were fearful that "coolie" labor would subvert native-born, or even white immigrant, standards. For this reason, among others, the Chinese Exclusion Act was passed in 1884, the opening moment in a process of anti-Asian racism that was to persist for three-quarters of a century.

There were even labor parties established in California around the turn of the century with the distinct purpose of organizing whites against Chinese. It was, as Herbert Hill has argued, a paradigmatic case of trade-union racism, the precursor of later attempts to exclude blacks from some of the skilled trades. But it also involved some nagging complexities that are with us to this day.

There were, so to speak, two bases for the hostility toward the Chinese: racist, i.e., a hatred of people of a different color and culture; and economic, i.e., a fear of competition from low-wage workers. Those two strands were often intertwined, but not necessarily. There was, for example, a bitter debate within the Socialist Party prior to World War I on this question, and some of the issues it raised are relevant to this day. There was one faction, led by Victor Berger, a traditional social democrat, that wanted immigration restrictions. The other side was led by the greatest socialist ever produced by the United States, Eugene Victor Debs, and fought such restrictions as "utterly unsocialistic, reactionary, and in truth outrageous." The party finally adopted a compromise that seemed to straddle the debate rather than to resolve it, but which, as Otis L. Graham, Jr., has pointed out, actually defined the position of most leftists ever since.

The compromise was the work of Morris Hilquit, a successful lawyer as well as a socialist leader, a man who obviously used his courtroom talents within the party. On the one hand, Hilquit's resolution said, "The Socialist Party favors all legislative measures tending to prevent the immigration of strikebreakers and contract laborers, and the mass immigration of workers from foreign countries, brought about by the employing classes for the purpose of weakening the organization of American labor, and of lowering the standard of life of American workers." Hilquit's facts were correct, whatever one thinks of his policy; business has always viewed immigration through the prism of private profit and anti-unionism rather than on the basis of any kind of internationalist principle.

But at the same time that Hilquit opposed unrestricted immigration insofar as it was a weapon of the union busters, he also condemned restrictions that were racist: "The Party is opposed to the exclusion of any immigrants on account of their race or nationality, and demands that the U.S. be at all times maintained as a free asylum for all men and women persecuted by the governments of their countries on account of their politics, religion, or race." There could be restrictions to fight capitalist "internationalism," but they could not be racist restrictions. That position was adopted, Graham notes, at a time when the population of the United States was approximately eighty million and that of the world less than two billion. The globe in 1981 had four and a half billion people, an increase of more than a billion and a half in twenty-one years; and Mexico, which has particular relevance to this problem, has a very high birth rate, doubling every twenty-two years. This is why the potential of the war between the poor and the ex-poor within our borders and those without is so great today.

If we go back to the period right before and after World War I, we discover that the United States violated *both* of Hilquit's principles; it was racist, and it manipulated migrant flows, particularly from Mexico, as a weapon against American workers.

The racist factor was no longer directed against the Chinese; it was now focused upon the "undesirable" immigrants from southern Europe. The Taft administration created an Immigration Commission that published a multivolume report whose ethnocentrism inspired the legislation after World War I. As David North and Marion Houston described that legislation in a study of undocumented workers: "If you lived in one of the blond-haired, blue-eyed European countries—or the relatively unpopulated New World—you could immigrate to the United States with ease (but few came); if you lived in southern or Eastern Europe you could apply (but the waiting lists were long); if you were from Asia, you knew you were not wanted."

At the same time, business employed Mexican nationals as a disposable work force to be used and discarded like so much human Kleenex. The Mexicans were unwanted up until about 1890, since the Chinese were available. But then the Chinese (and the Japanese, who were kept out at first by a "gentleman's agreement" between Japan and the United States) became unavailable, agriculture boomed because of reclamation, and European immigration decreased. The Mexicans were needed and used. With the Depression, the Okies and other victims of the Crash were now willing to take "Mexican" jobs, so the Chicanos themselves were repatriated. During World War II, many native-born Americans left the fields and factories, so the "Bracero" program—importing "strong arms" from Mexico, but on a temporary basis—was initiated. By the fifties, there was fear that too many Braceros were becoming permanently undocumented residents in the United States, so "Operation Wetback" was undertaken, reaching a peak of one million deportations in 1954. In 1964, the Bracero program was finally stopped altogether.

It would, however, be wrong to think of Chicano history in the United States solely, or even primarily, in terms of farm labor. By 1970, only 8.4 percent of the Chicano men in California were in the fields and almost 60 percent were in the factories. That is, ironically they had finally made it into the mainstream of American economic life at the very point at which the smokestack economy was beginning to crack and crumble. Chicanos are heavily represented in the auto and steelworkers' unions—and therefore in the ranks of the new unemployed. To compound this problem, the Mexicans across the border had been hurt by—of all things—the long-awaited reform of the racist immigration laws.

The first racist legislation in 1921 was primarily anti-Asian and anti–southern European. The 1952 McCarran Act compounded the outrage against Asians by defining an Asian not by the country of his or her origin (which was the case for everyone else), but on the basis of racial ancestry. An "Asian" was anyone whose ancestry was derived 50 percent or more from any Far

Eastern race! The 1965 changes ended that patently racist provision, which was good, and for the first time set a ceiling on immigrants from the Western Hemisphere (120,000 a year). In part, that was a response to pressure from the farm workers' union, which felt that it could not possibly organize a dual agricultural working class in which one component was constantly being enlarged by new entrants anxious to work at low wages. The law went into effect in 1968, and things became worse in 1972, when Congress denied social security to undocumented workers (they do, however, pay social security taxes!), and in 1976, when the last loopholes for the Western Hemisphere were repealed. As a result of these changes, people who had been in line for legal entrance to the United States were suddenly cut off.

There was an act of open hypocrisy in all of this: the "Texas Proviso" of 1952, which legally exempted employers from the legal proscriptions on harboring "illegal aliens." It is a crime for an undocumented worker to be in the United States—but not for a businessman to hire that undocumented worker. This bit of legal chicanery, as we shall see, has been indispensable for the exploitation of undocumented workers, and it is the legislative foundation for the return of the sweatshop. In short, it is often true that, as Michael Piore writes, "immigration has been initiated by explicit recruitment efforts by American employers or their agents."

Why are there so many undocumented workers in the Southwest? Because the Bracero program instructed many Mexicans in the possibilities of working in the United States, and the flow could not be turned off by fiat. Because Congress passed laws that suddenly changed the rules for legal immigration, and then decreed penalties for immigrants, but not for the businesses that exploited them, which forced the former underground. Because social, economic, and military revolutions are uprooting great masses of Latin Americans, and population growth leads to more hungry children. Because the collapse of the OPEC cartel undermined that famous Third World "middle class" (Venezuela, Mexico), and the strength of the dollar reinforced all the negative trends.

For poor workers in Texas and California and Arizona, these

massive economic tendencies were as mysterious as rainstorms had been to their ancestors. But the results were terribly real. The poor turned against one another within the United States, and some of the most exploited immigrant Americans had to organize against their brothers and sisters who were even more exploited. This helped make the return of the sweatshop possible.

II

Local 23–28 of the International Ladies Garment Workers Union (ILGWU—"the ILG") is located, just as one would expect, on the West Side of Manhattan, a few blocks down from the bustling garment district, where young blacks push racks of clothes through a permanent traffic jam. But this is about all that is in keeping with the standard image of an industry that is part of the legend of the Jewish and Italian immigrants. The walls of the union local have all signs in three languages: English, Spanish, and Chinese. I pass a room full of Chinese women studying English. This place is part of the new immigration, not the old.

And yet, ironically, tragically, Local 23–28 is faced with the problem that most people thought had been conquered by those older immigrant generations. Jay Mazur, the hard-driving and compassionate man who leads the local, tells me that the sweatshops have returned. Mazur and two of his staff members fill in some of the details.

The garment work force, they say, has changed radically over the last twenty or so years. In 1959, Local 23–28 had eight thousand members, perhaps half of them Hispanic (about 75 percent of the Hispanics being Puerto Rican). Now it has grown, partly through mergers, to 28,000 members, but the ethnic and racial composition has been utterly transformed at the same time. About 60 percent of the members today are Chinese; next come the Puerto Ricans, with 25 percent, and the rest of the membership is made up of people from the Caribbean, Central America, and Korea.

These developments, Mazur continues, can be explained in

part by the fact that Puerto Ricans often return to the island after a time in New York. Black men, he notes, had never come into the industry in great numbers, perhaps because it wasn't a "macho" place to work. The Chinese who do work in the garment industry are almost all legal entrants—the number of undocumented workers among the Asians, Mazur thinks, has been exaggerated—and they tend to be strong union members, with about 90 percent of them in organized shops. A copy of the local's newsletter has photographs of a giant demonstration in Chinatown in 1982, with 15,000 people marching, picket signs in Chinese, and Lion Dancers in the lead.

This is a very real accomplishment, although one qualifying fact has to be kept in mind: The American apparel industry pays low wages. In 1981, the average hourly take was $4.96 an hour, compared to $7.25 for the entire private sector and $8.53 in heavy industry (durable goods). The reason is that clothes in America are made in a small, fragmented industry that, particularly in recent years, has been almost completely open to foreign competition. Under the circumstances, it is remarkable that the union has managed to keep wages as high as they are. And the low wages also explain why Chinese and Puerto Rican and black women have the chance to earn them: Whenever you find an industry that has a high proportion of minorities and women, it is a guarantee that it does not pay very well.

Still, the shops organized by Local 23–28 are not sweatshops. There are well over five hundred of the latter in New York City, sometimes hidden away in the alleys and garages of the South Bronx, Brooklyn, and Queens, and in Manhattan itself. Franz Leichter, a New York state senator, described them vividly a few years ago: "It is not uncommon for thirty or more sewing machines, several steam pressing machines, and other equipment to be crowded into one small room. The crowded quarters are always poorly ventilated; many have no openable windows or doors except for the front entrance. The steam from the pressing machines makes the temperature and humidity even more intolerable. Most of the factories . . . have serious fire hazards . . . the windows are permanently barred, the fire doors . . . are locked shut. . . ."

The sheer physical misery of the sweatshop is not, however,

its defining quality. Indeed, Mazur surprises me by remarking that there are even a few of them that are air-conditioned. People do not have to sweat to be sweated, that is, to be cheated, humiliated, used. And what is critical for most of the sweatshops is that they have access to those undocumented workers. Not too long ago, Mazur remembers, a group of undocumented women workers came to the local asking for help. They were putting in a sixteen-hour day—from seven in the morning to eleven at night—for fifteen dollars a day. Shortly before they came to the local, even those pathetically small checks had been returned, marked "insufficient funds." When they complained to the employer, he told them he would pay them if they would only produce their "green cards," the work permits given out by the INS. The union was told the same thing when it checked out the story. The demand for the green cards was, of course, a barely veiled threat: Stop complaining, or I will turn you into "La Migra" (the Spanish nickname for the INS).

The trick is not new and is not confined to New York. In California, employers have been known to denounce their own workers to the INS so that they are picked up right before payday or on the eve of a union representation election. This is the fine—and intentional—fruit of the "Texas proviso": The employer, who is himself an antisocial criminal, has been exempted from a law that he can then use against the defenseless employee to keep him or her tame and docile under sweatshop conditions.

Who are the undocumented workers in the sweatshops of New York? Mainly, Mazur observes, people from the Caribbean and Central America, as well as some Koreans. The Puerto Ricans are, of course, legal by definition, and most of the Chinese have made documented entry, so they are the mainstay of the union. But the Caribbean islanders—from Jamaica, the Dominican Republic, and the smaller islands—are often without papers. So are the people who have made their way to New York from Central and even South America. They are themselves cruelly exploited, which is obvious enough. What is less obvious, but just as true, is that they are one of the reasons why the wages in the union sector are as low as they are, despite the advantages of organization. When, in a competitive industry, there are more than five hundred shops getting a super-profit from frightened and under-paid workers, it puts pressure on the companies that hire legal labor. Indeed, as we shall see, this is probably the one area where undocumented workers actually do bring down the wages of the legal workers.

Even though it is not a federal crime for an employer to harbor an undocumented worker in order to exploit him or her, it is still against the law to pay less than the minimum wage, which is precisely what these unscrupulous sweatshop employers do. But there have been huge cuts in the enforcement funds. In New York, unannounced inspections were abolished as far back as 1976. The Department of Labor only checks when it gets a complaint—from workers who are understandably afraid to complain. Not long ago, I even saw a sweatshop owner who was so brazen that he permitted the cameras from a New York television station to photograph his illegal operation. It was as if a Prohibition still had held a press conference.

All this has led to the return of one of the worst forms of exploitation, once thought to be long since ended: homework. A woman works eight or nine hours at her regular job, then she takes work home with her, putting in another five or six hours there, often assisted by her children. "Employers," Mazur says, "advertise almost every day in foreign-language newspapers. And homework is a big business, with established distribution routes and daily pickup and delivery service."

Does this mean that the undocumented workers actually take jobs away from American citizens or foreigners with work permits? That is a disputed, as yet unresolved question. One theory says that the undocumented do indeed replace indigenous workers; another says that they take the jobs the latter don't want. Mazur cites a U.S. Department of Labor study showing that 75 percent of the undocumented hold unskilled or semiskilled jobs at wage levels well below the American average. That, he argues, refutes the notion that they are "effectively in economic competition with native American workers."

I think that the evidence supports that conclusion. When, for example, the INS made an outrageous sweep of suspected undocumented workers in 1982—"Project Jobs," a blatant attempt to pit the legal poor against the undocumented poor—the people who were seized averaged about $4.81 an hour in wages. Even so, there is another problem. If there had not been a constant inflow of immigrants into the American economy over the years, business would have been forced to upgrade the lower sectors of the labor market. Since there would not have been a cheap, docile supply of people so desperate that they would happily do menial labor at the minimum wage, or less, they would have had to make those menial jobs much less so, more "American." That, in turn, would have made things much better for the blacks, the Puerto Ricans, and the other indigenous working poor. In fact, it has been possible to maintain a labor-intensive menial sector because of the immigrants, and to eliminate the intermediate jobs just above them. The ladder, so to speak, kept its lowest rung—the one so near the bottom that American workers didn't want to climb on it—but the next two or three rungs were destroyed. That could be one of the reasons why there is a native-born underclass.

That polarization I described in talking of the new black poverty is implicated in the new immigrant poverty as well. Saskia Sassen-Koob has documented that between 1970 and 1980, New York City lost 400,000 jobs (the outflow actually started in the sixties, and is larger than that), but at the same time, there was a 17-percent increase in nine white-collar industries, 40 percent of them in professional and relatively well-paid jobs. And simultaneously, there was the growth of sweatshops in the lower depths of the New York economy. The lower-middle and middle rungs of the American occupational structure are at risk; the top and the bottom grow.

To be sure, not all of the new immigrants work in sweatshops. There are the Korean grocers in Harlem, the Vietnamese restaurant owners in San Francisco, people working their way out of poverty in the classic, old way. So it is that one of the central themes of American conservatism has been to hold up the Asians as a shining example and to scold the native Americans for not being as resourceful as the Asians. This argument deserves careful attention.

III

In *Wealth and Poverty*, the best-selling work of conservative social thought that inspired the Reagan administration, George Gilder cheerfully announced that "there will be poverty in America for centuries to come." This prediction would not come true, he said, if this country closed its borders to immigration. In short, our assured supply of the poor is to come from the new immigrants.

Lawrence Mead, one of *The Public Interest*'s polemicists against the welfare state, was quite a bit more serious than Gilder (that is not too difficult). I quote him at length since he makes a classic statement of the conservative case. He is talking about people's attitudes toward work, community, and self-help: "What has changed most seems to be the willingness of disadvantaged workers to accept the jobs they are able to get, not the case of finding them. Unquestionably, low-skilled jobs are usually poorly paid, menial, and relatively unpleasant. But in previous eras, immigrant and low-skilled workers usually accepted such jobs in the hope that they or their offspring could improve their condition through hard work, saving, education, or political or trade union activity. Today's disadvantaged are more likely to shift restlessly from job to job, drop out and enter the underground or illegal economy where earnings are higher, or live off welfare or other programs."

A little later on, Mead is even less ambiguous. The underground economy is not mentioned; it is noted that the racial and poverty barriers to advancement have declined (which is simply not true, as we have seen: They have intensified as a result of the economic crisis). And the quintessential *Public Interest* conclusion inevitably emerges: Rather than those declining racial and poverty barriers being the problem, "it is more plausible today that the troubling behavior and condition of the disadvantaged is due to the social programs on which so many are dependent." In this perspective, I would add, it was almost providential that Congress in the seventies excluded the undocumented from social security benefits, even though most pay the tax. That, conservative theory suggests, was not an act of social cruelty but an excellent way to drive people to desperately hard work.

How does one deal with this argument as it relates to the new immigrant poor? Are at least some of them a living reproach to native-born workers who lack their moral fiber?

The first thing that has to be understood is that this phenomenon is in no way exclusively American. It exists in every advanced Western capitalist country and is, therefore, hardly one more baleful consequence of the Great Society. Between the end of World War II and the early seventies, the major capitalist countries of Europe (with the exception of Italy) became importers of labor. The "guest workers," as the West Germans called them, came from Portugal, Spain, Finland, Greece, Turkey, Yugoslavia, Algeria, the Sudan, and Morocco. Since they entered societies where there was a general labor shortage, they did more than just menial jobs, but they most certainly also did those. France and West Germany were the two economies that accounted for 70 percent of the total, but the highest proportion of foreigners was found in Switzerland, where, at the peak, they made up 35 percent of the work force.

Then, around 1973, the Europeans began to have second thoughts. The social costs of these foreign populations grew, and there were tensions between them and the native-born workers. So there was a conscious attempt to reduce dependence on the temporary immigrants. France, for example, even paid them to go home. But, just as with the Braceros in this country, those admitted for the economic convenience of the rich discovered new possibilities, even new necessities. The result was a permanent increase in the European labor force of about five million once-migrant workers and seven million of their dependents. Moreover, in a very familiar story, those who stayed were disproportionately young and had larger families. In time they will grow as a percentage of these societies.

By the late seventies and early eighties, these developments were placed in a new context: not the great postwar boom of the fifties and sixties, with its hunger for labor, but the economic crisis, with its soaring unemployment. There always had been racial and ethnic tensions between migrants and natives, but now they rose. In West Berlin, which has a huge Turkish enclave of 120,000 people, there are racist graffiti telling them to go home. In France, in the municipal elections of 1983, the right played subtly on racial prejudice in a number of contests (to be fair, the Communists had been the first to cater to working-class hostility toward the North Africans some years before). In Brussels, in May 1980, fifteen thousand demonstrators took to the streets in protest against apartheid in the capital of the European community. The war of the poor against the poor is not, then, simply, or perhaps even mainly, an American problem.

Mark Kellman has made an excellent analysis of what is happening: "All the advanced capitalist countries seem to have great difficulty filling both the pre-technical service-sector jobs that still loom reasonably large in providing the amenities of bourgeois life, and the low-skill remnants of mechanical production. The characteristics of jobs like [those of] restaurant dishwashers, gardeners, piecework assemblers, etc., are that they are episodic, there are no ascending skills or internal job hierarchies, and the labor markets for these jobs are competitive rather than union dominated or otherwise semi-monopolized because the training periods are so short as to allow for rapid replacement of workers. *These characteristics are incompatible with the socialized desires of the now-schooled proletarian workers, and the jobs are rarely filled by members of the dominant race or gender.*" (Emphasis added.)

American conservatives are outraged at this notion. Blanche Bernstein, the former New York City welfare commissioner and a hard-liner on the issue of welfare recipients not working, is typical. The undocumented, she says, are exploited, sometimes getting less than the minimum wage, without fringe benefits—but they are fulfilling a "vital economic function," one that indigenous Americans do not find "worthwhile." Aren't the hard-working immigrants proof that we have coddled the poor into laziness? It is not quite that simple, and not the least because the attitudes of the American poor are, as Kellman says, "socialized desires," not individual psychological aberrations. Indeed, they are the unintended consequence of government policy rather than personal flaws. Daniel Bell's *Cultural Contradictions of Capitalism* provides a framework in which these ironies can be seen quite clearly. (I make my own use of his insights, of course.)

For Bell, the cultural contradiction of contemporary capitalism results from contrasting needs of the systems of production and consumption. When it comes to production, advanced capitalist society requires discipline, science, rigor. Greater and greater investments in human capital are needed to prepare technicians for their role in a complex process. Pleasure must be deferred, for the virtues of the Protestant ethic are imperative. But when one turns to consumption, there is a startling change, particularly visible in the sixties and early seventies. Now, within the context of a popularized Keynesianism, self-indulgence is seen as an act of economic citizenship. The production for production's sake of a very gross Gross National Product demands consumption for consumption's sake.

Even under the austere and moralizing administration of Ronald Reagan, the White House waited breathlessly in 1983 for a "consumer-led" recovery from the worst economic crisis in half a century. Reagan's "supply side" economics, which were supposed to stimulate an investment boom that would be counterposed to the profligate "demand side" policies of the liberals, had failed. Even after the recovery of 1983, corporate plans for capital spending were relatively modest. In 1984, *Business Week* predicted, the machine-tool industry and the steel plants producing for the capital goods market might see slightly better times. That was all. What stimulated the upturn of 1983 was not the nonexistent investment boom on the "supply side" but a splurge of spending on the despised "demand side." The economic Puritans in the White House were saved by a return of cavalier patterns of consumption on the part of the fortunate citizens in the middle and upper reaches of the society.

Childhood, as David Riesman once remarked in a marvelous phrase, is now the time in which one is a "consumer trainee." The problem is that the media, which are in charge of the training program, transcend social class in their appeal, but the means of responding to the media are very much determined by social class (to borrow a concept from Charles Silberman). That is, the minorities and the poor are subjected to the very same socialization of desire as the middle class and the rich. They, too, are told to buy and buy and buy. Only they can't. The same holds true in the case of work. As the sociologist Robert Merton has noted, "the American stigmatization of manual labor . . . *has been found to hold rather uniformly in all social classes.*" (Emphasis added.)

One must hasten to add that, as we have already seen, there are simply not great masses of employable people on welfare; most recipients are children, and women doing unpaid labor taking care of them. But to the very limited extent that there are some few who prefer a government check to menial work, they are simply being good and obedient Americans. The United States has profited enormously from its consumption ethic—or, more precisely, the richest have made the most from it and the rest have benefited in the standard descending order—and it is impossible to confine that attitude toward life to one segment of the society, particularly when the "bully pulpit" of the President is so often transported to a pleasant California ranch. In addition, to call for compulsory work, as Lawrence Mead does in his *Public Interest* article, is rather bizarre when there are more than ten million Americans looking for jobs who can't find them.

Am I, then, advocating accepting the status quo uncritically? In no way, as the final chapter of this book will make clear. For now, I would only draw the policy implications from an earlier analysis: The goal of Southwestern growers and Northeastern sweatshop entrepreneurs—to have a class of imported menial laborers—is an economic disincentive that works against the modernization and "Americanization" of the lower indigenous poor. It is therefore no accident that many of those who promote the contrast between the migrants and the natives are those who profit from the exploitation of the differences between them.

Moreover, a part of that famous contrast is simply bogus, and one of the conclusions regularly drawn from it is quite naïve.

The bogus element is to imply that all of the immigrants are a homogeneous mass, which was more or less the case in the second half of the nineteenth and the first part of the twentieth centuries. The Cubans, as we have already seen, include people who became wealthy through a bloody dictatorship, as well as middle-class and skilled working-class refugees who brought a considerable human capital with them when they arrived. Ironically, the Cuban refugees were qualified for much more serious and comprehensive welfare programs—language training, assistance in job hunting, relocation—than any American welfare client ever received. Even the Indochinese "boat people," the victims of one of the most obscene acts of racist dictatorship in recent history, were mainly Chinese entrepreneurs. They have done in this country what they did in Vietnam.

To be more precise, the exceptional Vietnamese are able to do that. The Vietnamese community in Santa Clara County, California—the home of "Silicon Valley," the high-tech area south of San Francisco—grew to about 30,000 in 1978 and 1979 (more than 10 percent of the total population). Half of them work at production jobs where they earn only slightly more than the minimum wage. They work shoulder-to-shoulder with other new immigrants—Koreans, Thais, Samoans, Filipinos, Chicanos—in dead-end jobs.

The contemporary conservative model of social behavior misses these trends because it is economistic, i.e., it assumes that money is the only reason why people work and that it also explains how they work. That is naïve.

It has long been understood that cultures and histories affect the way individuals act. Max Weber, who defined the Protestant ethic and its role in the rise of capitalism, also analyzed the phenomenon of "pariah capitalism." There were certain groups—Jews in Europe, Indians in Africa, the Chinese in the Pacific—who represented the capitalist spirit and practice in precapitalist societies. The Jews, for instance, had the role imposed upon them by medieval Christians who both upheld the Church's ban on moneylending and wanted to borrow. Confucianism, which began as a philosophy and turned into something of a religion, was one of the few creeds not opposed to making money (most faiths rightly understood that commercial relations undermined traditional patterns). These groups were often pariahs, minorities within societies that both needed and hated them. For historical reasons, they established entrepreneurial patterns.

It is perilous to ignore such historical and cultural factors—and unconscionable to turn them into "racial" characteristics. Those Vietnamese and Korean families following a hallowed path by involving every member in long hours at what is, in effect, subminimum wage, or even unpaid labor in a small enterprise, cannot be taken as a model for America. To cite one simple but devastating reason: 84.5 percent of Asian families in the United States are composed of intact couples, and only 6.2 percent are families with children headed by a woman; the black percentages are 56.9 percent intact couples, 25.7 percent families with children under eighteen headed by a woman. There is, as we will see in the next chapter, a kind of black extended family, but it has been under attack in the United States for decades, in part as a result of welfare policy. Under these circumstances, to tell blacks to be "Asian" is to ignore reality.

Shortly after the War on Poverty began in the sixties, I met Herman Kahn, the futurist, at a party. What, I asked him, should the poor be trained to do? "Turn them into Japanese gardeners," he replied, only half facetiously. I was impressed by his wit and insight, and I was wrong. Japanese gardeners acted upon the same cultural values that made their society the only non-Western nation to become a great economic power; black Americans and Chicano farm hands are not candidates for the job.

But there is still another catch. The romance of the new immigrants assumes that the standard tradition is still in force—that the hard-working immigrant shopkeepers will, through enormous sacrifice and unpaid labor, make it possible for their children to go to college and become professionals and executives. It was, of course, never quite as easy as that theory makes it sound, but leave that aside. I have taught for more than ten years now in a great public university—Queens College of the City University of New York—where most of my students are the children of the older immigrant generation, trying to follow that legendary route to the middle and upper middle class. Many of them are finding it extremely difficult, because an elite path has turned into a crowded, jostling highway. When only 5 percent of a generation had a college degree, it was a ticket to a middle-class position; when more than 25 percent do, and there is a decline in middle-class jobs, the old rules no longer apply, not even for the second or third generation, and certainly not for the first.

In short, the conservatives have attempted to use the war of the poor against the poor as an ideological weapon, as a means of blaming the lazy native-born poor for not being as hard-working as the immigrants and the undocumented. At its very best, this involves misstatements of fact and highly simplified notions about human behavior. At its worst, it is an ingenious rationalization of the selfish interests of growers and sweatshop hustlers.

IV

One of the leading Hispanic members of Congress, Robert Garcia, a Puerto Rican from the Bronx, is a prime sponsor of a program to create "enterprise zones" in the United States. There have been a number of changes in the original bill, but the basic idea has remained. In designated "enterprise zones," the government would reduce certain business and individual taxes. In return, the companies would be required to hire 40 percent of their employees from the hard-core unemployed. When the bill came up a second time, there were those around the White House who wanted to add a cherished conservative panacea by suspending the minimum-wage law in the enterprise zones. That was turned down by Garcia and his co-sponsor, Jack Kemp.

Kemp and Garcia, the Republican advocate of supply-side economics and the Democratic representative of one of the poorest areas in the nation: an "odd couple" symbolic of an odd program of state-subsidized laissez-faire. The Kemp-Garcia idea is not, of course, confined to immigrant neighborhoods, old or new. It is proposed for the nation as a whole. But there are two reasons for looking at it here: First, it duplicates an earlier attempt to create an "enterprise zone," which was one of the significant causes of the problem of Puerto Rican poverty in the Northeast; and second, it is a well-intentioned scheme for institutionalizing a low-wage economy of the kind that so many new immigrants and undocumented workers inhabit now.

In the 1940s, there was a much-heralded plan for bringing Puerto Rico the advantages of the American standard of living. The colony the United States had conquered in the Spanish-American War was still living on a low but integrated level, producing sugar. "Operation Bootstrap," which was liberal in origin, was going to change all that. Labor-intensive industry would come to Puerto Rico because there would be cheap, subminimum-wage labor and various tax incentives. And business did indeed come, in the process undermining the island's traditional social structure and turning uprooted rural people into a major export, primarily to the American Northeast. But the promised positive transformation never took place, and business could leave once it had reaped the initial benefits. By 1960, the emphasis shifted to capital-intensive petrochemicals. Operation Bootstrap was finished—a strange prototype, one might think, for a scheme to deal with some of the displacement and poverty that Operation Bootstrap itself had helped to create in the South Bronx.

Most important to the present point, the concept of "enterprise zones" accepts the notion of legally institutionalizing an inferior work force. The government would give tax benefits that would, in effect, match the "subsidy" given by underpaid, undocumented workers in the sweatshops. But what kind of a business would go into such an area? Certainly not the mainstream corporations with a sophisticated work force. They would abhor the shabby neighborhood and, in any case, be unable to have a work force with 40 percent recruited from the long-term unemployed. There would be poverty jobs for poverty people. The proposal, then, is one that essentially adapts to the misery of the low-wage areas in American society, which are so often peopled by the new immigrants. Once again, American business would be able to evade the need to reorganize the very structure of work at the bottom of the society.

A second major proposal is explicitly concerned with the problem of the new immigrant poor: the Simpson-Mazzoli bill. It seeks to create effective sanctions against the employers who have been legally exploiting the undocumented workers at least since the Texas Proviso of 1952. But it seeks to put an end to the flow of the undocumented by requiring all workers to present an identification card so that those hiring them can be certain that they are legal. And it would provide amnesty for a good number of the undocumented who have been in the United States for a period of time.

Before going into my own critique of the bill, a word of warning. Precisely because we confront here one of those Hegelian conflicts of right against right, there are decency and morality on both sides of the argument. *The New York Times* supports Simpson-Mazzoli out of concern for the immigrant and the American poor; the American Civil Liberties Union has questioned its identification-card procedures because it does not want good ends accomplished through questionable means. And, to add to the complexity, a reactionary, Senator Jesse Helms, objects to the amnesty provisions altogether and presumably wants to deport some six million people, or at least try to do so.

And then there is President Reagan's own inimitable contribution to the debate. The President, as I noted earlier, is anxious to pay off his Southwestern agricultural supporters by giving them their promised supply of cheap labor. So he called for a "temporary worker" program that would bring in 50,000 Mexicanos, a retreat from a figure of more than 500,000 originally floated by the White House. Under the circumstances, it became clear that Mr. Reagan would have no chance of getting those "guest workers" unless he accepted the principle of amnesty.

He then supported that principle, to quote a famous phrase of Lenin, the way a rope supports a hanging man. The undocumented people who came into the United States before January 1, 1980, could apply for a temporary permit that might then become permanent in ten years. But these temporary residents would have to renew every three years, pay taxes but be ineligible for welfare, food stamps, or unemployment insurance, and would have to learn English, but would not be allowed to bring their families into the United States. Such proposals, and Helms's simple "no" to amnesty, are easy enough to reject. What about the serious measures?

The core proposal in Simpson-Mazzoli is the "counterfeit-proof" identification card. How such an item could be produced has not been explained, and experts like Delfino Zarela doubt that it could be done at all. Moreover, the identification requirement could be used to discriminate against Hispanics (why hire anyone swarthy who might get you in trouble with the law?) or, in the case of the more unscrupulous, could be used as a threat (the employer would not challenge an obviously counterfeit ID as long as the worker was docile). For these and many other reasons, I oppose Simpson-Mazzoli even as I acknowledge its humane intent.

This does not mean that one simply walks away from the problem. Three principles might become the basis of new legislation.

First, total amnesty. As Jay Mazur told President Carter's Select Commission on Immigration and Refugee Policy in 1980, "Those who oppose a total amnesty have only two alternatives. The first is the haunting specter of apprehension and mass deportation of millions of undocumented workers by a huge army and police force. The second is acquiescence in the creation of a permanent underclass, with all of its accompanying evils, within American society."

Second, special treatment for the people of Mexico and Central America, as well as for political and economic refugees from countries like Haiti. In the 1960s, we radically reversed our previous policy with regard to legal Mexican immigration, and the problem of undocumented workers is, in part, a result of that drastic, arbitrary action. In practical terms, the Mexican-American border is the main source of this problem. A decent policy toward Mexicans and the people of Central America, who have so often been victimized by our military and economic policies, makes obvious sense. It is also just.

Third—and here we come to the problem of controls—rigid

enforcement of health and other social requirements of hiring, as Congressperson Schroeder has proposed. Or, as I would urge, truly effective enforcement of the minimum-wage law in every state of the United States. In either case—or in both, for they are obviously not exclusive—the point would be to go after the illegal employer, not the "illegal" employee. If we were to adopt the exact opposite of the Reagan philosophy and insist that all inhabitants of the United States, whether they are documented or not, have basic economic and social rights, we would simultaneously strike a blow at the foundations of the American system of sweatshop labor in the factories and fields: low wages and frightened workers. If we policed the boss rather than the worker—if we merely enforced existing laws—we could take much of the economic incentive away from the real villains in the underground economy.

Finally, all that has been said begs the larger question. So long as the Western Hemisphere and the world keep uprooting people and turning them into refugees from their traditional lives, so long as the economic crisis continues to hurt the poor of the world more than the rich, just so long will the borders of this wealthy society be porous. The Third World is, as I pointed out some time ago in *The Vast Majority*, not simply "out there"; it is within and at the gates. As *The Economist*, hardly an idealistic journal, put it, "The United States immigration problem—if that is what it is—will never be solved, after all, until its neighbours attain its level of development. The laws of economic gravity are against it."

A commitment to a new international economic order is therefore part of the solution to the poverty of Los Angeles and New York and Chicago. I hesitate to say this, writing in the America of Ronald Reagan, where an obsessive anti-Communism will not even permit the government to see the suffering people of El Salvador and Nicaragua. But it is the truth, and until it is acknowledged, we will only find imperfect solutions to the new structures of immigrant misery; to the war of the poor against the poor.

8

Violent Men and Immoral Women

Two images of the poor probably have done more to set back the struggle against poverty than have all the efforts of reactionary politicians: a young black mugger knocking down an aging white woman as he steals her purse (the poor as victimizer rather than as victim); a welfare mother with a large family, pregnant once again (the poor as promiscuous and lazy).

When American poverty was rediscovered in the early sixties, the dominant stereotypes were positive: blacks responding to the nonviolent message of Martin Luther King, Jr.; Appalachians fighting against terrible odds with an indomitable mountaineer spirit. But then, in the middle of the decade, that and so much else began to change. There were the urban riots, the advocacy of violence by some of the militants, the general turmoil in a society going through an unsettling revolution in some of its basic values. It all seemed of a piece: the irreverent hippie freak youth with no respect for the flag or family; the spread of public pornography; the rising decibel level of rock music. And some who had wanted to help the poor were now afraid of them.

It is not the first or last time that something like this has happened. The French scholar Louis Chevalier has written of a transition from people talking of the "laboring classes" to speaking of the "dangerous classes" in the middle of the nineteenth century. That moment, immortalized in Victor Hugo's *Les Miserables,* was, Chevalier argues, associated with a biological crisis in which the most basic conditions of life of those at the bottom of the society were threatened by epidemics that bred a sense of desperation. In late-nineteenth-century America, there was an influential book that spoke of the "dangerous classes"—the Irish and the Germans; blacks, it was noted, were model citizens—and all of the evils for which they were responsible.

It would be foolish to deny that something had indeed changed, even though the public theories and perceptions about what it was were usually wrong or flawed. When I first came to New York City, in 1949, Union Square was a gentle place where radicals gathered to engage in spirited but nonviolent debate. The Lower East Side was then at the end of an era as the great point of departure for Jewish immigrants. There were Yiddish theaters on Second Avenue, and if life in the tenements was impoverished, it was proud and orderly. I lived for a while in a vibrant neighborhood on East Fifth Street, where everything closed on Saturday for the Jewish Sabbath and was open on Sunday. One could come home late at night and walk down those streets of the old-fashioned poor without the least bit of fear.

A mere fifteen years later I went back to what was now a black and Hispanic street to have a publicity picture taken in the middle of the afternoon. There was a palpable current of suspicion and hostility on Fifth Street, and I, who had been unafraid at two in the morning, was now concerned at one in the afternoon.

Union Square has turned into a huge drug supermarket. One side of the square is the province of the black dealers; the other side is the territory of the Puerto Ricans. There are strung-out, dazed young people everywhere, and sudden outbreaks of violence are common. Most of the time I walk all the way around the square rather than cross it directly.

Family disintegration among the poor is not as directly menacing as crime, but it has certainly provoked great anger, particularly among working people in the United States. Why, they ask, should we work long and hard when there is some welfare mother who is going out and getting deliberately pregnant in order to avoid taking a job? That, we shall see, is a question based on a largely erroneous interpretation of something that is quite real: a radical decline in intact families, particularly among the black poor. And then those workers say something else that is true: Why, they ask, do we pay a disproportionate share of the cost for those welfare mothers? They do. But the problem is not the welfare mother; it is the rich who evade their proportionate share of the cost.

On a somewhat more sophisticated level, there are those—for example, Bruce Chapman, the Director of the U.S. Census Bureau—who argue that the rise in the poverty rate in the seventies was, in considerable measure, primarily a reflection of family breakdown, not of the failure of the American economy. The implicit—and sometimes explicit—corollary of this thesis is that all liberal or radical attempts to deal with poverty through economic policy will inevitably fail. The causes of poverty, it is said, are psychological and cultural, not economic. Small wonder, these people say, that the War on Poverty and the Great Society didn't work. They were attacking the wrong problem with the wrong methods.

Indeed, there are some who hold that poverty is itself a culture. When that is said on the left, for example by the late Oscar Lewis, the intention is to emphasize the tenacity, the institutionalization, of misery in the United States. When it is urged on the right, say by an Edward Banfield, it is a tactic for making poverty something ephemeral and individualistic, a state of soul rather than a condition of the society.

All these themes are obviously interrelated: The decline in traditional families, so marked among the poor, and the increase in violent crime are the complex products of many of the same causes. But the personal psychologies of the poor are not merely individual; they are also the social consequences of massive economic trends, and if they obviously do not affect each person in the same way—there are many more poor people who are not criminal than who are—they do wreak havoc among entire groups of the population.

I

The discussion of crime and poverty in the United States is, more often than not, a battle between strawmen. Each side sets up a stunning, even idiotic, simplicity that it imputes to the other side and then shreds it to pieces.

A few examples. Robert Samuelson examines the links between crime and unemployment for the *National Journal*. Is there, he asks, "a direct connection between unemployment and crime?" This, he responds, overlooks the support system now in place for the jobless. (He himself is not aware that 50 percent or more of them did not get benefits in 1983, but that is not crucial here.) And "it insults most of the unemployed by assuming they could slip easily into crime." But who has ever suggested that "most of the unemployed" will quickly cope with their lack of work by becoming criminals? That is patently wrong. The serious statement, documented by Harvey Brenner of Johns Hopkins University, is that, over a period of five years, a sustained one-percent increase in the unemployment rate has, in fact, been associated with a 4-percent increase in state prison admissions and a 5.7-percent increase in homicides, and that there would seem to be a complex relationship between those statistics.

James Q. Wilson, perhaps the most serious and learned opponent of that relationship, wrote in *Public Interest* that there is clearly no causal relationship between deprivation and crime, since crime rates seem to have remained stable or declined during the Great Depression. But who is the foolish person who asserted that poverty is the only cause of crime, and that there is therefore a one-to-one link between the two? Wilson then goes on to point out that the decline in traditional religion is a factor in some of our social pathologies. I could not agree more, and have even written a book—*The Politics at God's Funeral*—which explores that point in rather great detail. But do these changes in moral attitudes occur in a vacuum? Might one suggest that the breakdown of stable communities as a result of cancerous urbanization is a (not *the*) cause of the decrease in religious faith *and* crime *and* family breakdown? Indeed, I believe my book showed that all of these factors are both causes and effects of one another.

On the other side, there are those who rightly argue that the completely cultural and psychological accounts of poverty are intended to downplay economic causes—and economic solutions. That is true. But some then conclude that the non-economic has no role at all, that any reference to the cultural or psychological is inevitably reactionary. Those who are guilty of that simplification generally have excellent motives, but it is a simplification nevertheless.

It is, then, with some trepidation that I set foot in an area covered with the scattered remains of strawmen.

To begin with—and the trend explains political attitudes as well as describing social conduct—there was indeed a major change in criminal behavior which, alas, occurred at almost the very same time as the War on Poverty. Charles Silberman—to whom this section is deeply indebted—writes: "Since the early 1960s, the United States has been in the grip of a crime wave of epic proportions." Between 1960 and 1976, the chance that a person would be a victim of murder, rape, robbery, or aggravated assault trebled. To make matters even more frightening, murder and rape had traditionally been crimes committed by friends (husbands, wives, lovers) or acquaintances (the neighborhood). But since the early sixties, murders by strangers have increased at double the rate of murders by acquaintances. In 1967, about half of the rapes in this country involved people who knew each other; by 1975, two-thirds of them were sexual assaults by strangers. Murder and rape are, under any circumstances, horrible, but when they become random they are all the more frightening.

Crime, just as James Q. Wilson notes, did indeed drop in the thirties, once Prohibition ended. It went up after World War II, but it was still well below the level of the twenties and the early thirties until the early sixties. If one adopts Karl Mannheim's theory that a person's idea of what the world really is dates from his seventeenth or eighteenth year, then when the War on Poverty began, only people over fifty years of age had any significant memory of a more violent time. Clearly, the War on Poverty did not cause the criminal explosion. The conservatives themselves would disdain such a "materialistic" thesis (in other areas, they themselves use this method, as we have seen). But, ironically, American attention was focused on the issue of poverty at the precise moment when violent crime increased radically. Small wonder that some people mistakenly regarded the latter as a consequence of the "coddling" of the antipoverty effort. But then another popular theory, that the new crime was a result of a more youthful population, didn't work either.

There is, historically, a link between age and crime. In 1960, youths between fourteen and twenty-four, who comprise 15 percent of the population, accounted for 69 percent of the arrests in the United States. That generation increased by 63 percent between 1960 and 1975, but crime went up by 200 percent. However, it is possible to make a sophisticated argument, seeing a point of "demographic overload" in that huge expansion of the younger generation. In that theory, something snapped, "the conventional means of social control broke down," and a 63-percent growth in the number of the youth generated more than a 63-percent increase in crime.

The raw statistics do not, however, catch the quality of the phenomenon. Silberman writes about what psychologists call "the absence of 'affect' ": "In the past, juveniles who exploded into violence tended to feel considerable guilt or remorse afterwards; the new criminals have been so brutalized in their own upbringing that they seem incapable of viewing their victims as fellow human beings or realizing that they have killed another person. 'They seem to have no ability to distinguish between someone shot in a movie and shooting someone themselves,' a youth worker told a New York State Assembly Committee. 'To them, everything is one big movie.' "

I talked about that alienated, psychopathic violence with Norman Thomas, who was six times the Presidential candidate of the Socialist Party, one day in the early sixties. There had just been a particularly horrible murder up in Harlem in which one youth had killed another for no apparent reason. Thomas said that when he had been a young Protestant minister in Harlem before World War I, he had been quite familiar with purposive, functional crimes, where a poor kid would steal an equally poor kid's coat. But this aimless brutality was something new and inexplicable.

The main victims of the crime wave, it must never be forgotten, are the poor and the minorities. When the Department of Justice did a study of violence and crime in the sixties, it found that the most terrorized single group in the society was black women. The reason was simplicity itself: The most victimized single group in the society is also black women. It is ironic that the poor as a group are blamed for a violence that they suffer much, much more than they inflict. One result of the stereotype that ignores this fact is what Christopher Jencks calls "statistical prejudice." Because it is true that blacks have a higher violent crime rate than whites, people—and employers in particular—treat all blacks as criminals, which is an absurd and racist reading of the numbers. Indeed, as Silberman points out, there is discrimination in the underworld itself: The professional criminals tend to be whites from working-class, or even middle-class, backgrounds; the "opportunist" lawbreakers, who take a chance when they see one, are, by contrast, predominantly from the poor in general and the minority poor in particular.

In saying this, I do not want to run away from the most disturbing statistic of all, i.e., that blacks have a particularly high crime rate. Puerto Ricans and other Hispanics in New York City share much of the poverty with the blacks (the 1980 census found that 32 percent of the people of Hispanic origin in the city were poor, as compared to 28 percent of the blacks). Yet in the early seventies—and Silberman, writing at the end of the decade, thought the trend still held—63 percent of the people arrested for violent crime were black, 15.3 percent Hispanic. In proportion to the population, the black rate was four times that of the Hispanics. It is clear that not only is it impossible to explain the crime of individuals simply by their poverty, but that there can also be a significant differential between groups suffering from the same poverty.

Why this differential between blacks and Hispanics? There

is a host of reasons why a racial explanation fails, but the simplest and most convincing is that blacks in Africa have a homicide rate about equal to that of Europe and therefore lower than that of *both* blacks and whites in the United States. "Violence," Silberman comments, "is something black Americans learned in this country." Between 1882 and 1903, for instance, 1,985 blacks were killed by lynch mobs. Even in the forties and fifties, as the black writer James Baldwin has eloquently described the experience, a black in New York City always had to be fearful of white violence. Baldwin himself was once severely beaten in a Greenwich Village bar for the high crime of being seated next to a white woman. This white terrorism effectively held black violence down over the years. To a degree suffered by no other group—with the possible exception of American Indians—black America has had violence thrust upon it. In the late seventies, black people were murdered in the United States at a rate eight times that of whites, raped two and a half times more frequently, robbed three times more than whites, and suffered one and a half times more aggravated assault.

It was not, however, mere fear that repressed a violent response to violence for so many years. The decency and humanity of blacks themselves were a factor, too. Booker T. Washington said, in his famous speech at the Atlanta Exposition in 1895, that if whites would only allow blacks to become hard-working artisans and mechanics, "you and your families will be surrounded by the most faithful, law-abiding and unresentful people that the world has ever seen." Granted, Washington was involved in trying to make the best possible deal with a racism he detested, but that sentiment was a commonplace among blacks. In A. Philip Randolph's Brotherhood of Sleeping Car Porters, the emphasis upon honesty was legendary.

Indeed, it is Silberman's reading of the evidence that the current pattern of black violence reflects a development that goes back only to the mid-sixties, i.e., that coincides with the general increase in violent crime in the United States. Since then, he writes, "the cultural devices that kept black violence under control [such as lynching] have broken down . . . and new cultural controls have not yet emerged." There is, I think, considerable value in the thought, but it raises an important question: Why did this breakdown in cultural controls occur when it did, in the mid-sixties?

The huge internal migration of blacks from the South, and from the rural South in particular, occurred in the forties and fifties. Was violence one of the responses to the traumas of a refugee population arriving in the decaying ghettos of cities that were no longer the staging areas for social mobility but were, to an increasing degree, urban reservations for marginalized people without a function in the society? That is certainly possible. Also, the mid-sixties saw not only the triumphs of Martin Luther King, Jr.'s nonviolent movement, but disillusionment with the War on Poverty as well.

I have written elsewhere of the last time I saw Dr. King, but I will repeat that account here, since I think the memory is relevant to the discussion. It was in the winter of 1968, several months before his murder. A small group of us who used to meet with him when he came to New York convened in a comfortable law office in Manhattan. I had the sense that Dr. King was near despair as we talked of the political problems confronting the movement. He had courageously broken with Lyndon Johnson over the war in Vietnam, but that had cut him off from the Johnson liberals and trade unionists as well as from the White House itself. On his left, the Student Nonviolent Coordinating Committee, which he had inspired, was moving to reject nonviolence and to question the goal of racial integration itself; there were Black Panthers and other militant groups talking about the need for armed struggle.

Martin Luther King, Jr., was a man deeply committed to both nonviolence and integration, and now he was being attacked, from both left and right, because of his most basic values. But he had not lost his sense of humor. When he asked me to draft a manifesto for the Poor People's March and I said that perhaps it was not wise for a white to be assigned that task, given the mood of militant blacks, he smiled and replied, "Why, Mike, we didn't know we were poor until we read your book." But what about the ghetto poor who hadn't read my book, or perhaps any book? They might have thought in the early sixties that poverty and racism were going to be abolished; they knew by the late sixties that they were not. Did that create a situation in which violence was the expression of an inner rage?

Let me carefully stipulate what I am not saying, because there is a great danger of misunderstanding here. People in the black community, or in regular contact with it, tell me that they have never encountered anyone who made the explicit link: I am furious with the racist society, therefore I will act out in criminal ways. And I am most certainly not adopting the theory that all blacks who engage in violence are radicals making a dramatic statement about their opposition to the system. Most of the criminals themselves don't believe it for a moment and, in any case, it is hard to see how a black murdering, raping, or assaulting another black is making a "statement" of any kind against white racism. What I am suggesting is that it is at least possible that there was a shift in the mood of black America that led to an explosion of pent-up violence.

To say that one can thus understand the unconscionable conditions that made a violent reaction more likely on the part of a rather small minority of black people is not to justify the violence. Indeed, for anyone who insists on thinking of this outburst as political, there is an inescapable conclusion that is hardly ever drawn: It was the worst, the most counterproductive politics one can imagine, for it severely retarded the progress of the great majority of blacks who were trying to achieve a minimum of decency without violence.

All of this should not be taken to imply that violence is unique among blacks, but only to argue that it is somewhat more common because blacks have themselves been the victims of violence more than any other group in the United States (again, with the possible exception of American Indians). The relation between poverty and crime holds without regard to creed or color, a fact that becomes all the more clear when one explores the idea of an "underclass."

The notion of an underclass is hardly new. More than a hundred years ago, Karl Marx described the *lumpenproletariat*—literally, the proletariat in rags—of early capitalist society. It was composed not of those proletarians who were disciplined by the new system and thus learned how to organize themselves and fight back as a class, but of functionless people, of those who had fallen out of society, who were its human refuse. Marx was profoundly hostile to this stratum—he thought that it supplied brawlers and street fighters for rightist leaders on horseback like Napoleon III—and he insisted that it was part of the underworld. In the 1960s, Gunnar Myrdal took something like that idea and used it to describe an emergent "underclass" composed mainly of young people who had been rendered superfluous and nonfunctional by the development of the economy.

In 1982, the journalist Ken Auletta published *The Underclass*, an excellent volume of reportage and observation, if somewhat flawed in its theorizing. Auletta understood, contrary to all the theses about permanent welfare dependency, that a majority of the poor moved in and out of poverty. But there was, he said, a minority, an ongoing underclass. It was made up of the long-term welfare recipients, the drifters, the street criminals who are often school dropouts and drug addicts, and the relatively nonviolent hustlers of the underground economy. The characteristics of this class, he reported, were not racial or geographic: it behaved in much the same way in white Appalachia, black rural Mississippi, Spanish Harlem, or Oakland, California.

Indeed, when Auletta told a group of black and Hispanic hard-core unemployed going through a special government work program about the white poor he encountered in Appalachia, one man said, "The most important thing I heard is that all races behave the same." This suggests to me that certain social and economic conditions—above all, the experience of becoming marginal, useless—create not a fate, but a greater likelihood that some (a minority) will turn to violent crime either as means to an end, a way of earning a living, or else as an act of sheer rage.

That is nonsense, James Q. Wilson would say. He triumphantly slaughters the strawmen I have already described: the theory, held only by foolish people who are irrelevant to serious discussion, that there is a one-to-one link between poverty and crime. But Wilson's comments on cultural factors, even though they lead to reactionary political conclusions, are worth thinking about and, in one notable case, actually help to document an analysis that is the exact opposite of his own.

The reason why crime declined, even during the brutal days of industrialization, Wilson argues, is that around 1840 the upper class adopted a set of Victorian values that then permeated down to the lower orders in the emergent cities. He cites Eric Monkkonen for the proposition that "bourgeois—that is, middle class—ideology acquired a remarkable degree of hegemony in England and America." So it was that "popular literature emphasized the values of thrift, order, industriousness, sobriety, the mastery of passions, and a deep regard for the future." These priorities were internalized by the great mass of people, and that was one of the reasons why social upheavals and transformations in the United States were accompanied by declining crime rates.

But then, starting in 1920, the educated classes in the United States began to repudiate the old values. By the contemporary period there was a "collapse of the Victorian popular culture and of the moral legitimacy of the institutions embodying it." There was the rise of a "Me Generation," a general conviction that the old constraints did not apply, that self-expression and acting out were good. When these notions permeated the world of the poor, they were a major reason for the rise in criminal conduct. The internal censors had disappeared. That, not poverty, explains the new violence.

There is obviously some truth in this argument, but it is put so one-sidedly by Wilson that he undercuts the value of his own insight. As far back as the eighteenth century, Voltaire and other Enlightenment thinkers were terrified of what would happen when the masses discovered the elite truth that the Judeo-Christian God did not really exist. According to legend, one night at dinner when his guests were talking about atheism, Voltaire dismissed the servants and asked the people around the table whether they wanted to be murdered by disillusioned butlers. Voltaire was, of course, as wrong as Wilson; most of those who stop believing in

God do not become criminals. That is about as silly as the idea that all poor people are, because of their poverty, violent. Monocausal explanations are no better when based on culture than they are when based on economics.

And yet, if one respects the complexities (which I explored in *The Politics at God's Funeral*), there is a relation between declining religious faith and individual conduct, and one possible consequence is an increase in crime. The "transvaluation of all values," Nietzsche said, would lead to an increase in social turmoil since it was the hated Church that had at least held the demonic powers in check. That process, however, was not the result of an irresponsible elite (which is Wilson's thesis and, indeed, *the* scapegoat of all neoconservative thought). It was a product of science, urbanization, of the hedonistic society that was the unintended consequence of a capitalism originally created by Protestant ascetics.

Moreover, the ways in which that cultural change affected various strata vary with the strata; i.e., the "cause" is both cultural and a question of social structure. The upper middle class responds to the loss of faith and Victorian values by cheating on its income tax, sniffing cocaine, engaging in extramarital sex. Its members do not become street criminals or prisoners. One of the ways that some poor people may interpret the new moral laxity is violence, but that is a distinctive response very much related to economic conditions. To turn this intricate process into a simple matter of cultural change initiated by a liberal educated class is not ultimately serious.

It is, however, purposeful. If the real causes of crime are "family structure, moral development, the level of personal freedom," and if these factors either cannot or should not be altered, then all the reformist solutions, the tough-minded as well as the tender-minded, will fail. Whether one offers the criminals carrots (jobs, antipoverty programs) or sticks (jails), nothing will change very much. But family structure, moral development, and the level of personal freedom are not free-floating values independent of social structures. I would argue that if transition of the black poor from the rural South to the cities had been accomplished with social supports—jobs and the like—there would have been different outcomes in precisely the areas that Wilson thinks are beyond the reach of government policy.

But then, Wilson's 1983 article lends unwitting support to Silberman's 1980 book. Wilson emphasizes the pervasiveness of middle-class values in American life, which is true. But he then forgets the crucial corollary that Silberman puts quite succinctly: "The distinctive features of lower-class life have their origins in the fact that American cultural goals transcend class lines, *while the means of achieving them do not.*" (Emphasis added.) Social class is the filter of cultural values. The liberating—or boring—hedonism of the rich becomes a bitter, frustrating incitement when it finally reaches down into the world of the poor.

Is the point, then, simply to explain the relationship between poverty and crime and to advise the society to endure the resulting violence until an economic and social utopia is built and people become nice? Not at all. Police means are necessary to protect society even from the terrible consequences of its own errors; street crime worsens rather than abolishes poverty and, more often than not, it targets the poor. Having said that, I hasten to add that increasing the number of prisoners is no solution, either. The United States has proportionately more people in jail than any country except the Soviet Union and South Africa. Moreover, those jails are primarily institutions for the criminal poor, and they hardly ever house the criminal upper classes. They are vile and degrading places that do not rehabilitate, but act as graduate schools in crime.

Along with effective police action, I believe we should adopt a very simple principle, i.e., that the only reason to lock someone up is the demonstrated probability that he will do violence to his fellow citizens if he is not incarcerated. Everyone else should pay his debt to society—and, wherever possible, to the victims of his acts—in some other way. Such a policy, I think, is not only morally necessary if one is to reduce the discrimination against the poor which is institutionalized in our prisons; it would also lower the crime rate.

Finally, I do not think that the abolition of poverty would

end all violent crime. I do think it would significantly reduce it, and do so to a much greater degree than any police force. In short, this is an area in which we need a nuance or two, not any more strawmen.

II

Family breakdown occurred at about the same time as the rapid increase in violent crime and for some of the same reasons. One result—one of the new structures of misery in the United States—is the "feminization" of poverty.

In 1960, 8.1 percent of white households and 20.9 percent of black households were headed by a woman. In 1981, the white percentage had risen to 11.9, the black to 41.7. Between 1950 and 1979, the number of children born out of wedlock in the United States quadrupled for both blacks and whites. In that same year, more than half of the black births in the United States were out of wedlock (the white figure was 17.1 percent). Among black women, teenagers accounted for 44 percent of those pregnancies out of wedlock.

This was not simply a poverty phenomenon. As is so often the case, the poor participated in a national trend, but since they were poor, they did so in ways that often hurt them more than anyone else. When a middle-class woman is divorced or separated, she does not go and apply for AFDC; a poor woman has no other alternative. But even here one must be careful, for there are, as Barbara Ehrenreich suggests, *nouvelles pauvres* living in suburbs who can be forced down into poverty when their marriages break up. In January 1983, I gave a talk in Marin County, California, a legendary, trendy upper-middle-class suburb of San Francisco. I had mentioned AFDC in passing, and after the speech, the daughter of an old friend, a young woman who had grown up in a comfortable environment, reintroduced herself and commented that it certainly was difficult to support her two children on AFDC.

Indeed, Mary Jo Bane and David Ellwood have shown that 75 percent of all women who go to AFDC do so because their living relationship changes (a husband or lover leaves or dies). And David Stockman, hardly a witness who exaggerates in these matters, approvingly quoted the Bane-Ellwood analysis that "divorce, separation, childbearing out of wedlock" are major causes of welfare dependence. In almost all of these cases, women are left with unsupported children and, contrary to the myth, it is not their decision, but the man's, that pushes them under the poverty line.

Thus the problems of the family life of the poor are a particularly cruel, exaggerated example of a larger trend that is transforming the family structure of all social classes. In 1980, the Census found that less than 20 percent of the households in Philadelphia conformed to the supposedly "normal" pattern of a husband-wife couple with children. In San Francisco the figure was 13 percent.

These matters are obviously difficult to discuss. On the one hand, this society still outrageously stigmatizes children born out of wedlock as "illegitimate," even though it is rather obvious that it was not the baby who engaged in pre- or extramarital sex. Coupled with this is the fact that here, as in the case of crime, there is a higher rate of black family breakdown (even when the figures are corrected for some very important simplifications to be discussed in a moment) than white. Such a statistic is clearly very easy to use in a racist argument, and that makes people wary of it for understandable reasons.

On the other hand, nonracists can use the data for politically reactionary purposes. In 1965, when Daniel Patrick Moynihan's analysis of black family breakdown was published, there was an uproar. Ironically, Moynihan had emphasized the social pathology in the black community—and ignored the strengths—for a perfectly decent liberal reason: He wanted Lyndon Johnson to act much more forcefully on behalf of the people in the ghetto, and he therefore painted the bleakest possible picture in order to buttress his policy recommendations. Indeed, it was Moynihan's memo that led Johnson to give the most antiracist speech ever delivered by a President of the United States, at the Howard University commencement in 1965. Among other things, it called for "equality of result" rather than "equality of opportunity," thus going far beyond the traditional confines of American liberalism.

Some of those criticisms directed at Moynihan came from militant, often young, black intellectuals who were beginning to come into their own at the time. They were, in my opinion, unfair in a significant number of cases. Martin Luther King, Jr., was, as usual, much more balanced and thoughtful than were some of Moynihan's vituperative critics. He agreed with Moynihan that there were trends in black family patterns that were heading toward a "social catastrophe," but he warned against the danger that "problems will be attributed to innate Negro weakness and used to justify neglect and rationalize oppression." I propose to be as realistic as King—and to avoid that danger.

All of those families headed by a woman were not poor. As a matter of fact, 70 percent of them were not, only 30 percent were. Even so, the decline in intact families, the epidemic of unmarried teenage poverty, the growing number of families headed by a poor woman, significantly changed the structure of poverty in the United States. In 1960, on the basis of the official figures, 65 percent of poor families were headed by a man under sixty-five years of age, 21.2 percent were headed by a woman (13.8 percent of the families were headed by either a man or a woman over sixty-five). By 1979, the percentage of male heads had dropped to 42.4, and of female heads had risen to 43.7. Adding in the fact that the aging poor are predominantly female, the feminine percentage of the adult poverty population had doubled in the years after the declaration of war on poverty!

So it was that in 1981, of the 859,000 people on welfare in New York City, 519,000 were children, 498,000 of them living in female-headed families. Why?

The momentous internal migration after World War II provides one part of the answer. It has long been common, as Herbert Gutman points out, for blacks to practice a kind of extended family pattern, with grandmothers, kin, and neighbors playing important roles. It was also common for first pregnancies to occur before marriage, and there was no stigma attached to them. That type of family life—which the official statistics, with their traditional

American bias, do not recognize—survived even when people moved to the cities of the North. There were, Gutman said, blocks in Harlem in which people from different parts of the South concentrated; there were people in Chicago who claimed to be able to tell where someone came from in the South on the basis of an accent. By James Q. Wilson's Victorian standards of morality, there was a fair amount of sin going on; in fact, there was an alternative style of family life that was true to its own (different) principles.

The problem is, that pattern seems to have broken down too. For the migrants arrived, as we have seen, at a time of declining job opportunity. There were those youth unemployment rates of 40 and 50 percent in Harlem and the South Bronx. How, the Puerto Rican leader Ramon Jimenez asked me, do you get family stability when all of those youths are milling around with nothing to do? It was not just that there was an increasingly permissive, hedonistic culture, as Wilson emphasizes; it was the impact of that culture on poor youths with uncertain futures, or perhaps no futures at all.

I would speculate that there is a rather large psychological element in the epidemic of teenage pregnancies among the poor. In many of the subcultures of poverty—the Appalachian white as well as the Hispanic and black—it is "macho" for a young man to get his girlfriend pregnant. And young girls, I suspect, living in a harsh and sometimes loveless world, subjected, as Silberman says, to all of the romantic values of the mass media but without the means of acting upon them possessed by the middle class, willingly court pregnancy as a way of finding love. In the process, they can sentence themselves to a life of poverty.

That happens, in part, because they are poor, or often both poor and members of a minority. It also happens because they are women.

Women in the United States occupy about the same economic position as blacks and other minorities. They, like the minorities, receive about 60 percent of the dominant (white male) workers' income. This result is not normally a consequence of overt sexual discrimination, i.e., a woman being paid less than a man working at the very same job. Rather, it is the result of the very structure of "women's work" in the United States. The vast increase in the percentage of working women took place after World War II (and, to a considerable measure, *because* of World War II, a period when it was necessary to recruit females to replace drafted males in the war industries). Mainly they took typically "female" jobs: typists, clerks, workers in the service sector.

The "female" jobs were almost always less well paid than the male, even when, as was often the case, the qualifications required were the same in both. But then, even when women did get professional positions, they were not paid as much as men. In part, this was because they tended to be segregated in the professions themselves. They were pediatricians, gynecologists, and psychotherapists when they got an M.D., not surgeons. These specialties, it will be noted, are appropriately "feminine," involving taking care of children, women, and emotional problems, rather than the "masculine" functions of repairing broken bodies or performing miraculous transplants. Women are also much more likely to be part-time workers than are men: In 1980, 67.3 percent of white males were full-timers all year, but only 43.3 percent of white women (the respective figures for blacks are 59.3 percent and 47.2 percent).

The plight of the female poor is to occupy a disadvantaged position within an already disadvantaged occupational structure for women. Take that enormous number of teenage pregnancies. Those young women will, in almost every case, become single parents and will receive little or nothing from the fathers of their children. That happens to them before they are even out of high school, and they therefore come into that women's labor market with much less training than anyone else. Some of them will despair of ever finding a job—not an irrational response—and will simply drop out altogether, becoming welfare cases. The "lucky" ones will find a menial, poorly paid job somewhere.

Why, it may be asked, the irresponsibility of the men? In part, it is a result of the cultural machismo that is so often found in the various worlds of the poor. But there is another possible reason, one that scholars have never fully explored. Samuel

Myers of the University of Pittsburgh and William Darity of the University of Texas have noted that the 1980 census showed that there were 420,000 more black women than black men, which represented a doubling of the gap since 1965. This is not a natural outcome—there are more males conceived than females—but a social and economic outcome. The black males, Myers and Darity conjecture, are more likely to be killed or sent to prison, or to lead lives so marginal that they have disappeared from the community. Whatever the cause, this imbalance sets up a demographic situation in which males are at a sexual premium, a fact that could well be a source of that macho attitude.

The point, however, is not to make the men scapegoats for the breakdown in stable family relationships. For even if they may have a somewhat privileged position in sexual relations because of those social demographics, poor males, again particularly if they are members of a minority group, are also at an enormous economic disadvantage. In the period of open racism on the job market—that is, until the 1960s—there were more openings for black women than for black men. Those openings were, to be sure, for domestic work and low-paid service jobs, but they did provide the possibility of steady menial work, something that was often denied the men. And when overt racism disappeared and new possibilities appeared in the sixties, the traditional entry jobs for male workers were no longer there in the numbers that had once prevailed. So there was very little economic possibility of playing the role of a father and husband.

All of this was compounded by the antifamily provisions of the welfare system. Until the 1960s, it was impossible for a family to get AFDC if there was a man in the house. There were even those notorious raids by the guardians of the public morality to see if they could find some woman cheating by living with the father of her child. (It made no difference if he was her husband; that was still cause for ineligibility.) Even today there are twenty-nine states in which a two-parent family, no matter how poor, cannot receive welfare payments or Medicaid. And even in a progressive state like New York it was not until 1976—and a court decision—that a family in which the man was receiving unemployment compensation could also apply for welfare on the mere grounds that it was in desperate need.

The predictable result of these policies was that the governmental policies of twenty-nine states forced families to break up in order to survive. And even in the more enlightened jurisdictions, the de facto policy is to aid only the broken family. This analysis is, in rather dramatic fashion, the opposite of the conservative account of the problem of the family among the poor. I take up their arguments, which are tediously predictable by now, for two specific reasons: Their refutation involves an important complexity; and their wrong ideas point rather clearly, if unwittingly, toward some important solutions.

George Gilder, as is usually the case, comes up with an analysis that is magisterial and absurd. "Once a family is headed by a woman," Gilder writes, "it is almost impossible for it to greatly raise its income even if the woman is highly educated and trained and she hires day care or domestic help. Her family responsibilities and distractions tend to prevent her from the kind of all-out commitment that is necessary to full use of earning power." All of this is topped off with a bit of mysticism: Women are compensated for this disadvantage because they have "glimpses of eternity in their wombs."

There is one grain of truth in this analysis: Highly educated and trained professional women are indeed put in a position of playing the traditional female role at home and the new role in the office. Cynthia Epstein dealt with this contradiction in *Woman's Place*. But Gilder generalizes this valid insight into a completely different proposition, i.e., that such women therefore cannot greatly raise their incomes. Female-headed families are poor in disproportionate numbers not because they lack money, but because of the gender of the family head with "glimpses of eternity" in her womb and no ability to cope with the pragmatic world.

But, as I have already noted, the Bureau of the Census figures for 1979 showed that about one-third of families headed by a woman—a more difficult case than that of the professional woman—were indeed poor. But slightly more than two-thirds were not. Indeed, about half of those female family heads earned between

$7,500 and $25,000, 10 percent were in the $25,000–$50,000 category, and just under one percent made $50,000 a year or more. These figures demonstrate that there is still a gender differential even for educated women (in 1981, women lawyers, whose percentage had doubled in the previous decade, earned 71 percent of male lawyers' income; women doctors and dentists earned 80.9 percent of the male income) *and* that the ability of trained women to increase their income was rising even as Gilder was writing his book.

The more serious theory comes from Bruce Chapman, the director of the Census Bureau. Writing in *The Wall Street Journal* in 1982, he argued that "there does seem to be at least a partial connection between the changes in attitude toward family life, the rise in single parent families, and high poverty rates." If white and black family composition had been the same in 1980 as in 1970, he comments, then white income would have increased by 3 percent and black income by 11 percent. It is not, he concludes, poverty that causes the breakdown, since "we saw no comparable trend, say, in the far worse times of the Great Depression." It is the decline in the traditional family that causes the poverty, not the other way around.

I have already dealt with that simplistic Depression analogy as it was presented by James Q. Wilson. One of the critical points to be made about family breakdown and the poor is very much like the one about crime. Single parenthood only creates poverty among those who are already on the edge; it is a disaster for a black teenage girl in a ghetto or a separated mother in a working poor family. That is, family breakdown can only have a poverty effect among certain disadvantaged strata of the society.

This points in the direction of some very important policy considerations. If economic structures are an important element in family breakdown—not *the* cause, any more than cultural and value changes are, but both a cause and an effect of those cultural and value changes—then different economic policies might lead to more stable family patterns (whether those take conventional legal or moral forms is, to my mind, irrelevant).

Before I develop that point, I must dispose of one last stereotype that keeps people from seeing it: the notion that welfare mothers are promiscuous and immoral women who have huge families in order to get more money from welfare. In 1977 the typical AFDC family had 2.2 children, which is fairly close to the national average. Between 1940 and 1968, when out-of-wedlock births trebled, they increased among AFDC mothers from 25 percent to about 33 percent, i.e., much less than in the country as a whole. Indeed, Harrel Rodgers has pointed out that a woman only "makes" money if she has one child. And in the state of Mississippi, with its munificent payment of $23 a month per child and a rule that says that there will be no additional money forthcoming after four children, the patterns are not different from other parts of the society.

So if the problem is not promiscuity—Blanche Bernstein points out that most of these mothers have had substantial and ongoing relationships with the fathers of their children—or laziness, what is it? Harrel Rodgers suggests a very interesting answer: If there were full employment, day care, and job training between 60 and 75 percent of the AFDC mothers could work. I got a sense of that reality in Maine in 1983 when I talked to some AFDC mothers at the headquarters of the Displaced Householder program directed by a Lithuanian displaced person, Ilza Peterson. In that state, one of the poorest in the country, a woman with one child gets $192 a month and rent is often in the range of $100 a month. That leaves $100 for everything else. Still, if you count in the cost of day care, transportation, and other expenses, a minimum-wage job still does not pay as well as AFDC!

One of the women wanted to be a police administrator; another spoke of how the whole job market is being pushed down as trained people are forced to take jobs for which they are overqualified. All of them, with full knowledge that in economic terms the decision is chancy, wanted to work. But the Reagan administration has, of course, adopted policies that tend to keep people on AFDC: high unemployment, cuts in benefits for the working poor, drastic reductions in work training. That is an almost scientifically designed program for promoting the welfare dependency that the White House says it abhors.

This is true even if every optimistic dream of Ronald Reagan—or any other politician—comes true. Full employment will benefit these women little or not at all as long as government policies frustrate those who want to work but are not given the realistic chance to do so. A rising tide, John Kennedy used to say, floats all boats—but it does not float the ones with holes in them. Similarly, if women are locked into welfare dependency not because they are lazy, but because there is no child care, then even the existence of job openings for them is not going to change their situation. A significant number of AFDC families, then, might be immune even to prosperity.

This has dangerous implications for the future. Alice Rivlin, then head of the Congressional Budget Office, pointed out in 1983 that one-fifth of the children in the United States are living in poverty, a rate much greater than the official figure for the nation as a whole. Unemployment and the great increase in single mothers were, Rivlin said, the chief cause of this development. It takes place, I would add, at a time when the roads out of poverty for all those young people are difficult or often impossible to find. It is at least likely that the policies of the Reagan administration have made a significant contribution to enlarging the underclass of the permanent and demoralized poor in the future. If that is the case, it could well lead to more violence and more family breakdown, and conservative America, which is the architect of this tragedy, will as usual blame it on the victims.

The psychological agony of the poor is not simply a characteristic of the interior life, but, in part at least, a public product that could be changed by different public policies.

III

It is now necessary to make some gentle criticisms of friends who have overreacted to the errors of our common (intellectual) foes.

There is an underlying method in the attitudes of analysts like James Q. Wilson and Bruce Chapman, and it was rather badly summarized by Edward Banfield in a controversial book of the 1960s, *The Unheavenly City*. Social class, Banfield argued, is not determined by money, work, relationship to the means of production, or any of the other objective indices. Rather, "the more distant the future the individual can imagine and can discipline himself to make sacrifices for, the 'higher' is his class." In this view, lower-class culture is pathological, possessing higher rates of mental illness not because it is the most stressful and violent place in the society, but because it is "present-oriented." The poor person is "radically improvident: whatever he cannot consume immediately he considers valueless." The lower-class household, he continues, "is usually female based. . . . In managing the children, the mother (or aunt, or grandmother) is characteristically impulsive: once they have passed babyhood they are likely to be neglected or abused and at best they never know what to expect next."

The conclusion? One does not explain poverty "as lack of income and material resources (something external to the individual)" but "as inability or unwillingness to take account of the future or to control impulses (something internal)." At times Banfield has intimations of the complex truth. For instance, he understands that the "present-orientation" of the immigrants from peasant cultures (Ireland, southern and eastern Europe) was related to their eternal battle merely to survive, a condition of life which requires that one constantly worry about the next meal. But for the most part he emphasizes an abstract, psychological definition of poverty, which makes the character flaws of the poor the main reason for their poverty. This is, of course, a generalized statement of the underlying methodology of the conservative analyses of crime and family breakdown.

But the notion of a "culture" of poverty need not be conservative. Oscar Lewis, the brilliant anthropologist who edited the tape recordings of conversations with Mexican and Puerto Rican poor people and made a major contribution to the understanding of poverty, proposed an idea from the left. According to him, the people at the bottom of the society developed their own institutions that allowed them to cope with intolerable conditions. The extended family, for instance, offends Victorian morality, for it deemphasizes the husband-wife relationship in favor of grandmothers, aunts, uncles, and neighbors, but it is well adapted to the realities of lower-class life. (Banfield's description of uncaring mothers is a caricature based upon the overgeneralization of the worst aspects of the recent increase in family breakdown.) As a "culture," this way of dealing with poverty is handed down from generation to generation.

There are very real criticisms that can be made of Lewis's theories. In *Tally's Corner*, Elliot Liebow argues that the patterns are not transmitted as a culture but are discovered anew as the younger generation confronts the same problems as its elders. And it can be argued that Lewis overstated the hermetic isolation of the culture of poverty, failing to see how it was precisely the presence of middle-class values in a stratum incapable, for objective reasons, of a middle-class way of life that was a great part of the problem. Whatever else one can say, it is clear that Lewis's intentions were to mobilize people to emphasize the resourcefulness of the poor and the institutionalized tenacity of their poverty. He was a man of the left who wanted to show that misery was a system, a structure, a psychology, *as well as* an economic result.

This last point is not always understood on the left, which sometimes confuses a Lewis and a Banfield. David Whisnat's *Modernizing the Mountaineers* is an excellent study of the efforts to end poverty in Appalachia. But he, for the very best of reasons, makes the error of counterposing the cultural-psychological to the economic-social rather than understanding their interpenetration.

Whisnat posits a paradigm that he derives from the writings of Daniel Patrick Moynihan:

Poverty
leads to
Cultural and environmental obstacles to motivation
which leads to
Poor health, inadequate education, and low mobility
limiting earning potential

which leads to
limited income opportunities
which leads to poverty.

He puts his own paradigm in sharp contrast to that of Moynihan:

Corporate monopolization of major resources
leads to
an inequitable and underdeveloped economic and political system
which leads to
Political powerlessness, economic and cultural exploitation, and environmental destruction
which leads to
poor education and social services, minimal income, hopelessness, and outmigration
which facilitates further
corporate monopolization of major resources.

I would argue that Whisnat's paradigm is the "God term," the original and initiating cause, while his version of Moynihan's paradigm describes a very real, if derived, system of poverty that takes on a certain coherence of its own. What is involved, I think, is not some abstruse discussion of the methodology of the social sciences, but a set of differences that have policy implications.

On the one hand, I think it important for those of us concerned with the elimination of poverty to recognize that its effects are, in part, individual and interior. Most of the people in poor black neighborhoods do not become violent criminals, and there are moral differences between those who do and those who don't, even though the higher propensity for a violent minority in these neighborhoods has to be explained socially and economically. There are, I submit, aspects of the interior self that are not going to be touched by the best of programs, and it is a very big mistake—political as well as intellectual—to talk as if it is a simple matter to transform psyches. Those intimate individuations of trends are, to be sure, affected by the trends themselves, but they assert a kind of human choice, even if a perverse choice.

On the other hand, it is terribly wrong to claim, as the conservatives do, that poverty is the expression of a kind of lower-class human nature that cannot be affected by any public policy. I know this from the history of my own ethnic ancestors. The Irish-Americans were, as noted earlier, the first minority group, the first people-class whose poverty was blamed on their nationality. They were, again, members of the "dangerous classes" of the nineteenth and early twentieth centuries, fearful fighters and drinkers and brawlers. (The racial and ethnic identity of boxing champions, it might be noted, follows the progression of immigrant groups and of black urbanization with almost a one-to-one precision.) They sat for the portrait of Banfield's lower-class type a hundred years before he painted it. But they changed. Andrew Greeley (who, admittedly, has a genius for finding statistics that prove the virtues of his own ethnic and religious group) has even offered data to show that the Irish are almost at the top of the social-class pyramid now.

What happened? A conversion experience in which an entire ethnic group abandoned its present-orientation and began to look and work toward the distant future? Or a process of social mobility, facilitated through an expanding economy, that allowed my grade-school-dropout grandfather to finish his life in a comfortable three-story private house in St. Louis? Obviously the latter. The question today is whether the people of the underclass—white, black, brown, and Asian—will be allowed the same opportunities as were given the Irish (and the Jews and the Italians and the other groups), or whether economic and social policies will lock them up in a world that has certain tendencies toward crime and disintegrating families. That is a political and economic—not a spiritual—issue.

These violent men and "immoral" women in the new structures of misery are not merely and simply social products. But they are mainly social products, and therefore society is responsible for the evil it has imposed upon them. If public policy could do so much to make these people what they are, it can also unmake the fate it has forced upon them.

9

Poverties

I call this chapter "Poverties" because, unlike those that went before, it makes no attempt at the analysis of a single problem, but shuttles between different, and not necessarily related, subcultures of American misery. In general I have singled out these areas for this kind of treatment because they define "traditional" kinds of poverty, i.e., the kinds that already existed twenty or twenty-five years ago. They do not fit into the general argument of a book focused upon the new structures of American poverty. They are the old structures, for the most part, and yet no account of poverty in the eighties would be complete without them.

Just because they are a venerable injustice, however, does not mean that they are easy to see on the very surface of the American life. I relearned that lesson in October 1982, when I blithely ignored advice I had been giving for about a quarter of a century.

I

I was on my way to give a speech at Starkville, Mississippi, and since I was working on this book I decided that I would be a poverty tourist. I told my faculty contact at Mississippi State University that I preferred to drive from Jackson to Starkville. I didn't tell him that I hoped to see, and even photograph, some obvious rural poverty. But I knew that welfare was the main source of income in thirty-one of Mississippi's eighty-two counties, that half of the five-year-olds in the state were not in pre-schools (although the state is now moving to change that), and that 35 percent of the Mississippians who tried to enlist in the Air Force were rejected. Wouldn't it be quite simple to get such a social problem to pose for a picture?

In *The Other America* I had written that poverty in general—and rural poverty in particular—lies off the beaten track. It is not obvious, which is precisely one of the reasons it is so often tenacious. As we drove from the Jackson Airport, I became uncomfortably aware that I should have heeded my own forgotten advice. The outskirts of Jackson could have been the outskirts of any city in the United States: the motels, the fast-food places, the low-rise businesses, that plastic homogeneity of Any City, U.S.A. Then we went down the Natchez Trail Highway, a pretty road lined with the ubiquitous pine trees of the South. There was a lovely reservoir named for a former racist governor, and then came small homes and apparently prosperous farms.

As we talked, my old knowledge slowly began to come back to me. The Delta is where the heavy concentration of blacks is found; shacks are not to be found on major arteries, because they can't pay the rent commanded by such important roads. But then it turned out that even some of the superficial well-being was not quite as it seemed. The chicken sheds at the seemingly prosperous farms were not owned by the farmers but advanced to them, along with the chickens and the feed, by entrepreneurs. Even the affluent farm owner, I remembered, is normally squeezed between the corporate input sector of the agricultural economy—the banks, the manufacturers of agricultural implements—and the corporate output sector—the processors, distributors, and giant export companies.

Social structure, I understood once again, was not to be seen; it had to be perceived. My act of stupidity on the road to Starkville might be paradigmatic of the attitude of the entire society toward rural poverty. Our eyes are so totally controlled by the stereotypes in our minds that we cannot see what we see.

For instance, it is well known that the American South is in the Sun Belt, which has been growing, and that it is better off than the Frost Belt of the North, which is in crisis. The fact is that the South, with less than a third of the population, accounted for 49.3 percent of the American poor in 1959 and 41.9 percent in 1978. Even that relative decline has to be put into a context, since part of it is explained by the fact that, though white out-migration stopped in a state like Mississippi during the sixties, black out-migration continued. As we have already seen, some of the worst aspects of black poverty in the cities of the North are consequences of the shocked lives of the black economic refugees from the South.

When one looks at the poverty rate in the non-urban parts of the South, however, there seems to have been real progress: from 33.2 percent in 1959, down to 13.5 percent in 1978. But the bulk of that improvement (from 33.2 percent to 17.9 percent) was made in the sixties, and in the mid-seventies the poverty percentage actually increased as a result of the recession of 1974–75. Since the statistics do not as yet reflect the economic catastrophe of 1981–82, the numbers are likely to have already gone up. But when it comes to the black and non-urban South, one does not have to be sensitive to statistical nuances to get a sense of the incredible deprivation: In 1978—a relatively "good" year—37.2 percent of the people living there were poor.

I finally got some sense of that reality on my visit to Starkville. The student who drove me to the local airport for the return trip took me down some back roads, and there were the broken-down houses that I had thought would be on the main highways for all to see. There was also a trailer camp, one of the important assembly points for the poor and the almost-poor. Indeed, when one looks at the 1980 census figures for "mobile home and trailer" percentages, they are very high in Mississippi, North Carolina, South Carolina, Tennessee, and West Virginia. And if one examines the states where more than 20 percent of the population had less than 125 percent of the poverty level, one finds that they are Alabama, Arkansas, Georgia, Kentucky, Louisiana, North Carolina, South Carolina, and Tennessee. Mississippi, as is so often the case, is the poorest of all, with 31.5 percent of the people below that level. Yet I could not see that last fact with my presumably trained eyes.

But then, if one looks not at the South in general, but at the poor black South, the reality becomes even more grim. The National Association of the Southern Poor describes the Black Belt as the area between Virginia and Louisiana with counties in which the black population ranges from 30 to 82 percent. Typically, Northampton County, North Carolina, had a per capita income of $2,673 a year at the end of the seventies, which was about one-third of the national average, and the three hundred other counties of the Black Belt had similar rates. These figures should not, however, be seen as shocking. Right before the Reagan cuts, the state of Mississippi provided a family of four on welfare with $120 a month—or $1,440 a year.

"The life of the people in the area reflects the very low income," the association's report continues. "They live in houses insulated by cardboard with tin roofs, in converted stables or chicken coops. Many have no toilets, indoors or out. Often they must transport water from long distances. Most babies are born without the assistance of any medical advice. The sleep of residents is sometimes disturbed by children crying from hunger; and our organization has witnessed hunger pacified by sugar and water for entire households, including babies, for periods of up to ten days."

The South, particularly the Southeast but even the Southwest, is not a happy Sun Belt with an affluent economy even in good times. Rather, a part of its growth has been based precisely on low-wage, anti-union practices. North Carolina, for instance, is a more industrialized state than many think; in 1980 it ranked seventeenth in value added by manufacture. It was, however, forty-ninth in the percentage of union membership (only South Carolina was lower). All of this is not to say that the South made no gains during the relatively good times of the fifties and sixties.

It did. It is to say that economic growth will have less of an impact there than it did historically in the industrial heartland—unless, that is, the American labor movement can finally make a major breakthrough into the region.

But what, one might ask, do unionism and industry have to do with *rural* America? A great deal. Here, again, stereotypes inhibit the eyes.

In 1945, at the end of World War II, there were about six million farms in the United States. By 1970 there were half that number, and their average size had almost doubled. In human terms, 24.9 percent of the American population was composed of farmers in 1930, 2.6 percent in 1981. What these statistics describe is the elimination of most of the subsistence farms as well as of most of the farm hands. Rural poverty, then, is often not farm poverty.

There are, for instance, sections of New York State that are "Appalachian." In part that adjective has to do with the landscape and the economy; in part it has to do with the fact that the definition of Appalachia in the 1960s was an exercise in politics having to do with the spending of money rather than the work of scholarly geographers. In Janet Fitchen's analysis of one of the small towns in this New York Appalachia, social decay "proceeded unrelentingly, with much the same inexorable sweep as was the case in the chestnut blight, which struck the same region and wiped out whole hillsides of stately and useful trees."

In the early twentieth century, agricultural decline, outmigration, debt-ridden farms, and people without skills adjusted to the industrial labor market. At the same time, the legendary social structure of rural America was subverted. The hamlets were impoverished, underpopulated, unable to carry out their traditional functions as centers of a vibrant, friendly community life. The people became members of the working poor, holding low-paying jobs in factories, in the highway department, in the low-skill, left-over jobs of an area that was no longer agricultural and not yet urban. That was much the same pattern I had encountered in Maine, where the subsistence farmers, the clammers, and the berry pickers had been driven by gentrification into the mill towns. It exists in Vermont where, only a few miles away from a fashionable ski resort, there are enclaves of bitter poverty.

The migrant workers face a different kind of poverty than do the exhausted agricultural areas of the Northeast. For one thing, they are extremely hard to count. For instance, the *Statistical Abstract* follows the legal definitions and, in effect, assumes that no Mexican agricultural laborers entered the United States after 1965. That is one improbable reason why it estimates migrants in 1979 at a mere 217,000. The best count, according to Richard Margolis, who wrote an excellent survey for *Rural America,* was made by the Department of Agriculture in 1977, which said that this labor force was one-third white, one-third Hispanic, one-third black, Oriental, and Native American. Margolis puts the total number at "more than one million women, men, and children who travel from place to place, yet have no place to call their own."

But then, where does one take note of the similar, but different, poverty of the Chicanos living in that thirties-style "tourist court" I saw in a tiny Nebraska town? There is a Chicano community of ex-migrants in East Kearney, Nebraska, a town of 20,000 people. It is on the "wrong side" of the Union Pacific Railroad tracks, in a neighborhood that spectacularly lives up to one of the classic patterns of poverty in the United States: bad roads for poor people. There are not simply muddy streets and trailer parks; there are no sidewalks. And yet the people living under these conditions have more stability and even amenities than do the migrants themselves. There are places, Margolis found, where at the height of the season a dozen people are stuffed into a single trailer and charged ten dollars a head per week.

There are even a few places where there is a minimum of decency for migrants. Farmworker Village is a 276-unit public housing project in Immokalee, Florida, built in the mid-seventies to show that, with money and imagination, migrants don't have to be treated like animals. It is both an exception and a "Potemkin village" for the government (Potemkin was a minister under Catherine the Great who rigged up villages with phony façades to prove that progress was being made), an exception to the rule.

Yet the point has been made: There could be decent housing for these people; we just don't care.

In the sixties and seventies, however, the farm workers in California did not accept that callous indifference. Under the leadership of Cesar Chavez, they organized and went out on strike, first against the grape growers, then against the lettuce growers. The resistance was fierce. Goons and the Teamsters Union were used to challenge and try to break the United Farm Workers; the press was manipulated. In the process, Chavez developed an extremely effective political network, and in 1975 the state assembly established an Agricultural Labor Relations Board, which, for the first time, gave workers in the fields rights already held by factory workers for thirty years. But there was also changing technology, pressure from undocumented workers, continuing grower resistance. At various points the media counted Chavez and his movement down and out—in the mid-seventies it was widely predicted that they would vanish—and were wrong.

And yet there were serious internal battles within the movement, between the farm-worker unionists in Texas and California, within Chavez's own staff. Even after incredible struggles and suffering—95 percent of the militants lost their cars during the grape strike—only 4.9 percent of the agricultural workers of the United States belonged to unions. And Ronald Reagan, who, as governor of California, had been one of the most determined foes of the movement—his obsessive hostility to legal aid to the poor is at least partly based on the fact that it helped farm workers against growers—became President of the United States.

The Reagan Presidency saw yet another trend: an agricultural depression. Here one leaves the marginal world of the Southern blacks, the New York "Appalachians," and the migrants, and enters the mainstream of American farming and the possibility of a new poverty. These are the women and men who accomplished such prodigies of productivity that not only fed the United States but yielded $44.2 billion in agricultural exports in 1981. And yet, in 1982, total farm earnings fell in actual buying power by 11 percent. The farmers were being ground down by the high interest rates that the Reagan administration and the Federal Reserve

Bank used to fight inflation. *The Wall Street Journal* reported that Farmers Home Administration foreclosures on farms doubled between 1981 and 1982.

During the Depression, militant farmers discovered a way to fight foreclosures. They would crowd into the auction and buy back the property for pennies, letting it be clearly known that any outsiders who tried to raise the bid would do so at their own risk. In August 1982, the "penny auction" tactic surfaced again in Minnesota (where the auctioneer caught on quickly and closed down the auction, but the foreclosed farmer managed to get a little time). This trend is somewhat analogous to the impact of the recession on relatively well-paid factory workers, as described in Chapter 3. It does not strike at the already poor; it hits at the very foundations of the lives of people who thought they had escaped from poverty, once and for all.

There is no point in exaggerating. The foreclosures of the thirties were in the tens of thousands; in the eighties, they are in the hundreds. In a sense, most of the poor have already been driven off the land. And yet, even if only a few of those dispossessed by a crisis that has tremendously devalued the value of land itself will become poor, it is one more sign of the ways in which the secure accomplishments of the past are now in danger of unraveling in an uncertain world. In Iowa in 1983, a college professor turned successful farmer told me that if young Iowans asked him what to study to prepare for a career in agriculture, he would tell them to take up business administration, not agronomy. Growing food is the easy part of the job; watching the ups and downs of the financial markets is more important.

That is the source of a possible new poverty and already the cause of a tremendous dislocation of families who seemed to have made it. Appalachia is, alas, a classic case of the old poverty, and generalizations about it that were true a generation ago still hold, even though it was an area singled out for special help in the sixties.

At first glance, Appalachia contradicts my insistence on how difficult it is to see poverty. If, for example, you fly into Columbus, Ohio—a city so quintessentially American that it is used by pollsters as a stand-in for middle America—and drive south, it takes little sensitivity to notice the poverty along the road. The highway itself narrows and begins to twist and turn; the fields and factories give way to hills and shabby little towns. By the time you reach Athens, Ohio, which is on the northern edge of Appalachia, you have made a transition into another world. The beauty of the landscape and the seeming quaintness of the people, the very otherness of the place, have tended to conceal the unromantic fact that it is very much integrated into the American corporate economy. Misery here is functional, not an accident; the glow is often tubercular.

Appalachia, as Herbert Reid put it, became an American cliché, beginning with its discovery as "a topic for literary exploitation and its subsequent cultivation as a field for benevolent work by Northern Protestant missionaries." The Southern Mountain Workers Conference, an institution created by Northern philanthropy and churches, said in 1927 that Appalachia was a place peopled by "those Anglo-Saxon, mountain-locked, one hundred percent Americans." The blacks, Indians, and immigrants were ignored. So was the fact that many people were already working in mines and lumber mills and did not spend their days singing folk songs in the hollows. It became the place where the notion of welfare dependency, of long-term reliance on AFDC, which is not the pattern in the country as a whole, was real. When Ken Auletta went to West Virginia to investigate "the white underclass," he found out that in the seven counties around Morgantown, the average AFDC mother had been receiving benefits for more than six years.

In those counties, Auletta reports, the average male has less than a ninth-grade education, and only 31 percent have finished high school. In 1977, the per capita income was $3,986—69 percent of the national average—and the poverty rate was three times that of the nation as a whole. Many lived in trailers; television was the only contact with the outside world.

John Kennedy glimpsed some of this deprivation during his 1960 primary campaign in West Virginia. He vowed that, if elected President, he would do something about Appalachia. So it was that the first poverty program of the sixties was the Area Redevelopment Administration (ARA) established in the Department of Commerce in 1961. It was supposed to stop the vicious cycle of economic and social disintegration so visible in Appalachia: Economic decline cuts local tax revenues, which makes the place even less desirable for new investment, which causes more young people to leave, which cuts the tax revenues even more, and so on in a downward and accelerating spiral. The Appalachian Regional Commission came not too much later. These beautiful but impoverished valleys were to be a great test case of the ability of government to solve such problems. It failed.

The ARA, as Whisnat points out, made a number of rather large assumptions about how change was going to take place. Jobs were going to be generated in the private, not the public, sectors; communities would be able to write overall economic plans (EEDPs); the benefits would go to the better off and then appropriately filter down to the poor through the mechanisms of the private economy. As the director of the Appalachian Regional Commission put it in 1970: "Unfortunately, development makes its first impact on upper- and middle-income groups. It has a trickle-down effect to the really hard-core poor."

When the War on Poverty began, there was a certain contradiction between that approach and the community organizing of the Office of Economic Opportunity (OEO). The Appalachian program was predicated on "modernizing the mountaineers," as Whisnat phrases it; community action was to try and help them make life viable where they were. That was not, however, the central problem. Organized political and economic power were.

Harry Caudill, whose haunting book *Night Comes to the Cumberlands* is a marvelous evocation and description of the mountains, understood this all too well. Caudill wrote of the 1964 Appalachian Regional Commission Report: "Growing acceptance of the programs by the governors was more important than finding solutions. They discovered that whatever aimed at effective reorganization of the decrepit economy ran afoul of established absentee-owned interests and the political structures they dominate. So the search turned toward palliatives rather than remedies." Caudill himself, for example, fought within the commission for the development of public power—which could assure that benefits would actually get to the intended recipients—but he was defeated by the private power forces. But then, public power was no panacea, as anyone concerned with Appalachia knows. In the mid-seventies, when I participated in a seminar at Athens, Ohio, with activists from the region, I was struck by the vehemence of the criticisms of the Tennessee Valley Authority (TVA), the very symbol of the most progressive accomplishments of the New Deal. There were people there from the Highlander School, long a source of radicalism in the area, and organizers from many other projects, and they were almost unanimous in their bitter comments. The TVA had originally been organized to deal with floods, to create cheap hydroelectric power and thereby to foster the development of the entire valley. In the early days there was a visionary faction within the Authority that saw it as pioneering new possibilities of cooperative living.

The visionaries were defeated rather early on, but the real transition came after World War II. The TVA began to switch from hydroelectric to coal policies, and in implementing them subsidized the strip-mining—which is to say, the environmental degradation—of eastern Kentucky. This was "modernization" with a vengeance—modernization dominated by forces outside of the region itself, by powerful coal interests and by the kind of imperialism that can grow in any large bureaucracy, private or public. (The TVA was later to become an ardent champion of the "breeder reactor" form of nuclear energy.) Caudill and others fought this strip-mining valiantly, but enormous environmental damage was done before the public knew what was happening.

I do not want to overgeneralize, to agree with Nicholas Von Hoffman that the TVA is "an idea whose time is gone." On balance, the people of the region are better off because of the TVA. But it did some terrible damage at the same time and proved that public property is not per se good or bad. The real question is who runs it and for what purpose. In the fifties an agency that had begun with high ideals began to adopt the methods and priorities of the private power sector. It thereby lent itself not just to economic development, but to a particularly destructive kind of economic development.

This was hardly a new pattern. Reid quotes Ronald Eller's research on industrialization and social change in Appalachia from 1880 to 1930. Eller wrote that "the persistent poverty of Appalachia has not resulted from the lack of modernization. Rather it has come from the particular kind of modernization that unfolded in the years from 1880 to 1930. By 1930 . . . most mountaineers, whether they remained on the farm or migrated to mill villages, timber towns, or coal camps, had become socially integrated within the new industrial system and economically dependent upon it as well. To say the least, this dependence was not on their terms—that is to say, it was not a product of mountain culture but of the same political and economic interests that were shaping the rest of the nation and the western world."

This point leads to Whisnat's basic, and powerful, critique of the Appalachian programs of the sixties. It was assumed, he argues, that Appalachia had problems because it was not integrated into the larger economy. In fact, the root cause of the region's troubles was—as earlier drafts of the 1964 Appalachian Commission Report recognized—precisely "its integration into the economy for a narrow set of purposes: the extraction of low-cost raw materials, power and labor and the provision of a profitable market for consumer goods and services."

In the memo that Paul Jacobs, Frank Mankiewicz, and I wrote to Sargent Shriver during the antipoverty task force of 1964, we made much the same point but generalized it. We criticized the basic, unstated thesis behind so many of the antipoverty efforts of the sixties, i.e., that there were victims but no victimizers. In this perspective, the basic infrastructure of the society, above all the corporate domination of resource allocation, was essentially benign and the poor were simply living in an unhappy corner of a sound and generous economy. It was against the political rules of the huge anticonservative coalition that Lyndon Johnson was building—it extended from Henry Ford to Martin Luther King, Jr.—to mention, say, that slums were an integral part of a housing industry devoted to building and rebuilding the homes of the upper and upper middle classes every generation, or that the strip-mining of Appalachia had something to do with the oil companies that so often owned the coal.

Jacobs, Mankiewicz, and I had tried to suggest—quite diplomatically, as I remember, but unmistakably—that there would have to be institutional change that might upset entrenched interests if there were to be a truly effective campaign against poverty. We were right, but we had no political power and little backing, even from the progressive forces in the society. Everyone in those days knew with a certainty that the old-fashioned structural and social class problems of the economy had been permanently solved. A Caudill had a much more significant constituency than we did, and real political effect, but the Appalachian case proved, unfortunately, that we were quite right.

And then, in the seventies, "Appalachia" began to expand. That is, the mechanisms of that downward cycle which everyone thought in the early sixties was as unique to the mountains as its folk songs began to appear throughout the Northeast and the Middle West. The rotting industrial base and declining tax base were now found in Michigan and northern Ohio as well as in West Virginia and Kentucky. The Appalachian poor had often fled to the auto and steel factories when their home counties could no longer provide them with the means of life. But now the mountain patterns appeared on the plains. Appalachia, which everyone had thought was a backwater, turned out to be the prototype of the future in Detroit and Pittsburgh and Cleveland and St. Louis.

—— II ——

In 1942, as a boy of fourteen, I spent two months at the Rosebud Indian Reservation in South Dakota.

I did not see what I saw. I was attending a Jesuit camp for middle-class youth, named for a famous missionary, Father De Smet. We lived at the St. Francis Indian Mission, sleeping in dormitories that housed the Indians during the winter, and riding every day across the dusty plains to the lush valleys nearby.* I was a child of my time and place and I did not know that I was living in the middle of a crime. And yet, looking back, my memories turn out to contain the essential images of that tragedy, even though I didn't know it when they were right there before my eyes.

I remember the young Indians who sometimes came into the Mission during the summer and ate the white bread as if it were cake. Occasionally a horse was stolen. Once one was returned that had been whipped with barbed wire and had become so shy of humans that she had to be destroyed. Someone said, "Isn't it strange that an Indian would do that to a horse?" And someone else replied, "Well, they've had their land taken away from them by the whites, and all they do is drink." Sometimes on our daily rides around St. Francis, we would see a tipi and wonder about the strange life that survived in such a place. On the Fourth of July I watched an Indian standing in the middle of the road taking enormous swigs from a whisky bottle.

Those images reflect a social history imposed upon the Indians by the cruelty and greed of white America. I didn't even know that I was staying in an institution that bears no little responsibility for this outrageous history—a Christian mission. And I had not heard of Wounded Knee, not too far away, where 128 Dakotas had been massacred by federal troops in 1890, ostensibly because of a misunderstanding about a religious dance, actually because of a policy of cultural genocide. I was thrilled when we went on a trip to Mount Rushmore and saw the gigantic heads of the Presidents carved in the side of the mountain. I didn't know that Rushmore had been sacred to the Indians and that the assertion of new American patriotism was the desecration of a Native American holy place.

I now know a bit of the history of what I saw. It helps explain why Indians, the indigenous people of the continent at the time

*There is a controversy of sorts as to which term one should use: "Indian" or "Native American." Since there are those in the population being described who use both terms, I will speak of Indians here, which is more familiar to most Americans.

of the European conquest, are the poorest of the poor in a land that was once their own. The experts estimate that there were between 850,000 and a million Indians when the white man came, and in the 1970 census there were 791,839. But that seeming continuity hides a tremendous disruption: In 1900, after two centuries of persecution, there were only 237,196 Indians, and Theodore Roosevelt wanted to be sure that final records were kept on the "vanishing red man." It is estimated that by the end of the 1980s, there will be more Indians than there were when the Europeans arrived.

Their poverty is extreme. Life expectancy is roughly twenty years less than whites; unemployment rates are stratospheric, and the 1970 census found that, on the twenty-four largest Indian reservations, 55.1 percent of the people were below the poverty line. Small wonder that those young Indians thought of white bread as cake. This is not simply the result of economic exploitation, although it plays an extremely important role. It is also the consequence of a policy that attempted to wipe out an entire culture.

In the late 1820s and the early 1830s, the whites of the Southeast coveted the Indian land. Ironically, the tribes involved—the Creeks, Choctaws, Cherokees, Chickasaws, and Seminoles—were so advanced that the whites themselves had named them the Five Civilized Tribes. The Creeks, in particular, had been ingenious in political as well as economic matters, with a system of town government and democracy that allowed them to absorb other tribes. No matter. There was a land boom on, what with cotton production up, and Andrew Jackson, a man of the region and an old Indian fighter, was in the White House. Eventually, 100,000 Indians were driven to the northern Louisiana Territory. One-quarter to one-third died along the way.

Economic motives came into play again after the Civil War. This time it was not a question of getting rid of Indians in the East, but of crushing them in the West, where they stood in the way of white America's continental destiny. Solemn treaties were concluded and broken, and after defeats or fraud the Indians were herded onto reservations where, in the words of an Indian Commission in 1872, it was necessary to reduce "the wild beasts to the condition of supplicants for charity." All of this was done on the assumption that Indians were a breed apart, even if a breed slightly less than human.

In 1887, the white man changed his mind once again. That was the year of the Dawes Act, which inaugurated almost half a century of federal commitment to the forced assimilation of the Indians into the American way of life. Reservations, after all, continued the "communism" that Senator Dawes found so objectionable; not so incidentally, they also contained some good land. That land was taken away from the community and allotted to individuals, who were to become yeomen or entrepreneurs on the white model. But, with money and outright fraud, the whites moved in, took two-thirds of the land away from the Indians, and created tens of thousands of refugees, some of whom drifted to the cities. The explanation about how lost land had demoralized the Indians, which I had heard in South Dakota in 1942, had more than a little, perhaps unwitting, truth.

In the process, the original Americans were finally supposed to get the right to become citizens if they "adopted the habits of civilized life." "These habits," Edward Spicer writes, "were assumed to be obvious as they were not further defined in the act or in other federal legislation, and they probably were obvious to the white employees of the BIA [Bureau of Indian Affairs]; civilized habits were their own ways of behaving, that is, speaking English, wearing hair and clothing in the fashion of the period, working six days a week, going to a Christian church on Sunday, and so on. Coercing Indian children if necessary into these ways was the ultimate objective of the assimilation program."

The coercion of children took a very organized form: the boarding school. Children were taken away from their parents and harmful "Indian" influences (sometimes rations were withheld from parents who refused the civilizing process for their offspring). Richard Pratt, the founder of the Carlisle Indian School in Pennsylvania—the whites called him the "Red Man's Moses"—boasted that he always assigned youth from different tribes to the same room. He explained: "This not only helped in the acquirement of English but broke up trivial and racial clannishness, a most important victory in getting the Indian toward real citizenship." This program of forced assimilation lasted from the 1880s to the 1930s.

Then, under the New Deal, John Collier, who had championed Indian rights, was put in charge of implementing the Indian Reorganization Act of 1934, which recognized the rights of the people on the reservations to self-government and even to their own culture. That lasted until 1953, when Congress decided that it was possible to "terminate" tribal status and to get the government out of the Indian business. Not many tribes were terminated, but two that were—the Menominee in Wisconsin and the Klamath in Oregon—just happened to have major timber interests. That policy was finally ended in the sixties, under Kennedy, and in 1970 Richard Nixon actually announced that "Indians can become independent of federal control without being cut off from federal concern and federal support."

In the sixties, something else happened. The Office of Economic Opportunity provided support for some community organizing among the Indians, and a young, militant generation, some of whom had gone to college, began to create an Indian civil rights movement that, in a series of controversial actions, finally focused public attention on the enormity of white America's guilt and responsibility. But that left a serious problem, one I encountered often in the sixties when I talked to Indian activists.

On the one hand, they were—quite rightly—appalled by the poverty to which their people had been subjected. They wanted the longevity, the living standards, of the larger society; they were outraged by what racism had done to them. On the other hand, they felt that Indian culture was superior to white culture, that it was based on a sense of community, of respect for the holiness of the land and water and air that had been destroyed by capitalism. But how can one have a capitalist level of life with a precapitalist level of technology? It is possible, I hasten to insist, to have a postcapitalist quality of life that is superior to the capitalist, not the least because it is respectful of the environment. But it must utilize the accomplishments of science and productivity, albeit in a completely new way. That quality of life, however, cannot be achieved on the basis of a primitive system of production.

The militants with whom I discussed this matter thought my point of view represented white, perhaps unconsciously racist, attitudes. I obviously do not agree, yet, having learned a little since I was a fourteen-year-old boy at the St. Francis Indian Mission, I went to work for some kind of synthesis that would end Indian poverty without assimilating them to white ways. For now, as Peter Mathiessen movingly describes them in his book *In the Spirit of Crazy Horse*, it was the "traditionals" among the Indians who were most torn apart by this unconscionable history: "Despised and exploited . . . they—many of them full bloods who spoke little English—were the people who suffered most from despair and apathy, poverty and unemployment, alcoholism and the random angry violence that besets depressed Indian communities to a degree almost unimaginable to most Americans who still imagine that the government takes care of the Indian."

In 1983, James Watt, the messianic enemy of the holiness of the earth, looked at the results of this history, so eminently capitalist in its rapaciousness, nearly fascist in its racism, and proclaimed that it demonstrated the evils of socialism. The spirit of Senator Dawes, fearful of our indigenous "communists," still haunts the land.

III

It might seem strange to include a brief discussion of the poverty of the aging in a book that talks of new forms of misery. Isn't it clear that in this area there has been unambiguous and irreversible progress? Yes and maybe.

The "yes" part is clear enough. In 1959, 35.2 percent of people over sixty-five were poor; in 1980, 15.7 percent. Indeed, between 1970 and 1983, the income of older Americans went up faster than that of those under sixty-five. One of the reasons for this change is that social security coverage was extended from 60 percent of the aging in 1960 to 92 percent in 1981. Another reason is that, during the sixties and the seventies, the benefit levels were increased and then indexed. The aging, then, were probably better protected against inflation in the seventies and early eighties than was any other group. So, yes, there has been progress and those who fought for it should be proud of their accomplishment. Now come the qualifications—and the possibility that the aging could indeed become the new poor, not so much in the near future (although that is possible, too) but in the early twenty-first century.

First, the qualifications. If it is true that "only" 15.7 percent of the aging are poor—a mere 3,853,000 human beings in their "golden years"—another 25 percent are on, or just above, the poverty line. In the Miami Beach area, where there are so many social security recipients, one watches them waiting outside of cheap restaurants to take advantage of specials, or sitting in front of shabby hotels. Many are not poor—that is a gain—but are within the magnetic field of insecurity and faced with all of the health problems that age brings. Older blacks and widows more than seventy years old are particularly at risk. *The Wall Street Journal* quotes an expert: "We're just giving them enough so they'll starve better." Second, the optimistic statistics do not emphasize the fact that more than 10 percent of those over sixty-five are getting Medicaid—even though more than half of them (1,700,000 people) are technically above the poverty line.

If the conservative proposals designed to assign a cash value to in-kind income prevail, the portion of the aging poor having their nursing-home bills paid for by Medicaid will be suddenly promoted into the middle class. On the other hand, there are those who attack the medical care programs for the aging on the grounds that they go far beyond the intentions of the original Social Security Act. In fact, Franklin Roosevelt's Committee on Economic Security, which proposed the social security bill, had said that the "second major step" in the social security process should be not simply health care for the aging, but the application of social insurance principles to the problem of health itself. And there are still major problems for divorced women, particularly those in their fifties who have spent their lives as homemakers. In fact, older women as a group are almost twice as likely to be impoverished as men.

The point is, progress has indeed been made, but it is not quite as unambiguous as some think. And the progress is not universally welcomed, either. This fact surfaced in the debate over the social security "crisis" of 1982–83. In early 1982, former Commerce Secretary Peter Peterson made the famous discovery that public expenditures for the poor were only a fraction of the outlays for the aging. To deal with the budgetary crisis, he said, it was necessary to think about cuts in this area. At the same time, it became known that some of the social security trust funds were in trouble. The air was filled with dire predictions of a breakdown in the system.

Peterson's point constitutes an ongoing danger, i.e., that some politician will, particularly at the end of the century, decide to balance the budget on the backs of the aging. But before looking at that possibility, it is important to understand that the crisis of the eighties was not a crisis of social security but of the American economy. During the seventies, both inflation and unemployment rose to very high levels. This put a special burden on social security. Unemployed workers do not pay social security (or any other) taxes; and benefits were indexed to correct for inflation. The system's revenues went down and its expenditures went up because the economy as a whole was in a period of "stagflation," which was inexplicable in terms of the conventional Keynesian wisdom.

This brings us to an ABC that is sometimes forgotten. Many Americans think that social security is a form of insurance, like a private policy. In fact, the system is not "funded" at all. That is, the government does not take—nor has it ever taken—the payments, invest them, and then pay the claims out of the monies actually earned, minus a charge for administration. Rather, it uses the taxes of the current working generation to pay the benefits of the retired generation. Unemployment among the young is thus a problem for the old. Moreover, the benefits are not proportioned to payments as an insurance policy. Two groups in particular, the rich and the poor, get welfare from the system, the poor because there is a certain minimum level of support, no matter what has been paid in, the rich because they are only taxed on a small portion of their income and therefore get maximum benefits at a very cheap (relative) price.

In the eighties, the "crisis" was a function of the mismanagement of the economy. If America had been operating at full employment with stable prices, the "crisis" would hardly have existed. As it was, that "breakdown" of the system was resolved by a compromise with one clearly reactionary factor. In addition to some sensible reforms, such as taxing the benefits of retired individuals receiving $20,000 a year and couples getting $25,000, the law postponed the July 1983 cost-of-living adjustment to January 1984. That "one time" postponement will affect benefits for years to come, and could even push some of the marginal people under the poverty line. Congressman Claude Pepper and AFL–CIO leader Lane Kirkland fought that provision and did eventually win some extra help for people receiving Supplemental Security Income. But still, a principle had been breached, i.e., there had been a slight rollback in the real income of people over sixty-five. They were penalized for Washington's inability to manage the economy.

What makes this particularly disturbing is that the real crisis will occur shortly after the turn of the century. In 1980, there were roughly five people of working age for every person sixty-five or older; by the year 2030, when the "baby boom" generation (1945–60) has retired, there are expected to be two and a half people between twenty and sixty-four for every retiree over sixty-five. On all but the most pessimistic analysis, the system will run a surplus until 2015, or even 2025, but then there is a danger of significant deficits. Mind you, all demographic projections are speculative; the baby boom itself came as a surprise.

This gets to a central point, one that the best people in the political movement of the aging have understood: To protect, and deepen, the antipoverty gains of the social security system requires that the society face up to structural economic problems.

The movement itself is one of the most exciting political developments in the United States in years. The original Social Security Act was, in part, a response to the organization of the aging by Dr. Townsend in the thirties. His plan, interestingly enough, was supposed to stimulate the entire economy, since the aging would agree to spend their benefits in the month they received them and thus help prime the pump for all. But after the agitation of the thirties there seemed to be relative quiet until sometime in the sixties or early seventies. I first encountered this new trend in Denver at a meeting of the Western Gerontological Society in the mid-seventies. There was a large audience, part of it made up of doctors and social workers, but part composed of the militant aging themselves. As people lined up at the microphone to criticize or applaud speakers, the confident and aggressive tone reminded me of the best days of the civil rights movement.

There was, for example, a very palpable response to the psychiatrist who attacked diagnoses of "senility" which allowed government to abandon expensive attempts to restore the aging to a meaningful life and permitted them to prescribe cheap tranquilizers for a vegetablized existence instead. In 1981, Ronald Reagan made a tentative suggestion to cut back on some social security benefits, and it was this same movement of the aging that rose up in protest and helped persuade every Republican in the United States Senate to reject the President's proposal. Reagan promptly backed down.

In October 1983, when I spoke at a Gray Panthers meeting in Seattle, what impressed me most was the understanding of the way in which the problems of the aging are linked to the fate of the economy as a whole. The conference was co-sponsored by the Washington AFL-CIO, and it had attracted activists of all ages. When I spoke of how the aging had to support the full employment of the young, there was an enthusiastic response.

Most of the older people in Denver and Seattle and at other meetings were not poor. They were middle class. But they were and are the front line of the forces defending the biggest single gain of the poor in the past twenty years, one that even Ronald Reagan has not yet dared to attack. If they build the kind of alliances talked of in Seattle, it is possible that this progress will continue for the indefinite future. But if the American economy continues to malfunction for another decade or so, it could well be that some unscrupulous politician will notice the figures that so intrigued Peter Peterson. When asked why he robbed banks, Willie Sutton said, "Because that's where the money is." And if a reactionary politician looks around for cuts, his eye will eventually alight upon social security. Because that's where most of the social spending is.

Finally, what about the 15.7 percent of the aging who, despite the gains, still are poor? It would be simplicity itself to raise coverage to 100 percent of the people over sixty-five and increase benefits so that everyone has enough to meet necessities. We have been sitting on the 15-percent laurel for a decade now (actually there has been a slight increase in the poverty of the aging since 1975). But why, in what is potentially the richest society in human history, should people in the twilight of their lives have to pinch the pennies of necessity? This is not a possibility of future poverty but a present reality, and it can be abolished anytime we decide to do so. We showed in the sixties and seventies that it is easy enough. If we care.

10

A Danger and a Hope

The Chinese ideograph for crisis is composed of the symbols for two words: danger and hope.

That accurately describes these times. The old poverty—the pace of social and economic time is accelerated and I am talking of the ancient days twenty and thirty years ago—seemed to be an exception to the basic trends of the society. Everyone was progressing steadily; a minority had been left behind. Therefore it would be a rather simple matter to deduct some few billions as they poured out of our industrial cornucopia and to use them to abolish the "pockets" of poverty. But the new poverty I have described in this book is quite different. It is, in complex ways, precisely the extreme consequence of tendencies that are transforming the entire society. To repeat, one reason why young men in the winter of 1983 had to ask New York City for beds for the night was that there were steel mills in South Korea, a fact that also menaced relatively well-paid trade unionists and even corporate executives.

This is the great danger confronting the new poor. If their plight is not an anomaly of the affluent society but the outcome of massive economic trends, why will the majority undertake the fairly radical changes that are needed in order to help a minority that is either not seen, despised, or feared? In the sixties, people thought that the struggle against poverty was going to be a lovely little war. But if, in the eighties, the poor and their friends explain that it is going to be a difficult and arduous struggle, who will respond, particularly when everyone is concerned about how it will affect him personally?

In that very real danger there is also hope. The majority of the people of the United States cannot possibly make themselves secure unless they also help the poor. That is, the very measures that will most benefit the working people and the middle class—the rich will take care of themselves, as they always have—will also strike a blow against poverty. That is by no means an automatic process; there are specific measures that have to be worked out to deal with particular problems of the poor. But basically the programs that are in the self-interest of the majority are always in the special interest of the poor.

Therefore, in this chapter I will not propose a politics based simply on morality and solidarity—not *simply* based on those values, but certainly based upon them. An increase in compassion and caring is essential, and for all of the simplifications of the early sixties, those were generous years, which does them credit. But in addition to affirming that we are indeed our sisters' and our brothers' keepers, it must also be said that the abolition of poverty requires programs—above all, full employment—that will probably do more for the nonpoor than for the poor. One is not asking men and women who have troubles enough of their own to engage in a noblesse oblige that is, in any case, patronizing. One appeals to both their decency and their interest.

I

But how is it that justice and self-interest are, in this miraculous case, in harmony with each other?

Full employment is good for almost everyone. That is a critical reason.

In the sixties, one of the most significant accomplishments of the decade came not from the War on Poverty as such, but from the fact that unemployment declined, with one insignificant exception, in every year of the Kennedy and Johnson administrations. So it was that the working poor constituted one of the two groups (the aging were, of course, the other) who made the greatest progress in the struggle to get out of poverty. And the harmony of justice and self-interest being asserted here as a possible future was a fact then. In a mere ten years the real buying power of production workers went up by more than 15 percent. In 1980, by stark contrast, the weekly wage had declined in real buying power to 1962 levels.

Would these patterns of escape from poverty in the sixties still hold in the eighties? Not for everyone; poor women are, we shall see, a special and very important case. But blacks, Hispanics, and other minorities, whether members of a marginalized underclass or part of the working poor, would gain. So would immigrants, and the question of undocumented workers would be put into a context in which decency would be an economic possibility as well as a moral imperative. The newness of much of the new poverty is precisely a function of an occupational structure that has destroyed many of the rungs of social mobility, the traditional escape routes from poverty. If a full-employment economy would begin to restore some of those possibilities, it would have a major and positive impact on these groups of the new poor.

Moreover, a full-employment economy is probably more effective at job counseling than are some psychiatrists and social workers. When it becomes the norm for everyone to work, people who were "unemployable" only yesterday suddenly turn out to be quite useful. World War II demonstrated this when it took women, blacks, and the long-term unemployed and put them to work in the arms plants; so did the European postwar boom, which showed that Greek and Yugoslavian peasants could do useful work in a sophisticated West German economy. Motivation is often not a matter of individual will but of social atmosphere. Full employment motivates work.

Full employment would even help reduce the levels of crime and violence in America. I am not proposing a strawman here, i.e., I am not suggesting that we disband the police and wait for jobs to abolish crime. I am saying, to frightened people as well as to the conservative cynics who tend that strawman and think they have actually done serious intellectual work, that a radical drop in the jobless rate will appreciably lower the number of muggings and assaults. There are other things that have to be done to protect society from violence. But this is certainly the most humane way of fighting crime.

Full employment would help a great number of the new poor; and it would benefit the nonpoor as well.

When the official figures admitted to more than eleven million unemployed and almost two million "discouraged workers" driven out of the labor market in 1983, that was obviously disastrous for those who had lost their jobs. But it also made things much worse for those who were still at work. The existence of a huge pool of idle people makes those with jobs fearful and helps drive wages down. It also sets off that vicious cycle where people clutch at every possibility and take jobs for which they are overqualified, and those they replace do the same until the least qualified at the bottom suffer the most. As a result, a pervasive sense of insecurity saps any spirit of militancy. It was not an accident that members of the United Automobile Workers turned against concessions to the companies almost the minute the economy improved a bit in 1983. So it is that a full-employment economy would not simply help the least paid, or the unemployed; it would set in motion a virtuous cycle that would improve the lot of everyone in the labor force.

This process would aid the successful members of minority groups as well as those in the underclass. The blacks and Hispanics who have risen in the occupational structure suffer from two contrasting problems: On the one hand, they are guilty because they have left behind so many despairing members of their own group; on the other hand, they suffer from that "statistical discrimination" which equates everyone in the group with its violent, and rather tiny, minority of criminals. Insofar as a full-employment economy would both reduce violence on the part of that minority and open up opportunities for the millions of the nonviolent poor who are black and Hispanic, it would improve the quality of life even for those who have already made it into the middle class.

In the case of women, these connections are even more obvious. Women and minorities in the seventies and eighties suffer from the same structural problem that is one of the main causes of the new poverty. There is no longer juridical racism and sexism in the United States; there is *occupational* racism and sexism. That is, minorities and women are paid the same for the same job (not, however, for equivalent jobs, where there is still a gap), but they hold many more bad jobs than do men or white Anglos. One of the consequences of the poverty of the underclass, of the immigrants and the undocumented workers, we have seen, is to remove any reason for business to modernize the bottom of the American economy. As long as there are plenty of frightened, hungry people willing to do dirty jobs for a song, dirty jobs will persist and sweatshops will thrive in the back alleys of the economy.

This situation has not simply hurt the people at the bottom; it has distorted and skewed the entire occupational structure. It has been one of the main reasons why there is a gap between the very bottom and the lower reaches of the stable working class. That is precisely the space that should be filled by people on their way up, but there is no incentive for business to create it. Women—and often minority immigrant women—are concentrated on the lower reaches. They are often the sweatshop and low-paid production workers. This is one of the major reasons for the "feminization" of poverty. But it is also a reason why so many of those intermediate jobs either do not exist or else are designed for low productivity and low wages. And there are even more women trying to fill that niche in the economy.

To be utterly utopian for a moment: a labor shortage in the United States would probably do more to eliminate poverty, sexism, and racism than all other policies combined.

Even the environment is implicated in this process. Ever since the economic crisis asserted itself in the seventies, it has been a standard corporate complaint that if only environmental restrictions were removed, the economy would boom. More often than not, that was a fraud, albeit a politically effective one. The Office of Technology Assessment has documented that Japanese steel companies, in the decade in which they took the lead over their American competitors, were paying environmental protection costs more than 60 percent higher than the corporations in the United States. But most people do not know that. And there have been very effective campaigns to roll back some of the gains that were made in the early seventies, quite often with the support of workers and their unions, concerned—understandably, alas—about their own jobs.

These trends also explain why there is often a certain listlessness in the college youth of America. One of the preconditions of that burst of spirit and generosity in the sixties—yes, of course, it sometimes was brash, immature, and unwise, but it was also essentially positive and good—was economic growth. There was a certain space that opened up, a feeling that one could take a chance for a year or two, that life was not, particularly for the young, totally determined by the pragmatic and the conventional. The volunteers for the Peace Corps and VISTA were one of the signs of those times. But then, with the economic crisis, everyone became practical; accounting courses grew in the colleges, literature and philosophy suffered. The culture was affected, not just the economy.

If there were full employment, I am convinced that would change. Young people in the seventies did not turn into cynics; they were forced to practice a certain cynicism and opportunism because there seemed to be no other alternative. But in my experience, as a professor at a great urban university, and as a speaker on countless campuses, I am convinced that the college youth of the eighties (and the seventies) are not that different from the generation of the sixties. They have simply not been given the chance to be as good as they can be.

If there were full employment, it would not simply give them the opportunity to move into better jobs; it would also permit them to make new kinds of decisions about work. And I suspect that if there were a new spirit abroad in the land that something could be done about poverty, the old idealism would reappear and one of the forms it would take would be a commitment to working with the poor. To this day I constantly meet people who had their lives changed as volunteers: fighting brown-lung disease in the South, helping dissident miners organize in West Virginia, living in a single-room-occupancy hotel with marginalized people in Seattle. Those who took this path did not simply reach out to the poor, important as that was; they also transformed their own lives for the better.

And finally, these things can have an international impact. In 1982 I testified on economic and social policy before a subcommittee of the American Catholic hierarchy. I talked of the report of the Brandt Commission and its core idea that a Northern commitment to transferring funds and technology to the poor of the world's South would also create jobs in the North. One bishop replied that he heard talk of the report whenever he was in Europe, but only rarely in the United States. And yet, living in France for a few months in 1983, I realized that Brandt's theme was practical politics. The French have made money out of aiding their ex-colonies. There is, I suspect, hope for the American poor if this nation would make a serious commitment to abolish the much greater poverty of the people of Asia, Africa, and Latin America.

II

I can hear the murmurs in the back of the hall: Fine, fine, but how do you propose to reach this promised land called full employment?

Not easily, be assured of that. Before I turn to the very difficult task of outlining a full-employment strategy (which I have detailed in *The Decade of Decision* and in my contribution to *Alternatives*, edited by Irving Howe) I should make two important preliminary points. First, the true utopians are the crackpot realists who now accept the notion that one can have a permanent labor reserve army of the unemployed amounting to eight or nine million people and still solve social problems. In the halcyon days after the Second World War, the official "full employment unemployment rate" was 2 percent; under John Kennedy and Lyndon Johnson it was 3 percent, with an interim target of 4 percent; in the seventies it became 5 percent; and in the 1983 Report of the Council of Economic Advisors, it was pegged at 6.1 percent. Indeed, the government did have the semantic decency to stop talking about full employment. The "full employment unemployment rate" became the "high employment unemployment rate," which then turned into the "inflation threshold unemployment rate."

One can make all kinds of sophisticated—and wrong—arguments that these jobless rates are necessary. (Conservatives thus unwittingly come to agree with Marx's analysis in Volume One of *Das Kapital.*) But when that is done, the theorists have the responsibility to publicly state their effective endorsement of an underclass in the United States and to take responsibility for the moral and criminal consequences of their decision. In fact, as *Business Week* and other serious business journals have acknowledged, the 6.1-percent rate is an optimistic target as far as the official thinkers are concerned. Their real expectation is that when unemployment comes all the way down to 7 percent—counting in the "discouraged workers" category that defines about nine million idle human beings—they will take anti-inflationary steps that will begin to put people out of work again. That means, among other things, the official institutionalization of the other America.

The utopians, then, are the ones who think it is possible to solve *any* of our basic social problems—racial, sexual, environmental, criminal—without deep-going structural changes. Business itself would profit if the measures urged here were adopted. In 1983 the Nobel laureate Wassily Leontiev published an extremely important article in *The Population and Development Review.* Until recently, Leontiev argued, capitalism has been creating its own markets, since the technology of its success has required more and more skilled workers. But now the technological revolution is changing all that. Just as tractors replaced farm horses, Leontiev writes, so computerized production is replacing human beings.

This means, he continues, not only technological unemployment but a basic shift in the distribution of income and wealth, a more polarized society with a well-paid elite and a poorly paid mass. Not so incidentally, I would add, it is precisely this trend that now makes the sweatshop viable in the United States. A very low technology and a very high technology become profitable at the same time because the middle is beginning to disappear. But if this is so, who will buy the products of the miraculous productivity brought about by the new technology?

I have located the new American poverty within an analysis of the sweeping changes in the world and national economies which cause it but threaten to disrupt the lives of the rest of America as well. So the program I summarize here is as radical as the problem I have defined.

In urging full employment to fight against that possibility, I am well aware that I am taking a position to the left of a good part of the Democratic Party and even of a stratum of ex-liberals who fought for the Humphrey-Hawkins bill in the seventies and are now somewhere in between a retreat and a rout. Moreover, there is an arguable case that my own ideas are "utopian." But what is unarguable is that if America accepts an official rate of 6–7-percent unemployment as necessary for the system, the problems of misery and social breakdown will increase in "good times" and become epidemic in bad times. My critics have a right to their point of view, but they should then come up with *their* solution. They might, for example, want to go back to Swift's "modest proposal" for dealing with the poverty of eighteenth-century Ireland: to kill and eat the babies of the poor.

My irony makes it clear, I hope, that the difficult program for full employment I outline here (and I stress the word *outline*) is both radical in American terms and the *only* realism if we are to confront the new American poverty.

There must be planning. That confronts us with two related mystifications, one from the simplistic left, the other from the shamefaced right. It is sometimes implied on the left that "planning" is the word for a magic panacea that will solve all problems. In fact, there is good planning and bad, conservative planning, fascist planning, Stalinist planning—and democratic planning. Having said that we must plan, one has hardly said anything at all. But then, the right has its own evasions in this area. It practices planning all the time, but it does not believe in what it does. Therefore it chants hymns to the providence of Adam Smith's invisible hand of the market, while engaging in the politics of the visible hand of state planning.

Ronald Reagan's Economic Recovery Tax Act of 1981 is a case in point. In 1982 the Council of Economic Advisors presented a marvelous commentary on that basic legislative triumph of Reaganomics. Americans, the report said, are consuming too much and investing too little as a result of past government policies. Therefore, current government policy has, through changes in the tax laws, made consumption more expensive and saving more profitable. (Of course, the poor, the workers, and the middle class are the ones who do most of the consuming; the rich, who have an excess of consumption, are the savers.) Then, with the market carefully rigged, the sovereign economic citizens are allowed to make their free choices.

All political tendencies in the United States, then—left, right, and center—are in favor of planning. All are trying to respond in a systematic way to a structural crisis—transformation of the international division of labor, unprecedented internalization of capital, technological revolution—that has all but overwhelmed whatever remnants of a free market still exist. Ronald Reagan has an "industrial policy" that says the government should, by legislative fiat, increase the amount of capital available to the private sector in order to allow it to respond to the radical challenges coming from a new world economy. The program is conservative in that it redistributes funds by shifting tax burdens from the working people and the middle class to the rich; but it is a conservative *planner's* solution since it does so by means of laws, not of markets.

I write at a time when it is unclear whether the recovery that began in the winter of 1983 will be long and vigorous or short and quickly menaced by inflationary pressures. However, one thing is clear: The investment boom that was supposed to follow upon the passage of the Economic Recovery Tax Act of 1981 simply did not take place. In 1983 the economy did begin to emerge from the recession, but it did so in the context of an investment bust, not a boom. The President was, of course, quick to take credit for the improvement, but the facts are at odds with the claim. Indeed, there is a plausible case to be made for the proposition that the "demand side" economics scorned by Mr. Reagan—that is, stimulation of consumer demand by means of increased government deficits—were his (temporary) salvation.

The point, however, is not to argue the merits and demerits of the Reagan policies in general. It is simply to establish that when I speak of the need for planning, I am talking of an approach common to every political tendency in the United States. The issue is not whether to plan. The real question is, who will plan, how, and for what purposes?

At the onset it is necessary to get some global sense of the problems and possibilities of the American economy. The United Automobile Workers have rightly pointed out that the work of Wassily Leontiev could be of enormous assistance in taking stock of the global needs of the economy. Leontiev has developed intricate "input/output" tables that illuminate and quantify the interdependencies of a modern economy. If, for example, the price of steel goes up, it affects the price of automobiles and that has an impact upon all the industries involved in one way or another with cars (rubber, glass, radios, etc.). With Leontiev's analysis and computer models, it is possible to calculate many of these exceedingly complex interactions. The Austrian socialists, who did exactly that, had the lowest inflation and unemployment rates in Europe in the early eighties.

But, secondly, computers do not make decisions, and there have to be ways of evaluating the numbers. Here the UAW proposes broader—and, to my mind, more accurate—criteria for assessing efficiency than Americans now use. In the United States more than in any other advanced industrial country, decisions on plant closings and relocation are made without reference to social cost. They are computed in terms of private cost and benefit only. In all other rich societies, including Japan, an employer cannot simply shut down a plant without any consultation. It is recognized that there is a social dimension to efficiency.

For example, a major plant closing will increase unemployment benefits at least temporarily, decrease taxes, including social security taxes, cause a fiscal crisis in the community in which the factory is located, affect all the related businesses that depend on that plant, and lead to an increase in alcoholism, domestic violence, and marital breakdown. In terms of a private calculus, it might make excellent sense to arbitrarily shut down and to impose many of the costs of that decision upon the taxpayers who will have to pay for the havoc that the shutdown wreaks. The UAW argues that planners must use criteria of judgment that take these broader consequences into account.

If that were done, for instance, it would become absurd simply to "write off" the smokestack areas of the Northeast and Middle West. Leaving aside the human cruelty in such a tactic—and the fact that high technology creates jobs for the high-paid and the low-paid but not for the in-between, which is where most Americans are—it would be extremely expensive to gut the heartland of America. Moreover, some of the glib generalizations about the end of the traditional industries, like auto and steel, mistake relative trends for absolute facts. Between 1959 and 1979, the manufacturing percentage of employment dropped from 42.1 to 20.6. But 20.6 percent of the (roughly) 105 million men and women in the labor force in 1979 was well over twenty million human beings. Even if the projections that envision a further drop to 19.5 percent in 1990 are accurate, there will be even more manufacturing workers than there are now (they will be a slightly lower percentage of a larger total).

If America, as part of a national economic plan, decided to meet just a few of its urgent needs, it could put even more people to work in the old industrial areas. The nation, it is well known, has a rotting infrastructure of bridges, sewers, and roads. It has, precisely in the Northeast and Middle West, destroyed much of the rail system. It requires, even if OPEC's problems obscured the fact in 1983, new, environmentally benign forms of energy. These needs are, for the most part, in the public sector, but they could be supplied by both the public and private sectors. A regionally owned public rail system in the Northeast and the Midwest could, particularly if America's chaotic and antisocial subsidies for transportation were given some minimal social rationality, create jobs for people now employed in—or laid off from—steel mills and automobile factories.

And there is also that international dimension of human need which is the focus of the Brandt Commission report. A serious transfer of funds and technology from the North to the South would create jobs in the North. The poor countries of Asia, Africa, and Latin America are not going to start tractor factories, at least in the intermediate future. They are going to buy them in the markets of the North. And just as the United States made money off the Marshall Plan—that was not the reason behind the Marshall Plan, but it was certainly one of its consequences—it could benefit if only it had the wisdom to be a bit more decent to the world's poor. And that, of course, would help the American poor as well.

All of this does not add up to socialism, although that is what the demagogues of the right will say about it. But clearly all of the proposals made here are not merely compatible with the existence of a private corporate sector; they will help that sector prosper. The New Deal, it should be remembered, benefited the entire society including those who most bitterly opposed it. (In honesty I should note that in other contexts I would also cite this as one of the structural limitations and inadequacies of a New Deal that, despite my criticism, I still retrospectively support.) What is being suggested is nothing more daring than trying to allocate resources to job-generating and truly useful uses.

One of the reasons that the society—and the new poor above all—is in such deep trouble is that American business has become inexcusably wasteful and speculative. In 1979, for instance, RCA said that it did not have $200 million to invest in a videocassette recorder, but it somehow found $1.3 billion to buy a finance company, and surrendered the videocassette market to the Japanese. That unconscionable diversion of real assets to intracorporate games was, moreover, partly paid for by taxpayers. Interest costs are deductible as a business expense, and most of the corporate takeovers of the eighties were accomplished with borrowed money, which reduced corporate taxes even more.

In this context I would propose policies that are both "pro" corporate and a limitation on corporations. If a company makes investments in wealth-producing assets that create jobs, I would favor government support and subsidies and, if that company did those things in areas of high unemployment and poverty, generous support and subsidies. But if a company wants to move out of an area in trouble, there should be advance notice, a public determination of social, as contrasted to private, costs and benefits, a requirement that the departing corporation take financial responsibility for the social damage it does, and a loss of all tax deductions for a move that is harmful to the society. In the same spirit, there should be prohibitive interest rates on money lent for takeovers, and lower interest rates on loans for first homes and cars. (The theory and practice of differential interest rates geared to public-policy goals has operated for more than a generation in the housing sector.)

The point is, poverty cannot be abolished, and all of our other social goals cannot be accomplished, if a welfare-dependent American industry insists on getting massive subsidies for speculative investments that do not generate jobs. If the billions lavished on mergers in the last ten years had been spent on meeting American needs, the country would be a much better place to live, the poor would be much fewer in number, and the workers and the middle class would be much better off.

But who is going to pay for all of these good things? With a Republican President presiding over a deficit that is 6 percent of GNP—and demanding that there be a constitutional amendment to outlaw what he is doing—how can one talk about bold new departures in the name of the poor?

The first part of the answer to that question is easy, both analytically and politically. I noted it in Chapter 4. If, as the

Reagan administration says, a percentage of unemployment increased the federal budget, in terms of lost revenues and additional costs, by $25 billion, then the 3.3-percent increase in the jobless rate from the President's inauguration till the end of 1982 cost $82.5 billion. If one takes the AFL-CIO estimate of a $30-billion loss for each percentage point of unemployment, then almost half of Reagan's estimated 1984 deficit is accounted for by his own use of joblessness as a weapon against inflation in 1983. And conversely, if one followed a vigorous full-employment program, it would partly finance itself. It would, in Lyndon Johnson's characteristic phrase, "turn tax eaters into taxpayers."

That, so to speak, is the "sixties" part of the answer: Growth finances itself; it is a solid investment for the government to make. But—and we now move into a more difficult area—in the short run there could indeed be budgetary constraints. Presidents, even liberal Presidents, are after all not entirely focused on that long run in which, to paraphrase Keynes, they are no longer the President. How to deal with the problem here and now? The eighties, I believe, must give an answer that the sixties never dared to mention: through the redistribution of income and wealth.

The federal tax system, as we have seen in this book, is a maze of welfare handouts for the rich and the very rich. In 1981 and 1982, the Congressional Black Caucus—which speaks on behalf of one of the most important groups of the poor in the nation—produced meticulously documented counter-budgets as alternatives to the Reagan proposals. In each case, the Caucus restored all of the program cuts that weighed so heavily on those in need and took away, in rather modest amounts, some of the subsidies to the rich, thus coming in with a deficit lower than the President's. Remember, a few capital-gains deductions are worth several times the entire federal expenditure for Aid for Families of Dependent Children.

Thus far, I have been talking about macroeconomic measures that would reduce poverty by means of full employment. Is there any role for the poor themselves to play in this process?

At first, the precedents seem to be discouraging. The War on Poverty had its famous statutory declaration that there must be "maximum feasible participation of the poor." In part, as Daniel Patrick Moynihan has shown, there was "maximum feasible misunderstanding" about what that meant. But there were community elections for poverty councils, and the turnouts were absurdly low. Doesn't this show that the poor are not really interested in making the decisions, but only in getting the results—and the money? Wasn't "maximum feasible participation" a demand imposed on the program by intellectuals intrigued by the theory of alienation, rather than a need of poor people concerned with the struggle for daily bread?

Yes and no. There was, no doubt, more than a little romanticism in the early days of the poverty program. Some wrongly thought that the poor were the revolutionary proletariat that the organized workers refused to be. That was, and is, silly. It totally overlooks the way in which poverty demoralizes and disorganizes the people at the base (and in which the discipline of industrial work leads to self-organization in unions). But it would be equally wrong to see those low turnouts for community-action elections as proof of the eternal passivity and indifference of the poor.

Most Americans, particularly those who do not have secure middle-class comfort, are quite practical about elections. They seek not ideological vindication, but solutions to problems. Therefore, as Walter Dean Burnham has shrewdly suggested, the lack of participation on the part of the poor may be the result of a rational assessment of a hopeless political situation created by the rich. In the 1880s and 1890s, wealth in the United States was challenged by a populist movement with the vision of a cooperative commonwealth and a visceral hatred for banks and railroads. At the same time, the wrenching transition from free enterprise to monopoly capitalism involved chronic recessions and urban resistance over a period of twenty years. Therefore it became necessary to hold down participation if the status quo was to be protected.

Between 1848 and 1896, the mean turnout in Presidential elections was 75 percent. It dropped to an average of 65 percent between 1900 and 1916, and to 52 percent between 1920 and 1928. During the Great Depression—the time of political reform and union organization—voter participation rose, and it averaged 60 percent between 1932 and 1960. Now it is just above 50 percent. Why that big drop from the nineteenth to the twentieth century? A number of things happened, Burnham argues, to produce the "system of 1896" as the wealthy began to defend themselves against the poor farmers and workers. The Southern planters took over control of the Democratic Party, while industrialists became dominant in the Republican Party. Participation was reduced by law—poll taxes, property requirements, elaborate conditions for voter registration—and the machines were deprived of the patronage that had made them a kind of politically controlled welfare institution.

I summarize briefly, but the point is clear. Voter participation was made much less meaningful, and the turnout declined as a rational response to a new situation. In the postwar period, Burnham points out, the people who didn't vote were, precisely, the poor, the minorities, the less educated, the lower-paid strata of the working class. They were the "hole" in the American electorate and they did not see any party or leader who made it worth their while to get involved. These patterns, I think, are related to the experience of the community-action elections in the War on Poverty. People did not get involved because it was not obvious to them what difference it would make if they did. And, it turned out, they were right.

In the recent past there has been evidence that when the poor do see a point to participation, they participate. In the Chicago, Boston, and Philadelphia mayoral elections of 1983, there were massive turnouts of black voters. Suddenly the old patterns did not seem to apply. It is, of course, true that nationality and race have often proved, contrary to Marx, much more potent and emotional means of political mobilization than class. And yet the fact remains that those elections showed that poor communities could be effectively organized. If, as *The Economist* noted in 1983, blacks began to vote at the same rate as whites, that would change American politics. And if, I would add, there were a poverty program of the eighties that did not stall on takeoff—which is more or less what happened in the sixties—there might even be maximum participation of the poor in their own struggle.

I do not insist upon this point out of some abstract attachment to the notion of participation. The ways in which decisions are made affect what decisions are made. If, say, there is the kind of planning that resolved the New York City crisis, dominated by bankers and the establishment, it makes it all but inevitable that the sacrifices imposed will be primarily upon the people and the poor. But there is yet another condition of effective participation. In a society more and more dominated by experts and computer printouts, the technology of decision-making excludes, by its very nature, a stratum of people who lack education.

To facilitate significant participation at the base, meaningful participation has to be made possible. This sounds like a tautology, but it is in fact a summons to a most basic reform. If there is to be planning, and the wealthy and powerful have a monopoly on experts and computers, then that planning cannot be participatory. There have to be public resources made available for counterplanning. The Congressional Black Caucus could come up with its imaginative counterbudgets in 1981 and 1982 because members of Congress got large allotments of federal money for staff. But what about a community of poor people in a rundown neighborhood, in a Los Angeles *barrio* or in the South Bronx? They have a grasp of what needs to be done, but they are unable to translate that into the technical language of contemporary political and economic debate. But if they could hire and fire their own experts, they would have not simply the right to participation in planning, but the possibility as well.

These are just a few brief thoughts on the kind of macroeconomic program needed to deal with a new poverty that is so often based upon stagnant or crumbling occupational structures. There are some basic reforms I have not mentioned—a reduction in income is one—because they require an analysis that goes beyond the boundaries of this chapter. There are others I have omitted because they are genuinely radical, such as paying for all necessities collectively and making them available free, e.g., providing medical care based upon medical need without reference to money. In this latter case, I simply want to avoid a debate over questions whose relevance is not immediate. What I have done, I hope, is to give some general idea of the kind of macroeconomic program that is needed to deal with the new poverty.

I do not apologize in the least for having ranged so far afield from the poor themselves in a good part of this outline. That, in a sense, simply reflects one of the most basic themes of this chapter, i.e., that the plight of the new poor is implicated in the crisis of the world economy, that the solutions they need are the same as the solutions that are in the interest of the entire society. But there are also specific measures that relate to the new poor, and it is important to note at least a few of them here.

For the working poor—indeed, for American society in general—the institution of a national health program would make an enormous difference. Why is it that an American worker loses health coverage when he or she loses a job, while a Canadian worker who belongs to the same union, watches much the same television, and roots for teams in the same baseball league, does not? Moreover, national health would allow the government to gain some control over the single most inflationary element in the budget. Even after almost all other prices fell as a result of Ronald Reagan bringing the economy to its knees in 1982, medical costs continued to increase as if nothing had happened. Our system of third-party insurance paying the costs of fee-for-service medicine ingeniously combines the worst of capitalism and socialism in a single stroke. Ending that muddle might save money as well as increase health care.

The stopgap measures proposed during 1982 and 1983 provided for temporary health care for the unemployed. That, obviously, is better than nothing, and one should support it enthusiastically. But there must come a time when this country will finally put an end to its shameful exceptionalism as the only advanced nation on the face of the earth without national health care.

Not only should all the benefits taken away from the working poor be restored—food stamps and Medicaid in particular—but a new principle should be adopted: No one who works full time should be poor. Full employment would have a tendency to move the labor market in that direction, by bidding up the cost of work for everyone. But the nation should not wait for this effect. The minimum wage and the various support programs should be set at levels that guarantee a nonpoverty income for every working citizen of the United States.

There are a number of things that can, and should, be done for the uprooted poor of the great cities. Those among them whose central problem in 1981 and 1982 was the lack of a job would be enormously helped by full employment. But the more marginal people, many of them out of the labor market, need other kinds of assistance. If there were a national commitment to affordable housing for everyone, with a special emphasis upon the poor, it would be possible to counter the negative consequences of gentrification, in Maine as well as in New York. Indeed, Ronald Reagan's Director of the Office of Management and Budget, David Stockman, had privately come up with an excellent idea before the publication of an excessively frank interview forced him to retreat. He favored, according to that interview, a "mansion cap" where the interest deduction on a mortgage would be limited to $10,000. That would continue a rather significant subsidy to the working people and the middle class; it would require that the rich actually pay for their own housing.

If one would add that the subsidies should be confined to a single place of residence—when there are rotting tenements in the South Bronx, vacation houses should not be underwritten by the government, as now happens—and if there were a commitment to affordable housing for all, the 90 percent of the society that is neither rich nor upper class would benefit, but so, particularly, would those homeless people who have been run out of the single-room-occupancy hotels. This, however, still leaves the problem of the discharged mental patients who frighten so many people and do unwitting harm to themselves. In their case, there is no alternative to keeping the promise that was made a generation ago, and has been systematically broken ever since. They need small-scale community centers, professionally staffed and spread throughout the cities, that can help integrate them into the life of communities as far as that is possible.

The minority underclass is, so to speak, divided into two components: those, often men, who have been utterly marginalized by an occupational structure with no place for them; and the women heads of family with children. The first group would obviously be helped by the achievement of full employment, but the effect would not be automatic. Many of these people, as Ken Auletta showed, have been so psychically and emotionally alienated that they would have a strong tendency to resist a process that would benefit them. It is, as Auletta's book demonstrated, possible to have special programs to bring them back into the community, but that takes considerable money and an enormous amount of sympathetic support. What is the alternative? To institutionalize a stratum of excluded people who will haunt the margins of the society and occasionally strike out at a frightened citizenry. That cost is infinitely higher than serious job-training programs. Moreover, one should not forget that Auletta described attempts to work with these people under the deteriorating economic conditions of the seventies. In a full-employment environment, the effort would cost somewhat less and succeed more often, because the new atmosphere in the society would motivate people to want to work.

Women who are heads of families will not, it should be remembered, automatically benefit from full employment. Many of them are so tied down by the unpaid labor of child care that they cannot even consider taking a menial job that, given travel and other costs, would actually end up lowering their incomes. Therefore this stratum of the new poor needs not sermons on the glories of work, but programs making it possible for its members to go out in the labor market—child care, above all—and guarantees that when they *do* work, it will raise, and not reduce, their income.

The immigrants and the undocumented workers need, above all, the enforcement of minimum-wage and other labor laws now on the books and systematically ignored. The crime for which employers should be arraigned is not that they hired undocumented workers. That would make it even more likely that Hispanics would suffer increased discrimination. Rather, they should be held responsible for not meeting minimal standards in their relations with any worker, whether documented or not. That would destroy the sweatshops—it would deprive them of their ability to threaten exploited workers with deportation if they complain—

and it might put some limits on the cynical exploitation of such workers by the growers and the building industry of the Southwest.

At the same time, there should be a special program for legal immigration by Mexicans and Central Americans. This, as I have indicated, would be an act of realism as well as decency. And if full employment were realized, one of the main impediments to such a policy—the fear of American workers that they will be shouldered out by hungry competitors—would disappear.

Crime, as I have already insisted, has to be fought by the police as well as by social programs. But the prison system of America, one of the most expensive and cruel institutions for the poor and the minorities, can be reformed here and now. The principle should be that no one is sent to jail unless he or she is found to be a threat to the peace and physical safety of the society. It is time that the United States stopped running postgraduate schools for criminality, which turn those who have made an initial mistake into permanent members of a criminal class.

Finally, there is a series of reforms outlined by Rudolph Penner, the Director of the Congressional Budget Office, in testimony before a Congressional committee in the fall of 1983. Penner, a conservative, did not advocate these measures, but he did a considerable service simply by identifying them. We could create national minimum-guarantee levels for AFDC, much as was already done in the SSI program. Then state participation in the AFDC program for unemployed, intact families could be made mandatory. That would take local government out of the business of promoting family breakup.

Contrary to some of the more ominous suggestions of the Reagan task force on hunger, food-stamp benefits should be extended to the working poor, and to childless individuals and couples not now allowed to participate in the program. Food stamps have been a triumph, and the nation must not only reject the conservative proposals to turn this function back to the tender mercies of states that already provide utterly inadequate funds for AFDC; it must also see to it that food stamps are available to *anyone* threatened by hunger.

Medicaid should be automatically provided for all poor families with children. In 1985, Penner notes, this would give coverage to an additional twelve to thirteen million adults and children. And child-support enforcement could be expanded in order to deal with the personal and social tragedy of deserted, impoverished women. These are a few of the possibilities envisioned by Penner, and they are all worthwhile.

So there are very specific programs that speak to the needs of the new poor. But what are the politics of achieving them?

The underlying concept of that politics can be stated simply enough. The nation is in a structural economic crisis, the most severe that we have known in almost a century. The overwhelming majority of the nonpoor are at least threatened by the same massive trends that have done so much to create a new poverty. The programs that are in their interest, above all full employment, are profoundly in the interest of the new poor. At the same time, there is no single group in the country that can, by its own unaided effort, resolve the crisis for itself. If all of the trade unionists (20 percent of the work force) or all of the blacks (12 percent of the population) or all of the poor (15 to 20 percent of the nation) mobilized independently, they would clearly fail. On the other hand, there is a community of interest between middle-class feminist activists and impoverished female heads of families: both need the transformation of an occupational structure that, in radically different ways, penalizes both. The building-trades worker, the underclass member, and even the distraught former mental patient have a common interest in affordable housing.

And there are also new possibilities for organizing the poor themselves. The welfare state itself, as Richard Cloward and Frances Fox Piven have pointed out, opens up the possibility of mobilizing people who have suffered cutbacks in recent years. The changes in registration rules, many of them a legacy of the civil rights struggles of the sixties, have lowered some of the barriers to the participation of the poor so carefully preserved for half a century by Northern Republicans and Southern Democrats. Moreover, helping the poor into this coalition in their own name counters one of the most pernicious effects of the recent reductions in social programs, i.e., the tendency to set poor against poor, black against white, men against women, workers against the poor, and so on. So long as those at the bottom and middle of the society squabble over insufficient resources, all lose. There has to be genuine cooperation and a commitment to generating sufficient resources that will allow all to win.

This is one of the many political reasons why full employment is such a critical demand. It will not automatically eliminate all of the structures of misery that have grown up in the past two decades. But it is clearly the precondition for doing just that.

It is wrong, however, to put all of this simply in economic terms, with an emphasis on the intersecting self-interests of different groups. There is a moral dimension to the issue as well. As noted, the idealism of the sixties and the cynicism of the eighties are, in considerable measure, social products. Economics and ethics are not located in separate and sealed compartments. If there are economic policies that make moral concerns more likely, then a powerful lever for the organization of people in the battle against the new poverty is human solidarity. In the sixties, many religious people found a new relevance for their faith in the civil rights movement, in the War on Poverty, in the struggle against America's unconscionable intervention in Vietnam.

That spirit did not disappear. It continues in the resistance to the Reagan social cuts, in the disarmament movement, in the fight against intervention in Central America. But I am convinced that there is an even greater idealism in this society waiting to be made possible. The young, in particular, need a vision that transcends the mindless hedonism of so much of contemporary life.

But good spirit without a solid program is not enough. And here I have what might seem to be a strange fear: that we may suffer in the future from Ronald Reagan's radicalism and principled politics. Reagan is, let there be no doubt about it, an authentic radical. In 1980 he said, quite rightly, that there were new and fundamental problems, that the solutions of the past generation would not work. He, more than any other President in my lifetime, translated his campaign program into a legislative agenda and, in many cases, into laws. One of the reasons why the American people seem to forgive him so very much is, I think, that they recognize in him a man of principle, even a utopian.

But his utopia is, whether he knows it or not, a cover-up for the *realpolitik* of the rich and corporations. It also didn't work. Could Reagan's failure discredit the notion of a principled and programmatic politics? I think so. I can easily imagine the adepts of a stale wisdom arguing that any attempt to think things through, to meet economic and social problems in a systematic fashion, is doomed. Ronald Reagan could, in short, make "muddling through" popular again.

But muddling through is not good enough by half. The forces that are reshaping the American economy and society are extremely radical and will not respond to unrelated reforms on the fringes of massive problems. We have no choice but to redefine the nature of work, because if we don't do it consciously and in the name of specific values, it will be done for us from on high, in the worst possible way, with a new joblessness rather than a new leisure. In that case, the greatest costs will be imposed upon the most vulnerable, a response to the crisis that is already under way.

An antipoverty politics must be coalitional, with full employment as a central goal, and must awaken the latent moral idealism of the nation in the service of a very specific program.

Will it happen? The danger that it will not is great; the structures of misery are much more menacing today than they were in the sixties. There could be a revolution without revolutionaries, an unwitting transformation of the conditions of human existence that would preserve the worst of the past in a fantasy future. There would be custodial care for the suffering of increasing numbers of superfluous people, and electronic security would become a growth industry, protecting the elite from the sporadic, unorganized violence of a disconsolate, demoralized stratum at the bottom of the society. The gulf between the two nations—that of the rich and that of the poor—would deepen, since there would be an occupational void in what had once been the middle ground of the economy.

The pattern would be international—but then it already is.

In Europe, there are immigrants of the second generation now, young people who have lost their parents' homeland but have not been allowed to find their own. Unemployment threatens the gains of welfare states much more generous than our own. There is homelessness and aimlessness. The dirty jobs are being sent to the Third World, the high technology is reserved for the rich countries, and Africans starve while Americans spend billions to create an artificial food scarcity as a way of maintaining farm income. The danger in that Chinese ideograph of crisis is palpable, already here.

But there is reason for hope. In the sixties, the best people thought they were doing something for "them"—the blacks, the Appalachians, the truly *other* Americans. But now, more and more people are discovering that they, too, are "them." I do not mean to imply for a moment that the majority of Americans have become poor or will do so in the near future. I merely but emphatically insist that there is a growing sense of insecurity in the society, and for good reason. The very trends that have helped to create the new structure of misery for the poor are the ones that bewilder that famous middle of the American society, the traditional bastion of our complacency. And perhaps that middle will learn one of the basic lessons this book has tried to impart: A new campaign for social decency is not simply good and moral, but is also a necessity if we are to solve the problems that bedevil not just the poor, but almost all of us.

If we do understand that point, perhaps we will do something more profound than simply to discover an enlightened self-interest. Perhaps in the process we will discover a new vision of ourselves that rises above our individual needs and unites us in a common purpose. Perhaps that pilgrimage toward the fullness of our humanity will begin once again.

Index